Women in the West

When Montana and I Were Young

A Frontier Childhood

Margaret Bell

Edited and with an introduction

by Mary Clearman Blew

With an afterword by Lee Rostad

UNIVERSITY OF NEBRASKA PRESS : LINCOLN & LONDON

First Nebraska paperback printing: 2003

Library of Congress Cataloging-in-Publication Data
Bell, Margaret, 1888–1982.
When Montana and I were young: a frontier childhood /
Margaret Bell; edited and with an introduction by
Mary Clearman Blew; with an afterword by Lee Rostad.
p. cm – (Women in the West) Includes bibliographical
references. ISBN 0-8032-1325-5 (cloth: alkaline paper)
ISBN 0-8032-6214-0 (paper: alkaline paper)
1. Bell, Margaret, 1888–1982 – Childhood and youth.
2. Frontier and pioneer life – Montana. 3. Frontier and
pioneer life – Canada. 4. Women ranchers – Montana –
Biography. 5. Abused children – Montana – Biography.
6. Montana – Biography. I. Blew, Mary Clearman, 1939–
II. Series.

CT275.B5595 A3 2002 978.6′03′092–dc21 [B] 2001041060

IN MEMORY OF Grace Stone Coates, Joseph Kinsey Howard, and H. G. Merriam, all of whom tried to bring *When Montana and I Were Young* to publication.

CONTENTS

Introduction

At a meeting of his newly formed Montana Institute of the Arts in 1947, probably in Great Falls, Montana, the legendary University of Montana professor H. G. Merriam was approached by a middle-aged woman with a manuscript under her arm. Unlike many professors of creative writing, Merriam was generous with unpublished writers. A former Rhodes scholar and founder of the influential journal *Midland* and, later, the *Frontier*, Merriam had devoted much of his life to discovering, encouraging, and publishing the work of otherwise unknown writers in the Northwest. "Out of our soil we grow, and out of our soil should come expression of ourselves, living, hating, struggling, failing, succeeding, desponding, aspiring, playing, working – being alive," he had written in an early edition of the *Frontier*, arguing for the writers of the Rocky Mountain West to stop imitating the literary traditions of the eastern United States or Europe and to uncover their own material in their own region. "It is not cleverness or sophistication or sheer brawn or realism or romanticism or pessimism or sentiment that we want; it is all these – life honestly seen and felt, and passed through a healthy imagination."[1]

The woman who approached Merriam that day had certainly seen and felt a great deal of life. At nearly sixty years of age, her face was lined and her hair graying to steel, but she walked like a lifelong horsewoman, with the straight back and muscle tone of a much younger woman, the kind of ranch woman about whom it's said in the West, *They look fifty when they're thirty, and when they're eighty, they still look fifty.* Her face, as Merriam would have noticed, was a contradiction – the stoic looking-into-the-wind features, the taut mouth that gave little away, and yet the eyes, magnified and softened behind the thick lenses of her glasses, that revealed the eagerness of the would-be writer. Her name, she said, was Margaret Bell – Peggy

Bell – and she had been born in Great Falls in 1888 and lived most of her life on ranches in Montana and Canada. The manuscript she carried was a memoir of her first eighteen years.

In her own way, Peggy Bell was as much an advocate for regional art and literature as was Merriam himself. What with her scant four years of formal education, she knew little and probably cared less about a European cultural tradition, but she had known and admired the cowboy artist Charles M. Russell from childhood and shared his love of the prairie landscape, the unfenced freedom of the open range, and the customs of the lost cattle frontier. She knew that she had experiences as deep and tales to tell as valid as any man's, but she also knew that she was up against dimly perceived forces of culture, gender, and class that silenced women like herself and her friend the self-taught artist Evelyn Cole, oil painting her stiff murals of cowboys up in Chinook, Montana.[2] Peggy Bell probably had never heard of feminism in 1947 and would have disdained it if she had, but she was certain of a couple of things – first, that she had survived her childhood in spite of the abuse inflicted upon her from a man's world, and second, that she'd grown up to be a better cowhand than most men she'd know. She was determined to get her life story told.

By all later accounts, Peggy Bell was an engaging raconteur whose humor and natural sense of storytelling could keep an audience entertained for hours. At that first meeting, H. G. Merriam probably was attracted by her wit, but he also would have been struck by her background, recognizing that her unique and absolutely authentic material grew "out of our soil . . . living, hating, struggling, failing, succeeding," just the kind of material that for years he had been seeking out and encouraging. He introduced Peggy to his friend Joseph Kinsey Howard, the Great Falls newspaperman, charter member of the Montana Institute of the Arts, author of the acclaimed *Montana: High, Wide and Handsome*, and editor of *Montana Margins*, an anthology of little-known Montana writers. More importantly for the eventual outcome of her memoir, he also put her in touch with another protégée of his, a poet and writer of short fiction who lived in the tiny community of Martinsdale, Montana, named Grace Stone Coates, who Merriam thought might be able to help Peggy Bell rewrite and revise her memoir for publication.

Grace Stone was a Kansas-born woman who came to Montana to teach school and ended up marrying a storekeeper named Henderson Coates. As Mrs. Coates, she settled down, more or less uneasily, behind her husband's mercantile in Martinsdale in a house identical to the one his brother and sister-in-law lived in. The other Mrs. Coates disliked Grace, who avoided social obligations in order to write her poetry and short stories and was thought very odd for doing so.

Today, Grace Stone Coates's name has been forgotten by everyone except a handful of Montana bookworms and John Updike, who chose her short story "Wild Plums" to represent 1929 in his *Best American Short Stories of the Twentieth Century*. But in the late 1920s and early 1930s, Coates was publishing poetry in magazines as well known as *American Mercury* and *Poetry*, and no fewer than twenty of her short stories, most of which had first appeared in *Midland* or the *Frontier* under the auspices of H. G. Merriam, were cited during a single seven-year period as Distinctive or Honor Roll stories by Edward J. O'Brien for the annual *Best American Short Stories*. The Caxton Press of Idaho published her two collections of poems, *Mead and Mangel-Wurzel* in 1931 and *Portulacas in the Wheat* in 1932, and Alfred A. Knopf published her collection of short stories, *Black Cherries*, in 1931. All three books, of course, have long been out of print.[3]

But after 1932, for whatever reason, Coates's publications suddenly dwindled and ceased. Her last published short story appeared in the summer 1935 issue of the *Frontier*. A worried Merriam urged her to stop wasting her time writing for local newspapers and submit a novel to Knopf: "If you are going to continue as a writer – and you must do so – it is time that another book by you should appear."[4] She did have a large manuscript for a novel, Coates replied. "Your comment to Mr. Knopf moved me . . . Oh, I have a glorious idea if it just works out."[5]

But by 1947 Coates's correspondence with Merriam had become less and less frequent, and she no longer spoke of the novel. Merriam may have been hoping as much to rekindle Coates's creative spark as to assist Peggy Bell when he put the two women in touch with each other. And he had another, unspoken reason for bringing them together: both women were writing, from personal experience, about childhood abuse.

At first the Bell-Coates collaboration seemed to go well. Coates invited Bell to stay with her in her Martinsdale home while they worked together on Bell's book – "she spent the past month with me, and we got something done on her projected book," Coates wrote to Merriam. "We are both tough, so we survived the close association in an inconvenient, non-modern house."[6] But the going was hard:

I'm interested in her manuscript, but it is almost impossible to do anything with it at a long distance from her. All one can do is to state more felicitously what she has put down; and she hasn't put down on paper the necessary things. Her book has a dreamlike quality, in that characters appear and disappear without motivation, as in a dream; they are unnamed; she lives 8 years without one word of household conversation – even her little sisters remain just that – little sisters, sometimes one, sometimes two, sometimes three; and after she has reduced them to one, sometimes two of them appear hand in hand at the crest of a dreamlike hill. What she hasn't put down is a wealth of humor and entertainment that relieved the "almost unbearable agony" of her story. (I quote from Sloan Associates.) It is a disservice to her for well-wishers to lead her to believe she has an acceptable mss. at this time.[7]

After their month of intensive work, Bell went home to Great Falls, and Coates continued her desultory journalism for local papers. Her interest in Bell's manuscript continued, however. In May 1949 she wrote to Bell, apparently in response to an advance offered to her by Harper's:

Would you consider coming over here again for a month, say? I know I was upset and nervous when you were here before, and probably disagreeable; but that was because I had one idea in mind (not to let you be a household drudge) and you had another (not to let me be). But I wouldn't be embarrassed about my house this time – it's my house and my business if I want to let it look like hell – I can do your book with you but not without you. I know what you are up against – just what [Joseph Kinsey] Howard and you and I didn't want – a romantic [sic] fictionalized story interest – but we can do it if we have to – even if we have to take sex hormones to get in the mood![8]

But in September of that year, Coates wrote to Merriam:

Mrs. Bell is a fine woman. Any service I have given her, if such it was, has been free. I did re-type and correct her entire mss., and told her she now had a beginning to work on – that she had a skeleton to work from. But she is determined and headstrong, and in spite of my expressed opinion that she whould [sic] wait about submitting her mss until she had it as perfect as she knew how to make it, she let Howard send it to his publishers, and others. I advised her to stop chattering abut [sic] her book until she had one, and not to associate my name with it until I gave her permission; and on top of that prohibition appeared an item she had given the [Great Falls] Tribune, that GSC etc. was cooperating with Mrs. Bell etc. . . . She wrote me she had been in Mis-

soula, and received invaluable information, instruction and renewed enthusiasm; and I refrained from writing her that that was good, if she considered lack of enthusiasm her main deficiency.[9]

And that was that, at least for the collaboration. Peggy Bell apparently never availed herself of the invitation to spend another month in Grace Stone Coates's house, although correspondence between the two women continued sporadically until at least 1957. Coates continued to write for local newspapers until 1963, when she left Martinsdale for a nursing home in Bozeman, Montana. Childless, she had outlived her husband by many years, and her mind was fading. She died in Bozeman in 1976, forgotten and alone, and was buried without a memorial service or even an obituary notice in the newspapers. Her papers were lost or scattered.

Peggy Bell, on the other hand, never stopped trying to get her story told. Her letters and papers contain a sad litany of near misses, of publishers who might have but somehow did not make her an offer for her book. Over the years she lost the typescript of the manuscript she and Coates had labored over during the summer of 1947, so in her old age she started over. In a nursing home herself, with the help of a retired schoolteacher, she rewrote her entire memoir and added it to her massive magpie stack of letters, clippings, essays, and keepsakes. She died on 19 September 1982 at the age of ninety-four.

Thus far the story of Peggy Bell and her memoir has been about the vanity of human wishes, or at least the vanity of those humans wishing to be remembered as writers. Now it turns into a detective story.

During her later years in Martinsdale, Grace Stone Coates befriended a young woman who, like herself, had come to the small ranching community as a new bride with a college education. Lee

Rostad returned Coates's friendship by listening to her reminiscences, reading her work, visiting her in her nursing home, collecting what she could of her scattered papers, and eventually writing her biography, which also includes a number of Coates's poems.[10]

In the mid-1990s Lee received a phone call from a friend who had found a box of papers in the garage of a house he had purchased from Henderson Coates's niece Marion. Would Lee be interested in looking through the papers? Indeed Lee would; and there, among letters and other scraps of writing, she found a book-length carbon copy of a manuscript entitled "A Child Remembers" in a font she recognized as Grace Stone Coates's manual typewriter and paginated Coates – 1, Coates – 2, Coates – 3, and so on. The carbon had been used and overused to the point of transparency, making the text very hard to read, but Lee thought she might have come upon the manuscript of the novel that Coates had told Merriam she had written. She showed it to the editor who had published her biography of Coates. He told her that it wasn't the sort of project he could take on but that he knew that Mary Clearman Blew, over in Idaho, had always been interested in Grace Stone Coates, and why didn't Lee ask Mary to take a look at her find?

When Lee sent me the manuscript, I read only a few pages to be virtually certain that it had not been written by Grace Stone Coates. For one thing, it read like a memoir, but it certainly wasn't a memoir of Coates's childhood in Kansas. Also, Coates was a polished, mannered, some might even say facile writer, and this manuscript was, to say the least, awkward, with spelling and punctuation errors, repetitions, and digressions that made it sound like what it claimed to be: the narrative of an uneducated woman named Peggy Bell who had been born in Great Falls, Montana, in 1888. The bad carbon nearly drove me crazy, but, fascinated, I stayed with it to the end and realized that, whatever else, Lee had come upon a powerful and unique story.

After talking it over with Lee, I sent the manuscript to Dan Ross at the University of Nebraska Press. He had his staff perform a technological miracle by running the faint carbon pages through a scanner, which raised the print to legibility, and then submitted the manuscript to outside reviewers. In a few weeks he sent me their reports.

Both reviewers pointed out the weaknesses of "A Child Remembers," particularly when viewed as a novel. "The plot is apoplectic," wrote one. "Incidents are not developed, major changes in the family's circumstances are treated as casually as an anecdote. . . . Transitions are not clear."[11] "As a 'novel,' it is not very well written – unpolished with an abrupt and poorly developed ending," wrote the other.[12] And yet both reviewers were clearly fascinated, as I had been, with characters and details. Both were disturbed by the horrific physical, psychological, and sexual abuse that the narrator describes, and both believed that, taken as a memoir, the manuscript was impressive. "If the book can be categorized as 'nonfiction,' have a good introduction, be well-edited so that it reads smoothly, and have autobiographical connections, I think it would be an important addition to women's autobiographical writings," concluded the second reviewer. "The strength and endurance of Peggy is wonderful. Her descriptions of ranching, farming, and horses seem realistic and show a dimension of frontier life that is unrecorded."[13]

"Can you identify a historical Peggy Bell?" was Dan's question to Lee and me. I thought it sounded like the proverbial search for the needle in a haystack. Lee and I had both grown up in Montana, but neither of us had ever heard of her, and for all we knew, "Peggy Bell" was a pseudonym or a complete fiction. But Lee has not lived her life on a Montana ranch with blizzards, droughts, hail, and grasshoppers for nothing. She listened stoically over the long-distance line between Idaho and Montana as I made some halfhearted suggestions about homestead records and the records of the Catholic

Church (Peggy had written about her three years in a mission school near Okanagan, Washington, and her subsequent year as a novice in a Vancouver convent) and said she'd see what she could do. I came home a week later to hear the voice of an uncharacteristically excited Lee on my answering machine: "I've found Peggy Bell!"

Montanans are fond of saying that they all live in the same small town with one awfully long street, and Lee's discovery of Peggy Bell is a case in point. After some false starts in the State Library in Helena (she didn't know that Peggy had remarried a man named Dobin, confusing the records), Lee happened to attend a writing workshop where she ran into Cindy Kittredge, the director of the Cascade County Historical Society in Great Falls. Had Cindy, per-chance, ever heard of a Peggy Bell? Why yes, said Cindy, Peggy Bell was a very well known personality in Great Falls. She was active in the Montana Cowgirls Association, she was the grand marshal of the Bicentennial Parade, she had been inducted into the Cowboy Hall of Fame.[14] "In fact," added Cindy, "you're probably acquainted with Peggy's granddaughter, Diane Volk." And indeed, as it turned out, Lee sat on a museum board with Diane. At the next board meet-ing, she handed Diane a copy of Peggy Bell's manuscript, saying only, "You may find this interesting." Later Diane said that she had read thirty pages when suddenly it dawned on her: "My God, it's Granny!"

Lee's task would be to research Peggy Bell's life and to verify as many of the details of her memoir as she could. My task would be to edit the manuscript into readability. As it turned out, Peggy Bell had been a compulsive saver of letters, clippings, notes, and pages and pages of manuscript, all of which had ended up in the archives of the Cascade County Historical Society. In this trove, Lee found the second version of "A Child Remembers," this one entitled "When Montana and I Were Young" by Margaret Bell-Dobin, paginated

MBD. The second version contains some of the episodes of the Coates carbon and some that the Coates carbon doesn't, as well as many errors in sentence structure, punctuation, grammar, and spelling, heavily corrected in ink by, perhaps, the retired school-teacher who had visited Peggy in her nursing home and taken her turn at trying to wrestle the book into readability. Occasionally, a note indicates sentences added by typist C. M., and long sections about the cowboy artist Charles M. Russell appear to have been edited and retyped, perhaps by C. M.

After struggling with my scholarly impulses, which would have had me prepare a sort of variorum edition, with notes referring back and forth between the two versions, I reminded myself that it wasn't as though I was working with, say, the Quarto and First Folio versions of *King Lear*, so I balanced my obligation to Peggy Bell's text with my obligation to contemporary readers. Following the lead of Grace Stone Coates and C. M., I regularized spelling and punctuation, and usually I took their advice on grammar, although I winced and stayed with Peggy when I came upon a sentence that started "You would think . . ." and found that C. M. had amended it to "*One* would think." I pared out the repetition and also the material that struck me as extraneous (for example, eighty pages, mostly anec-dotal, about the life and career of Charles M. Russell). When I had to choose between one version of a story that Peggy told and another, I went with the version that sounded the least worked over and clos-est to her voice. I tightened sentences and added transitions where they seemed necessary, and I used consistent names for family members. In a very few instances I rearranged paragraphs and epi-sodes for the sake of the narrative. I used as a guideline the advice I would have given Peggy if she had been looking over my shoulder while I edited. My goal, first and foremost, was to do justice to Peggy's story by producing a readable and coherent narrative from her various versions.

What is it about Peggy Bell's memoir, I have asked myself, that has lured so many – H. G. Merriam, Joseph Kinsey Howard, Grace Stone Coates, the retired schoolteacher, C. M., and finally me – to devote hours and months to bringing it to light? Why should this story be heard?

To begin, readers will find in *When Montana and I Were Young* a unique documentation of frontier childhood in Montana and Canada during the twilight of the cattle frontier, the last of the vast unfenced northern prairie, and the beginning of the homestead movement that eventually would transform the West.

Statehood was still a year ahead for the Montana Territory when Peggy was born as Margaret Olson in Great Falls in 1888 to a cowboy and a nineteen-year-old hotel waitress. In later years she would claim to have been the first white baby born in Great Falls. Although the town had been established some fourteen years earlier, in 1888 Great Falls was still a raw village where families who wanted fresh milk kept a cow and grazed her with the town herd. One of Peggy's earliest memories had to do with chasing her family's milk cow until her legs gave out. Knowing that her stepfather would beat her for losing the cow, she despaired, but she was rescued by a young Charley Russell, who brought her and her cow home and gave her his own picket rope.

At the age of eight, after her mother's death, she was caring for three younger half-sisters and herding cattle on her stepfather's homestead in Canada, and at seventeen she was breaking horses to ride and drive on her uncle's ranch near Sand Coulee, Montana. In her memoir she describes in detail how to bridle a workhorse taller than she is, how to sharpen the sickles for a horse-drawn mowing machine, how to milk a dozen cows twice a day, how to keep a fire going in a wood stove, how to poison and skin coyotes, how to cut the feet out of a pair of hopelessly worn socks and sew them up for mittens. Ranch-raised myself, I constantly have been brought up short by the exactitude of her detail, by terminology and expressions that I thought I had forgotten.

Second, *When Montana and I Were Young* is written from a viewpoint unique among women's frontier narratives, which typically describe the landscape and the living conditions from the point of view of a cultivated newcomer – say, the point of view of Isabella Bird, Mary Hallock Foote, or Mary Austin. A good comparison in time and place with *When Montana and I Were Young* is Nannie Alderson's *A Bride Goes West*, which describes the narrator's shock and disillusionment when, as a young bride from Virginia, she came to live on a cattle ranch in eastern Montana in the 1880s. Peggy Bell, on the other hand, born a generation later than Nannie Alderson, writes not as a shocked outsider but from her own center. Born and raised on the prairie, Peggy is incurious about the world beyond her own and never yearns after a different life in a different place. Hard work is what she knows and expects; in fact, she is proud of how long and how competently she can stack hay, for example, or seed wheat. She fears coyotes in packs and the wrath of her stepfather, Hedge Wolfe, but she loves animals and open spaces, and when she daydreams, it is about escaping Hedge and owning a good horse and a ranch of her own with plenty of feed and water for her cattle. She never whines, never pities herself, never asks more than the chance to stand on her own feet without being brutalized.

To her lack of curiosity about a larger world, add her lack of interest in the abstract, as illustrated by her experience with religion. Although she lived for four years in a mission boarding school and entered a Vancouver convent as a novice, and while she writes about her respect for the nuns and her affection for some of her devout schoolmates, she has little to say about religious faith but trusts in her own common sense and experience as an outdoorswoman. Lost in the woods after a school outing, the nuns ask all the girls to pray for rescue, but Peggy and an Indian girl get their bearings, find the trail, and hike out to bring help for everyone. Similarly, she says nothing about the rituals of devotion she must have experienced in the convent but describes every piece of her novice's habit, remembers the children she cared for in the nuns' orphanage, and looks down her nose at the poor old workhorse that the nuns think will be a treat for her to ride.

Nor is she drawn to romantic passages about landscape. She lives with the familiar, not the exotic; she doesn't see dramatic sunrises or sweeping prairie vistas; she takes for granted the plant and animal life but reports on the quality of the grass for feed, the time it takes to plow and harrow and seed, the changes in the weather that will affect her and the horses and cattle she cares for. She is specific and loving but unromantic in her descriptions of livestock:

I always had one cow that was crazy about me. The last pet cow I had in Canada was a big, wild-looking dark red with a black neck and head.... Her affection had its drawbacks. Range herding in the summer, I went out with the cattle about seven o'clock in the morning, and they would graze until ten or eleven, then lie down and chew their cuds during the heat of the day. I would hurry to finish whatever mending I had with me so I could sleep. But my pet cow always figured that I needed cleaning up about that time, and she would come over and start licking me. She didn't object to my wearing clothes, but she did object to my having anything tied in my hair. Many a time when I was asleep, she got hold of my braid with those lower teeth of hers, trying to pull the string off. She would pick me up by the hair, and when I hollered, she would moo-o-o in the most consoling manner.

Above all, Peggy's is a story of survival, of growing up poor and female in a frontier world controlled by men. Her mother divorces a drunk to marry an abusive gambler who separates her and her children from her extended family, literally works her into the grave, and then inflicts unspeakable physical, emotional, and sexual abuse upon Peggy and her younger half-sisters.

The child abuse described in *When Montana and I Were Young* will linger long with readers, partly because it is so shocking, but largely because it is described in such a matter-of-fact and unadorned voice that never asks for pity. Hedge Wolfe, the stepfather, is one of the really memorable villains of western literature, a man so irresponsible and lazy and mean, and yet with more lives than a tomcat when it comes to escaping the consequences of his behavior, that we can hardly help but admire his instinct for self-preservation even as we despise him for his manipulations, his mania for control, his secretiveness to the point of not even allowing Peggy to know the date or year of her own birth. A classic abuser, at one point he moves the family practically overnight because a neighbor has asked questions.

Spare the rod and spoil the child was a saying that seemed common sense fifty or a hundred years ago, and some contemporary ideas of physical child abuse probably would have baffled Peggy Bell herself. But even allowing for changing mores and the exaggerations of recollection, Elliott West in *Growing Up in the Country* notes that enough child abuse is mentioned in frontier reminiscences and memoirs to show that it certainly was not unknown and cites Mari Sandoz's bullying father in *Old Jules* as an example.[15] Elizabeth Hampsten, in *Settlers' Children*, quotes the psychohistorian Lloyd De Mause to the effect that the history of childhood is "a nightmare from which we have only recently begun to awaken. The further back in history one goes, the lower the level of child care, and the more likely children are to be killed, abandoned, beaten, terrorized, and sexually abused."[16] In her own research, Hampsten says, she has been struck by how often the violence described by De Mause coincides with the recorded experiences of settlement children: "It is as though in personal and family relationships the settlement experience briefly leapt backwards through the centuries."[17] Linda Peavey and Ursula Smith, in *Frontier Children*, follow Hampsten in asserting that one of the strongest impressions some children retained of their home life was of beatings and overwork.[18]

It is likely, then, that the punishment and work piled on Peggy Bell were extreme but not unheard-of. But consider this description of one of the beatings inflicted by Hedge:

As soon as he had finished eating, [Hedge] told me to go out and get the bellyband off the harness. This was an extra-heavy strap, about two inches wide with no buckles, that he always used to beat me with.

I brought the strap, and he said, "Now pull off your duds, and I'll tan your hide for you."

When I got down to my undershirt, I hesitated, and he jumped up and jerked my shirt off. "So you won't mind what I tell you? Maybe you will after I get through with you this time."

He started beating me from one corner of the room to the other. Mother went into the bedroom with the little girls, who were frightened and crying, but Hedge hollered at her, "You come out here and shut that door."

Mother came. He handed her a little light strap off her valise and said, "Help me give her a good trimming."

I was covered with stripes already. I was tender-skinned, and in many places he had drawn blood. Mother hesitated, but when he roared, "What's the matter with you?" she, too, started beating me – a thing I'll never forget, even though Mother has been dead for many years.

This is not a beating in the heat of anger or one brought about by stress or alcoholism, which Elliott West suggests was the cause of much of the abuse of women and children on the frontier, but an example of sadism. It is also a sustained abuse that continued from Peggy's early childhood until her midteens, when she finally escaped. But the most intense pain here is psychological; the betrayal of the mother, forced though it may be, is what remains with Peggy all her life.

As for the sexual abuse that Peggy endures from Hedge and his brother, she herself unwittingly offers an explanation that may account for the absence of such experiences in other frontier memoirs and reminiscences. When a sympathetic neighbor woman is horrified at her bruises and scars, Peggy remembers, "I wanted to tell her there was something worse than this, but how was I going to say it? I thought of telling her that Hedge was like a bull, always chasing me, but what if she asked, 'What for?'"

Peggy has been victimized not only because she is small and female but because she lacks the very language with which to tell her story to a potential rescuer. Isolated as she has grown up, kept from contact with adult women or even with older girls, the only words she knows to describe what is being done to her are the words she has heard used to describe the breeding of livestock, but she knows they are inappropriate. She has been silenced as literally and effectively as though she had had her tongue cut out, and I would posit that her determination to possess language and to tell her story in later life came from being robbed of language as a child.

How much of *When Montana and I Were Young* is fiction?

I believe that Grace Stone Coates, working with Peggy Bell in the 1940s, made different assumptions about Peggy's text than a reader seasoned by the memoir decade of the 1990s would have made. Although Coates herself wrote from personal experience, she felt no need, in her short stories, to stick to the literal truth of "what really happened," and she apparently saw no need for Peggy to do otherwise. "I know what you are up against – just what Howard and you and I didn't want – a romantic [sic] fictionalized story interest – but we can do it if we have to – even if we have to take sex hormones to get in the mood!" she had written in May 1949.[19] This sounds very much as though Peggy was determined to write one kind of book, and Coates, thinking of the expectations for the conventional novel of the time, wanted her to write another kind of book.

Among the Bell papers is a nine-page sketch entitled "Qu'Appelle?" headed "Grace Stone Coates, Martinsdale, Montana," but with Margaret Bell's name as author, which has been adapted from an episode in *When Montana and I Were Young* and which begins, "I knew, as soon as my stepfather told Beck instead of me to climb down from the wagon, round up the cows and bring them in, that things would not turn out as he expected. I knew she would not come home with the cows, knew it clearly and strangely as a thing that already had happened." Peggy's version of the same incident is told in a matter-of-fact, "I-knew-that-was-going-to-happen" tone with prosaic details, but the sketch implies a paranormal experience linked to the historic Qu'Appelle trail and concludes, "All that evening, while we were getting supper and eating it and clearing it away, and in bed that night after Hedge had gone to take the mare and saddle and lantern back to the section house, over and over we questioned and listened, hungry for the tiniest crumbs of the adventure; until at last we drifted into sleep, a question half asked, half answered, on our lips. But all she told us seemed like something I had heard before, and forgotten."[20] "Qu'Appelle" is an interesting example of Coates's mannered style superimposed upon Peggy's text – "knew it clearly and strangely," "over and over we questioned and listened" – and gives another glimpse into the struggle between the two women for control of *When Montana and I Were Young*. Little wonder that their collaboration did not continue.

Peggy knew she was not writing a novel. She was not above stretching the literal truth for the sake of the story, but she also wanted readers to know the "truth," in a larger sense, about her childhood, and she did not want that "truth" distorted. Some of her story can be documented through historical records or corroborated by family members. Grandma Travers and Uncle Mike are real people who ranched near Sand Coulee, Montana. Hedge Wolfe is also a real person who eventually returned to Canada and settled down (although Hedge Wolfe is not his real name, and his descendants dispute the abuse that Peggy describes). We can be reasonably certain of the general outline of Peggy's life.

We can also be sure of her precise details. When Peggy describes how her dress used to tear apart at the waist when she jumped bareback on a horse, and how, after she repeatedly sewed bodice and skirt back together, her skirt got progressively shorter in front until the back hung down like a tail, we can be pretty certain that we're hearing from someone who has jumped bareback on a horse while wearing a dress. In the truly dreadful episode involving strychnine poisoning, a modern toxicologist has confirmed the accuracy of the symptoms and the description of the strychnine itself.

My personal opinion is that the romantic interest introduced toward the end of *When Montana and I Were Young* is fiction. The young men do not correspond to known individuals in Peggy's life, and their characterization is suspiciously close to the romantic suitors of conventional novels of the 1930s and 1940s, the writing for which Grace Stone Coates prescribed "sex hormones." Not everyone who has read the manuscript agrees with my assessment of Peggy's suitors, however. "Oh, they might be real!" exclaimed one reader, protesting my dash of cold water over the young men; and, of course, they might be.

On a sparkling June afternoon in 1999, Lee Rostad and I lunched with Peggy Bell's granddaughter, Diane Volk, in her home overlooking the Missouri River in Great Falls, Montana. During our discussion of her grandmother's memoir, in which Lee and I raised questions about family feelings and issues of privacy, Diane returned again and again to how much Peggy had wanted to have her story heard. "I know that Granny is up in heaven at this minute, cheering because you two have brought her book to light," Diane said, finally, "and I think Uncle Martin will feel the same way."

Martin Bell, Peggy's only surviving child, did indeed give his gracious permission for the publication of his mother's memoir, and Lee and I thank him and Diane. We also owe thanks to many other people and institutions, in particular, Cindy Kittredge and the Cascade Historical Society; the Montana Committee for the Humanities, which provided Lee with a grant to finance some of her research; Norma Ashby of Great Falls, who interviewed Peggy on her television show; Dr. Patricia A. Talcott of the University of Idaho, who provided helpful information on toxicology; Susanne George-Bloomfield of the University of Nebraska-Kearney, whose suggestions were invaluable. To this list add Phil Rostad, whom we thank for his patience; my many graduate students at the University of Idaho who have taught me so much about reading and writing memoir; and all my daughters and surrogate daughters who run in and out of my house but almost always respect my quiet time to write.

In editing *When Montana and I Were Young*, with Grace Stone Coates looking over my shoulder, as it were, I have often felt the frustration that Coates expresses in one of her letters to H. G. Merriam: "she [Peggy Bell] talks about 'cute aprons' and 'dainty fragrance' and some of her sentences are longer than Mrs. Bloom's soliloquy."[21] However, I have also shared Coates's admiration for Peggy's toughness, lack of cynicism, and determination, and I have shared H. G. Merriam's certainty, as he writes back to Coates, that "both Joe Howard and I thought there was something there that should not be dropped."[22] Lee and I are particularly grateful that the University of Nebraska Press has made it possible for Peggy's story finally to be told.

MARY CLEARMAN BLEW

Notes

1. H. G. Merriam, "Endlessly the Covered Wagon," reprinted in Steve Smith, *The Years and the Wind and the Rain: A Biography of Dorothy M. Johnson* (Missoula MT: Pictorial Histories Publishing Company, 1984), 35.

2. Margaret Bell, notes and letters regarding Evelyn Cole and her ill-fated statue of Charles M. Russell, Cascade County Historical Society, Box 1, Folder 4. "Does anyone realize that one of the entries in the statue competition is a woman?" she demands in a letter to the *Great Falls Tribune*.

3. Richard Roeder, "Grace Stone Coates, Forgotten Poet and Writer," unpublished essay, in the collection of Lee Rostad, circa 1985.

4. H. G. Merriam to Grace Stone Coates, 9 September 1934, Merriam Papers, University of Montana, Box 18, Folder 18.

5. Grace Stone Coates to H. G. Merriam, n.d., in the collection of Lee Rostad.

6. Grace Stone Coates to H. G. Merriam, 7 November 1947, in the collection of Lee Rostad.

7. Ibid.

8. Grace Stone Coates to Margaret Bell, 30 May 1949, in the collection of Lee Rostad.

9. Grace Stone Coates to H. G. Merriam, 16 September 1949, in the collection of Lee Rostad.

10. Lee Rostad, *Honey Wine and Hunger Root* (Helena MT: Falcon Press, 1985).

11. First reviewer's report, in the possession of the University of Nebraska Press.

12. Second reviewer's report, in the possession of the University of Nebraska Press.

13. Ibid.

14. Lee Rostad and I have heard repeatedly that Peggy Bell was inducted into the Cowboy Hall of Fame and that her friend Evelyn Cole traveled with her to Oklahoma City to be present for the ceremony but that one of her nieces was the only member of her family to attend. However, according to the records of the Cowboy Hall of Fame, her induction never took

place, and Peggy Bell's is not one of the names on the official wall of plaques commemorating what some have called the "Rich Western White Guys' Hall of Fame."

Among Peggy Bell's papers is an undated clipping, probably from the *Great Falls Tribune*, that reads as follows:

State Cowgirls Join National Hall of Fame

Three members of the Montana Cowgirls Association are the first modern women members of the National Cowboy Hall of Fame.

Announcement and presentation of Hall of Fame certificates were made during the association's banquet Saturday night.

Members of the Hall are Margaret Bell-Dobin, Great Falls; Elizabeth Giffin Cheney, Stanford; and Fanny Sperry Steele, Helmsville.

It was explained they have full voting privileges in the Hall, located near Oklahoma City, Okla.

All are pioneer Montana ranch people. Mrs. Dobin was born in a log cabin on the site of the present Paris store in downtown Great Falls. Mrs. Steele is a former national champion bronc rider, and Mrs. Cheney is a well known rancher.

Only other woman in the Hall of Fame is Sacajawea, the girl guide for the Lewis and Clark expedition.

It is possible that Peggy Bell herself was the source for this information. It is also possible that some confusion has arisen about "being inducted" and "being in" the Cowboy Hall of Fame, where displays are crowded with the photographs and memorabilia of the famous and not so famous. I searched unsuccessfully for Peggy Bell's picture when I visited briefly in the fall of 2000 and unsuccessfully also for the picture of my cousin Clem "Noisy" Killham, whom I have likewise heard described as "being in" the Cowboy Hall of Fame.

15. Elliott West, *Growing Up in the Country* (Albuquerque: University of New Mexico Press, 1987), 152.

16. Lloyd De Mause, "The Evolution of Childhood," *History of Childhood Quarterly, Journal of Psychohistory* 1, no. 4 (spring 1974): 503–75.

17. Elizabeth Hampsten, *Settlers' Children* (Norman: University of Oklahoma Press, 1991), 17.

18. Linda Peavey and Ursula Smith, *Frontier Children* (Norman: University of Oklahoma Press, 1999), 65.

19. Grace Stone Coates to Margaret Bell, 30 May 1949, in the collection of Lee Rostad.

20. Margaret Bell, "Qu-Appelle?" unpublished and undated short story, in the collection of Lee Rostad.

21. Grace Stone Coates to H. G. Merriam, 7 November 1947, in the collection of Lee Rostad.

22. H. G. Merriam to Grace Stone Coates, 10 November 1947, in the collection of Lee Rostad.

When Montana and I Were Young

1

I suppose my babyhood was normal up to the time my father and mother separated and she returned to her former work as a waitress.

My mother, Truleen Travers, was only sixteen when she emigrated from Ireland to New York and, in answer to an advertisement in the *Sun,* Waitresses Wanted, made the long trip from New York to the Montana Territory. The decision was easier for her, perhaps, because her older brother Mike was already in Montana, working in the gold mines in Helena.

My father, Sy Olson, was born in Norway and had come west when he was seventeen, drawn by the glitter of the gold camps. He found no gold, so he hired out as a cowhand. His first job was wrangling horses, but he was soon a full-fledged cowboy who loved his work. Horses and cattle and the range held a fascination for him, as they did for hundreds of others – as they did for me, and always will.

Mother was often embarrassed by the attention showered on her in the woman-hungry Montana Territory. One of her persistent admirers was Jerry Koiel, the tall, handsome foreman of the C Bar C spread, until one day when the dining room rush was over and Truleen had sat down in the kitchen to rest her tired feet and have a cup of tea.

She asked the cook, "I wonder why that little Indian woman has been waiting out there so long?"

"Maybe she is hungry and waiting for a handout. Here, give her this."

As he spoke, he handed Truleen a sack of scraps from the table. Mother gave him a questioning look.

"Go ahead!" he insisted. "Give it to her. Scraps are a lot better than nothing. I often give the Indians the best of the scraps. It's a hell of a lot better than going hungry."

Mother picked up the sack and went out to do as she was told. When their eyes met, the young squaw burst into tears.

Mother asked, "What's the matter? Are you sick?"

"Yes, me much sick here."

"Why? What happened to you?"

"You know him, Jerry?" the little squaw asked in a trembling voice.

"Not Jerry Koiel?"

"Yes, you see, this him papoose. Jerry, him like white squaw too much. Him no come home no more."

Mother was trembling. She took a few seconds to get control of herself. Then she nodded her head and said, "Your Jerry will go home tonight."

She took another good look at the infant, just to be sure she was not suspecting Jerry unjustly. The hungry child was now munching on a piece of roast beef and was very happy, making the resemblance even more pronounced.

When Mother returned to the kitchen, the cook asked her, "What was the little squaw trying to tell you?"

Mother was so unnerved that she was afraid to reply, so she scraped plates, making so much noise that her voice was barely audible. "She said her man doesn't come home anymore, and she is worried about him."

The cook said, "I know what she means. Now that there are a few white women coming into the territory, some white men have forced their squaws, some with big families, to go back to the reservation. It's a damn shame, because the poor kids don't feel like they belong in either camp, and they grow up trying to brazen their way through life. Many become troublemakers between the whites and the Indians, but on the other hand I know some half-breeds who are fine people, artists and painters. I also know some white men who stayed with their squaws and even sent their children to the Old Country to be educated."

The Chinese dishwasher did not talk as much as the cook, but he was much wiser. He knew Mother was the white woman involved, so he watched her closely to see if she would send Jerry away. Mother knew he was watching her, which helped to strengthen her determination. All evening she rehearsed what she was going to say to Jerry, but when she met him face to face, she blurted, "Jerry Koiel, go home to your hungry wife and child and never speak to me again," and slammed the door in his ashen face.

At a Saturday night dance some time later, Mother met the dashing happy-go-lucky young cowboy who was to become my father. She had had offers from older men, men of means. Some of them later became prominent in the state's affairs, but my father was a lad of promise and promises. He was popular, with a good singing voice, and he knew a lot of songs. He also played the mouth organ, which was an asset on those long dark nights on the fall roundup when some of the boys would request a lively tune that would help to dispel their loneliness, and some wanted a song that would bring back happy memories of home or their girlfriends. Sentimental songs were the most popular. Sometimes he would actually sing some of the boys to sleep.

Father had a poise and urbanity that was seldom found among cowboys. I have been told he acquired it by frequenting the dance halls of the frontier. Wherever he got his polish, Mother admired it. When he would come calling on her to take her out for a drive, he would hire the classiest driving team in Helena. He was no slouch on the dance floor, either. He and Mother often received compliments when dancing together. Once they won first prize at the Grand Ball on New Year's Eve.

After the spring roundup, my parents moved into the little old log house where I was born, 319 Central Avenue, Great Falls, Montana Territory. Mother worked at the Park Hotel, which gave her some advantages that many other expectant mothers did not have. When she met young Doctor A. F. Longeway at the hotel, he gave her some helpful advice and brought me into the world when the time came.

I took after my father in build and looks, also in his way of getting on the good side of animals. I got my first riding lessons when I was two years old because I was always running away, or maybe I should say toddling away. Montana's prairies were still covered with tall grass and wildflowers, and the bright-colored flowers held a great attraction for me. I never tired of picking them, but Mother was afraid that I would run into a rattlesnake in the thick grass.

Father suggested sitting me on his old saddle horse. Mother was afraid that I would go to sleep and fall off and get hurt, but I never did, although I did come very near several times. By the time I was five, I could ride well enough to bring in the milk cows, and at seven I broke my first broncos – but those years belong to the darker side of my childhood.

The days of the big cattlemen were soon over, and my father, with many other cowboys, was laid off permanently. Some of the boys took up homesteads and tried to get back into the cattle business in a small way, while other diehards, like my father, turned to gambling.

Father drove the hack for the hotel for a short time. He also worked in a livery stable, hitching and unhitching livery horses and taking care of transient trade that came in, but neither of these jobs was to his liking. I must tell you about a practice that was common in those days in Great Falls. All the hotels of any importance had a nice hack, with the hotel's name on it, that met the trains. Each driver would call out the name of the hotel he was representing and in the most courteous manner help each guest into the hack. The drivers' attire was immaculate. Being immaculate didn't bother my father, but the stiff manners the drivers were to assume was not for him. He said he felt like he was making a damn fool of himself in front of his old cowboy friends, who would often be on hand at the depot to make fun of him.

Father was given one last fling at his favorite profession when he was hired to ride on the last big roundup for one of the big spreads in this part of the country. That fall they had six weeks or more of perfect weather, and they were almost done with the roundup, but when the wind started, it blew a gale. Rain soon turned into snow as the wind shifted to the northwest. Within an hour after the wind shift, the weather turned bitter cold, with wind and snow increasing to blizzard velocity.

The cowboys tried desperately to hold the cattle, but the driving snow was making it almost impossible, while the cattle were making desperate efforts to break away and find shelter from the storm. When darkness added to the fury of the storm, the cowboys had to give up and get back to camp themselves before they were hopelessly lost. As it was, they had difficulty making it back to camp.

Nobody in camp slept much that night as they buried themselves in their blankets, thanking God for their tarps. At daybreak it was still snowing, but the wind had died down, making visibility a little better. Nobody was anxious to give up the shelter of their bedrolls, but they all knew they must when the cook hollered, "Come and get it!"

Cooks on the roundup camps of those days were a cantankerous lot, especially the good ones, who made everybody cater to their whims. This morning in particular the cook was up first as usual, and as he got ready to make breakfast for a big bunch of hungry men, he waded around in snow up to his knees. He started to cuss, first himself for taking such a job, then the weather, and next Weary Willie, his woodchopper and water boy.

He and Willie shoveled the snow away from the wagon. While the cook struggled to start a fire, Willie cut more wood and went to the spring for water, but just as he made it back to the wagon with two full pails, he tripped and fell. The cook let loose a string of cuss words that would do credit to a muleskinner: "Of all the lazy, lousy, stupid excuses of a man, you are the worst. Pick your worthless carcass up and get me that water before the damned fire goes to waste."

His profanity was so strong that some of the cowboys got up with the intention of telling him what they thought of him. But they looked around at the mounds of snow and realized that under each mound of snow was a man. In their fear that their friends might be smothered, they forgot about the cook and hurried to see if the boys under the snow were still alive. To everyone's surprise, they were.

The cook never knew how close he came to being worked over when he added, "Hell, you couldn't kill them sons of bitches with a Gatling gun."

About nine that morning the wind shifted to the southwest and started blowing the snow back in the opposite direction, creating a ground blizzard. But shortly after ten the sun came out, and the foreman, a half-breed Blackfeet, and my father headed for the breaks of the Missouri River. When they came to a steep, treacherous bank, they hated to look over it, but sure enough, there was a sizable bunch of cattle, quite a number with broken legs, humped up and shivering on a narrow strip on the far side of the river and surrounded by perpendicular rock walls.

The foreman said, "We will have to shoot anything that can't crawl out of here, but not until we get them across. How in the hell are we going to do that?"

The half-breed said, "The river is not very deep there. If they got over, we get them back."

"We could if we could get behind them, but can't you see how crowded they are, struggling to keep out of the water? That water is pretty damn cold, and that's where we'll be until we get them started across."

Their horses went slipping and sliding down the steep bank, its projecting rocks marked with hair, hide, and blood from the frightened animals that had tried to keep on their feet as they were being pushed down into the river by the herd behind them.

"Kid, your horse is good in the water, so you stay here ready to lead them across if we can get them started."

They hollered and whistled and threw rocks into the bunch, which only made the cattle crowd closer to the bank, trying to climb over one another.

My father's horse was getting enough of standing up to its belly in the icy river and was giving him a bad time and splashing water all over him. Finally, my father hollered, "Why in the hell don't you try shooting them out?"

"Because I was afraid of losing too many. But I guess that is the only thing we can do. Here we go. Fire into the rocks behind them."

A shower of rocks together with the report of the six-guns startled the wild cattle so badly that they rushed into the river. Some of the smaller animals were crowded off their feet on the boulder-covered bottom and carried away by the swift current, but all the strong stuff made it across and also made the difficult climb out of the canyon.

The cripples struggled to follow the other cattle, more cripples than the cowboys had shells to shoot them with.

The foreman said, "I think we should try to cut their throats by shooting for their jugular veins, otherwise it might take a half a dozen bullets of this caliber to finish one off."

Father said, "Hold my horse, and I'll see if I can't scare some of the strongest of the bunch. Once they lose their footing, they will roll right back down into the river."

Still, a few landed on a small strip of sandbar.

"Now let's do our best shooting and get out of this hellhole," the foreman said, and soon the old Missouri was running red as one animal after another in its death struggle pushed into the water and was carried downstream to be snagged somewhere where the Missouri widened and was shallow in the fall of the year.

After all the fall work was done, the cowboys always rode into town to celebrate. This fall they felt that they had a better reason than ever for wanting to drown their troubles in bourbon. The C Bar C, like many other spreads, was being forced out of business for lack of range and water. It was a gloomy bunch that headed for town that day, but after a few drinks the world must have looked a little brighter to them. My father didn't drink, but he enjoyed a good time and stayed with the boys until train time.

In our young little town, the novelty of meeting the passenger train had not yet worn off. Fifty-four cowboys joined the regular crowd at the depot that day, most of them noisy. The biggest puncher of the bunch was called Tiny. He always rode a good-sized Morgan horse, which he was very proud of. He rode up beside the engine and sized it up.

When the engineer came out of the depot, ready to pull out, Tiny said, referring to the engine, "It looks like you have a pretty damn good horse there, but I'll bet you the drinks for the boys that my horse Sandy here can beat yours to that tarpaper shack up ahead."

The engineer took a minute or so to take in the situation and then said, "Young fellow, I don't want to disillusion you, because you evidently don't know much about my horse."

"You are right about that, but you know nothing about my horse, and I am ready to prove that to you," Tiny insisted.

8

"You don't mean to tell me that you would risk your neck racing a train over that rough prairie just for a drink of whiskey?"

"It's not rough for a surefooted horse like this. Let's go."

The big chestnut, Sandy, seemed to know that their honor was at stake. He made good his owner's boast with enough time to spare for Tiny to swing around and throw his lasso over the engine's smokestack. All the other cowboys raced along on the other side of the train to be on hand when the engineer stepped down to pay his bet and congratulate both the rider and the horse. The train pulled out with a fifty-four-gun salute and many waving passengers.

As Father glimpsed a group of passengers going into the hotel, he thought of Mother and their baby and rode up alongside the foreman and said, "Put my horse in the barn. It's about time I went up to see my wife."

As he made his way home, he tried to get a rough count on how much money he had spent in such a short time and was surprised at the total. But Mother was not so angry about the money he had spent as hurt that he had spent several hours in town before he came to see her.

"After almost two months, I expected you would rush up here to see us, first thing."

"Under ordinary circumstances I would, but we ran into a hell of a lot of bad luck and needed a few drinks to forget and try to get back to normal."

"Did all this bad luck happen after you came into town?" she inquired, sarcastically.

"Oh no! You must have had some of that snowstorm that all but put the finishing touch to the cattle business!"

"Yes, that storm was a bad one. I was wondering if you had to get out in it."

"We were out in every bit of it, and we had one hell of a time."

This was the last celebration my father's outfit had together, and there was much forced laughter that tried to hide an aching heart, knowing that the life they loved was over and they would have to adjust themselves to a new way of life.

Adjusting seemed to be the order of the times. Fort Benton, the great distribution center, the head of navigation for the vast Montana Territory as well as Canada, was fast losing out to the incoming railroads, which in turn were putting the big freighting outfits out of business. Most of the freighters had met the riverboats at Fort Benton and picked up the freight and hauled it overland by horse and wagon to the various towns in the Territory and Canada, and when the freighters went out of business, there was no longer much demand for horses. As a result, the two horse ranches south of Great Falls went out of business. Tom Carter owned one, and old Major Fields owned the other.

Father went to work for a short time breaking horses for the owner of a livery stable who was doing a big business locating homesteaders. During the winter when work was slack, Father was often told to help the livery stable boys clean the stable and haul hay when it was needed. This kind of work irked Father, because after all he was a full-fledged cowboy who had served his apprenticeship a long time ago. When spring came, he was off looking for a riding job of any kind.

He found a job once in a while, breaking a horse or two for a rancher or maybe just taking the rough off some old horses who needed breaking again after a rest, but these jobs barely kept him in spending money. He never had any money to give Mother and often stayed away from home for that reason. To make a long story short, he turned to gambling. In the saloon atmosphere, he began to drift lower and lower, morally and financially, until Mother could no longer stand the embarrassing gossip that came to her almost every day. She finally divorced him and accepted full responsibility for my care and support.

He led a life of indolence after they separated, sometimes driving a hotel hack to pay for his room rent but never working steadily. He never married again. All these things I must have learned through hearing my mother and grandmother and uncle talk of him. I have no baby memories of him. By the time I met him again, I was older than my mother had been when she married him. Like my mother, I was fascinated by his love of good horses, his charming attentions, and his ample assurances; and like her, I lived to wish my first impressions of him had been true.

Knowing how gentle and timid my mother was, I have often wondered why she stayed in the West after her first experiences. Almost the day of her arrival, she saw two men kill each other. She and another waitress had gone to the store to buy muslin for aprons. As they passed a saloon, the door burst open, and two men rushed out, shooting. Both fell. Other men came rushing up, and the two girls, too frightened to move, stood clutching each other.

Blood was spurting from a wound in one man's throat. Someone bent over him to stanch the flow with a handkerchief. The cloth was drenched in a moment, and Mother tore open her parcel and offered her muslin. The man held it over the wound a moment or two, then rose gravely and handed the bloodstained cloth back to her. "We don't need it anymore, Ma'am, thank you."

Automatically, Mother took the muslin, and the girls hurried away. They shrank from carrying the cloth, yet they didn't want to drop it on the public road, so they took it to the hotel to burn it. The cook laughed at them. "That's good American blood," he told them. "It makes it all the better. Give it to me, I can use it for a dishrag."

Mother was horrified and dropped the cloth in the stove. She said it burned with a strange odor she would never forget.

2

I don't know how much later Mother met Hedge Wolfe, a sturdy young Canadian wrestler who was causing quite a sensation in our little town by betting any man fifty dollars that he couldn't give him a hold and then throw him on his back. Hedge was so quick and experienced that he seldom lost to anybody.

My earliest recollections of him are a blur, but of one of his visits I am sure. It was my first awareness of the man who became my stepfather. Mother was still working and living in the Park Hotel, and she had bathed me. I even remember the glycerin soap that she used because it looked transparent and so much like candy that I tasted it. I was standing on a chair in front of the mirror while Mother dressed me and combed my hair, and I was completely happy.

There was a rap on the door. Mother opened it, and a stranger entered.

Mother turned from me to him. She seemed to be very happy. The stranger came nearer. I tugged at Mother to make her turn back to me and got a stern scowl from the invader. I stamped my foot at him, which seemed to aggravate him more. His scowl frightened me, and I stood staring over my mother's shoulder with jealous resentment, while his pale cold eyes looked into mine with malice.

Mother continued to work at the Park Hotel until shortly before my first little half-sister, Beck, was born. From then on her life would be just a series of moves. But she was deeply in love with Hedge and completely in his power until her death at age twenty-eight, when my third half-sister, Rose, was still a baby. It is one of the unsolved mysteries of my life how she could have loved such a man.

Shortly after marrying Hedge, Mother used her little savings to buy a gentle team of horses, a buckboard, and a set of double harness. She didn't have enough money to pay for it all, but the man she bought everything from knew her well and let her debt go on Jaw Bone, as they used to say. Hedge promptly decided to take the team and make a trip back across the Line, as going to Canada was called in those days. He told her he would make some money boxing or wrestling. By this time Mother was expecting a baby and begged him not to go, but he promised to be back soon. She waited and waited for him to at least write a letter, but none came.

Finally, Mother sent a train ticket to her mother, who had just arrived in New York from Ireland. When Mother explained her circumstances, Grandma Travers lost no time, and both she and the new baby arrived before Hedge did.

I liked my grandmother from the start. She had more time to talk to me than the chambermaids in the hotel did, and she taught me the words to songs I loved to sing. She took me everywhere with her. I just loved her and still do, although it's years since she left us, God bless her.

Grandma Travers was very handy at making anything in the clothing line and soon had readied all the baby clothes that Mother needed. She also did sewing for other people and washed and ironed men's white shirts. She was kept very busy until a Chinese laundryman came to town and charged less than she and other women did. Grandma didn't lose as many customers as some, because the hotel let her do her laundry with theirs, but some poor women had only a bucket or a wash basin to do their washing in, so they couldn't get the white shirts very white. They were the ones who lost their business to the Chinese.

I can still hear her chuckling as she told of her first brush with the strange customs of the West.

Her trunk had not arrived as soon as she expected, so she made several trips to inquire at the depot, which at that time was in west

Great Falls. The first time she went, she could not find the depot, so she made her way to a boxcar where a man was busy with a handful of waybills and asked, "Will you please, sir, tell me where the depot is?"

"Yes, Ma'am!" the agent answered politely. "You're in it."

But the trunk had not arrived, and it did not arrive until Grandma had made several trips and become well acquainted with the depot agent. On her last trip, she took me along. There were not many children in Great Falls at that time, and the agent was surprised. He asked, "Where did you get the kid?"

Now Grandma was surprised and looked around to see a kid before she replied, "My good man, I have no kid, nor have I seen one since I came west."

Pointing to me, he asked, "What is that?"

"Sure and you don't mean the child?"

"Yes, we call them kids, or papooses, if they happen to be on the darker side."

With a deep sigh Grandma admitted, "We are never too old to learn."

"That's what the Chink found out."

"Pray tell me, what is a Chink?"

"The kind of person you won't see around here anymore. We loaded the only one we had on a raft without any oars and sent him down the river."

"Did he drown?"

"Well, that I couldn't say for sure, but we never saw him again, and the raft went over the falls."

"Why did you do such a terrible thing to the man?"

"His laundry prices were putting the women out of business, bless their hearts, and we wouldn't stand for it. We wanted to make them happy."

Grandma had her own ideas about drowning a man because his

14

prices were cheaper than anyone else's, but she was discreet. "A body has to be very careful what he does around here" was all she said.

"You bet they do," the agent continued. "I've seen plenty of white men bite the dirt."

That was another expression new to Grandma. "I never heard of anybody biting dirt," she said.

The agent grinned. "Oh, that's just a way of saying he cashed in his checks, or died. We have no jails out here, and wouldn't be bothered herding criminals anyway. We give 'em a quick trial, and if they're guilty, we banish them or hang them, and no fooling with them. That's why we are all good people here."

"It wouldn't pay to be otherwise," was Grandma's cautious reply as she bade the agent good-bye.

As soon as we got home, Grandma asked Mother if the Chink really drowned.

Mother said, "No, he didn't. Your son Mike happened to be standing on the riverbank. It was just getting dark, but Mike said he heard the splash when the Chink dove off the raft into the river and swam to the opposite shore, and he saw his outline when he climbed up the bank, so don't let that worry you, Mother."

(In fact, the Chinese had gotten ashore and run to one of the city offices that was still open and got some dry clothes. Then he walked all the way back to Helena, where he came from. It's not surprising that few Chinese came to Great Falls for years after that.)

"Tell me, my child," Grandma asked, "did your brother Mike ever take a hand in such terrible things?"

"That question I cannot answer, because Mike, like most of the men who have tried to make this country livable, seldom discusses these things. One reason is because sometimes you don't know who the enemy of the law is."

"I suppose that is true."

"What if you had been here when the road agents were terrorizing the whole country, and one of your relatives had been murdered and robbed, and nothing was done about it! I think the vigilantes, who made the first cleanup around Virginia City, were *heroes*! Imagine the courage it took to track down that organized gang of outlaws in thirty- and forty-below-zero weather! Of course, the road agents scattered as soon as they knew the vigilantes were after them, but the vigilantes kept on until they caught and hanged all the ringleaders."

Grandma had not met her new son-in-law, because he was up north across the Line. No one knew why he had gone, not even Mother, but she assumed he was on a business deal of some kind. "You won't lose any money on your team," Hedge had kept reassuring her, so she expected him to come back with plenty of money, or at least enough to take care of the family until she was on her feet and working again.

I was so happy with just Mother, Grandma, and the baby that I didn't see why Mother wanted Hedge to come back. As far as I was concerned, he could stay in Canada. Grandma had her doubts about him. As soon as Mother could do for herself, Grandma looked for ways of earning money. Besides sewing and washing men's shirts, she took care of another confinement case and made a complete layette for another expectant mother. She was very handy with her needle, doing all this work by hand, even to making a wedding dress. She was thrifty, too. She would take old dresses of Mother's and quilt two worn-out skirts together into a petticoat for me.

Hedge must have come home broke when he finally did arrive. He was in an ugly mood, more surly than ever, and angry because Grandma was with us. It was Grandma's first experience with Hedge, and she never got over it. She and Uncle Mike talked afterward, how Hedge treated Mother so harshly that she was afraid to ask for the money she needed. Then he would make her so miserable that she would be quick to give him money when he asked for it to get back in his good graces.

The evening he came home, I made a mad dash for the door with one arm in my coat, but Grandma called me back and said, "I want to see if the stage brought us a letter from your uncle Mike. He's coming to see us and get your grandma a homestead of her own. Now get your bonnet and don't run down the stairs. You might fall and get hurt."

Once outside I was a child again, bouncing all over the rough boardwalk and giving Grandma a bad time, as she wanted me to walk like a little lady and not ask so many questions.

When we came back, we could hear Hedge finding fault with Grandma living with us. Hedge always referred to Grandma as "the old woman," and he implied that Mother was feeding her, when the fact was that Grandma often helped us out with groceries. (He called me Spindleshanks, because I was so thin.)

That evening Mother and Grandma talked things over. Mother explained that a hotel was no place to raise children, especially now that her husband was home, but that she could keep working at the Park Hotel if Grandma would stay with the children. So the next week Grandma went house hunting. All she could find was a three-room shack across the river, close to the toll bridge. It would be inconvenient for Mother to get to work. She would worry about me, and paying a twenty-five-cent toll twice a day would be expensive, but she and Grandma were forced to take whatever they could find. The former tenants had made and left a boat, and Mother thought she could use it to cross the river and save the toll part of the time.

The tenants had also left a lonesome little water spaniel, and he almost turned himself inside out for joy when we came. Grandma told me that I was all for renting the house just to get back to the dog and that I could hardly go to sleep that night wondering whether the dog would be there when we got back.

Mother had to borrow the money to pay the rent. That meant she must go back to work whether she was able to or not. She also had to buy a cookstove and a few bare necessities. She never had trouble getting credit, but she always had to work and pay for everything herself.

Grandma scrubbed the shack spick and span and had us moved into it before dark. I had a fine time playing with the friendly little spaniel, and he paid for his keep by herding me away from the river.

Hedge came home before long, without any money, but this time he didn't come alone. He brought his nephew Pete, just down from Canada. Pete was the only man I ever saw Hedge get the least bit friendly with. They used to play checkers on a homemade bench that had been in the house before we moved in. Grandma had scrubbed it nice and white, and Pete drew a checkerboard right in the middle of it, and Hedge got Mother's button can and sorted out the black and white buttons. They sat and played checkers by the hour until they got tired or hungry. Then Hedge would ask Grandma what she had in the house to eat. Grandma always laid down her sewing and prepared something for them, although she had to grit her teeth to keep from telling them to get out and earn something.

I never heard my mother and grandmother say a good word about Pete, but I liked him. He was good to me and could do what nobody else could. If I could find him an old newspaper, he would fold it up and then, with his fingernails, make me dolls and horses and such. He never used scissors. He would look out of the window and say, "Get me some paper, and I'll make that lady carrying water from the river," or he'd make a long string of Indians crossing the Missouri on horseback, looking just like the horses did when they were swimming and then came out all dripping wet and shaggy-looking.

In a small community like ours, everyone knew everybody else's business. Mother had to stand the cracks they made about her husband, how lazy he was, how he gambled away every cent he could get his hands on, and what a fool she was to put up with him. They nicknamed him the "Canadian Maverick." Any man who really wanted to work could always get a job, if nothing else as a brakeman on the railroad. Many a good man swallowed his pride and went to work on the railroad until he could find something better, but not Hedge.

Hedge had sold Mother's gentle little team while he was in Canada and spent or gambled away the money. But still she gave him ten dollars so he could go to look for work in Sand Coulee. Jim Hill owned the coal mines in Sand Coulee at that time, and the little coal camp was booming, with gambling wide open and money flowing like water through the saloons on payday. Hedge knew this, which was why he was so anxious to get there.

About this time Mother's brother Mike came from Helena to visit us. He happened to arrive while Grandma was alone with us children, so she had a chance to unburden her fears about Mother's failing health and her worthless husband.

Uncle Mike was furious and said so, with much profanity.

"Mike, Mike, where did you learn such foul language? You never swore in the old country!"

Mike was too upset to worry about his language. He kept on muttering, "The dirty, lazy son of a bitch. I'll show him he can't treat my sister that way, not while I'm around! What the hell is the matter with her? Has she lost her mind?"

Grandma sighed. "Everybody in town can see what Hedge is but her."

Uncle Mike wanted to start right out looking for Hedge, but Grandma persuaded him to wait until Mother came home. That only made it worse, because Uncle Mike was shocked by her frail condition and the change in her appearance. Mother tried to cover up for Hedge, saying that her weakness was due to her recent confinement and that she would be herself in a short time. She would do anything rather than have unpleasantness between her husband and her brother.

They waited for some time after supper that night, but Hedge didn't show up. Mother went to bed, but Grandma and Uncle Mike waited until two o'clock in the morning. Finally, Uncle Mike couldn't stand it any longer and said to Grandma, "Mother, I'm going out and find that son of a so-and-so. It will be better that we have our meeting away from the house, because I don't intend to handle him with kid gloves."

Grandma tried to talk him into going to bed and dealing with Hedge in the morning, but he was too angry to sleep. He went looking for Hedge and made the rounds of almost all the saloons before he located him at a faro bank table with several hundred dollars in front of him. That made Mike change his plans in a hurry. He had intended to tell Hedge just what he thought of him and work him over with his fists, but now he decided to get the money instead.

He drew his revolver and very quietly stepped up behind his brother-in-law, pressing the weapon against his ribs. "Hedge, I am taking this money to your family, which you have so shamefully neglected."

As he spoke, he scooped up the money with his other hand, filling his overcoat pockets. Hedge never moved but turned pale as he always did when he was angry – unlike Uncle Mike, whose face got red when he was in a rage. To everyone's surprise, Hedge never went for his gun. Instead, he just dug up some more money and went on with the game.

The green cowboys who had lost the money roared with laughter. One of the boys said, "That kind of a gamble calls for a drink."

Hedge paid no attention until the young fellow said, "You there, the big loser, I thought you might need a drink."

"I don't drink," Hedge replied.

That short answer didn't sit well with the cowboy, who said, "I don't mind a man beating me in a card game, but when he refuses to drink with me, I've got no use for him."

"I told you I don't drink," Hedge said. And it was the truth. He never drank as long as I knew him, not even tea or coffee.

An old half-breed in the game who still had hopes of winning said, "Come on, it's your play. Good whiskey won't go to waste while I'm around." With that, he reached over and drained Hedge's glass with one gulp.

Mother had gotten out of bed when Mike left, and she and Grandma had another cup of tea while they sat by the fire, worrying and speculating. At last, they heard somebody coming. Grandma opened the door, and there stood Mike, all smiles.

"Come in, my son! Did you find him?"

"You can bet your bottom dollar I did."

Mother, worried about Hedge, asked, "What happened? Did you have any trouble?"

"I sure as hell didn't, and this is what I relieved him of." Uncle Mike began emptying his pockets on the kitchen table while both women watched in amazement.

Finally, Mother asked, "Mike, did he have all that money on him?"

"You're damned right he did, every cent of it and more. After I took this, he pulled more money out of his pocket and kept on playing."

To Grandma's practical mind, this was gratifying. Now they could put in their winter's supply of grub and fuel without skimping or weighing every precious dollar before it was spent. But

Mother's worries increased. What would the aftermath be? She knew Hedge would not let go of all that money without a fight.

Uncle Mike wasn't taking any chances on keeping the money in cash. He knew Hedge would eventually get it back if it was left in Mother's hands, so while he was stacking the double eagles he said, "We will go across the river and pay any bills that you owe. Then we'll put in a winter's supply of grub. Have you got any coal left?"

"No," said Grandma. "I've been gathering driftwood, but it's getting scarce. We'll need coal to hold a fire when cold weather comes."

Mother began to cry. "Mike, please, first thing, give Mother the fifty dollars she loaned me. She's been doing everything around here, all the work and the sewing – she ought to be paid for that, too."

Grandma spoke up and said, "Get your groceries first. I don't need it yet."

"Yes, you do. You need overshoes so bad. I felt sorry to see you coming in with your feet all mud and wet every time you have to go to the river for water and wood. Give her the money, Mike."

Nobody slept much that eventful night, what with counting and recounting the money, which amounted to something over five hundred dollars (I have forgotten the exact amount, although I have a very good memory, and even now I can remember things that I wish I could forget), and worrying that Hedge might show up any minute, although as it turned out, Hedge didn't come home again until Mike had gone back to Helena. But the next morning Pete dropped in, just in time for breakfast as usual, pretending to be looking for Hedge.

Mother invited him to sit up to the table and eat breakfast with us. Then she asked if he would stay and mind the baby while we went to town. Pete was always more than willing to mind us kids when Mother and Grandma were both working in the Park Hotel, and he agreed. But I got to go on that never-to-be-forgotten shopping trip because I needed shoes, and Uncle Mike, who liked kids, insisted on taking me along. He also wanted Mother to see a doctor, but she promised him she would do that on payday.

Grandma always said she thought that five hundred dollars prolonged Mother's life. And every time I hear the story about Cinderella, it makes me think of that shopping trip. What a day that was! I think even Mother forgot her troubles while they bought yards and more yards of calico and outing flannel for Grandma to make dresses and nightgowns and petticoats for us all. (She made our underwaists and panties out of flour sacks. Flour came in fifty-pound sacks and hundred-pound sacks in those days. Only salt came in small sacks, like they have today.) They bought blankets, stockings and socks, a few face towels, oatmeal by the hundred pounds, I think five hundred pounds of flour, fifty pounds of navy beans, a box of dried apples, and a case of Eagle Brand condensed milk. (That was supposed to be for the baby, but I took a taste every chance I got.) Another thing I liked was the case of tomatoes. I sure liked canned tomatoes. They got ham, bacon, a slab of salt pork (more often called sowbelly), sugar, a wooden pail of jelly that looked much prettier than it tasted, laundry soap, salt, and a keg of syrup. The keg was tin-covered, with a thin layer of wood to keep the tin from wearing out when the keg was jostled about in the freight wagons. It must have been a good-sized keg, because it lasted us a long time. When we finally got to the bottom of it, we found a dead mouse.

I mustn't forget to tell how Hedge reacted to the holdup. He came home later and never mentioned it, just sat down to the supper table and ate a hearty meal like the rest of us. So all of Mother's worries were for nothing.

Hedge got a job hauling coal for Sam Dean, who had a little mine near Sand Coulee. Sam said that Hedge could use one of his big wagons, and Hedge bought a team of old plugs to do the job until he could afford a good heavy team.

Making those old plugs do a job turned out to be easier said than done. They were never able to pull a load of coal up Graveyard Hill. Sometimes other coal haulers would stop and give Hedge a pull up to the top. If they didn't, he would have to unload half his load and pull it up the hill, then go back down for the other half. If the road was dry, he might have easy going until he got to the Gibson Flats, where he often got stuck, or to the Sand Hills, where the road this side of the cemetery was often tough going. He was so disgusted with his team that he would knock hell out of them every time another hauler passed him.

He knew he couldn't make money without a good team. He tried to trade off the old plugs, but nobody wanted such worn-out old horses. Finally, a man who owned a livery stable and furnished horses to homesteaders offered him a heavy team of geldings. They were not well matched; one was short and chunky and the other rangy. The bill of sale said nine and ten years old, broke to work double, branded JC and JU on the shoulder, but it didn't mention dependability or gentleness, because these horses had been in several runaways and were looking for a chance to run away again. Any excuse, they were off. Dashing through the streets, kicking, trying to free themselves from the wagon until it upset or snagged. (Once a horse experiences the excitement of running, he will always try it again. Even if he is hurt in a runaway, he will still run again and again, endangering lives and often breaking up the wagon and the harness.)

Uncle Mike had already filed on land, and now he was worried about somebody jumping his homestead. He had neglected it, and the deep grass grown up around his shack proved that nobody had lived there for a long time. So he quit his job in Helena and came over to live on his homestead and get the patent to it. Grandma was delighted when he surprised us with a visit. He hired a livery rig to drive her out and show her his land and also a homestead site adjoining his. Grandma was so eager to file on it that she could scarcely wait until the land office opened the next morning.

After showing Grandma her land, Uncle Mike drove her to his tarpaper shack, the only improvement he had made on his homestead. Grandma was not easily frightened, but she was surprised by the numerous rats and mice that scurried for cover when Grandma and Mike opened the door of that shack. Excelsior from the mattress and flocking from the two old sougans littered the floor. (Sougans were cheap comforters, much in use in those days. They were too short to cover a man's feet, and it was said that they drove men crazy, struggling night after night to cover their feet.)

Uncle Mike exclaimed, "Well, I'll be damned. Who would expect such destruction from such little sons of bitches!"

"It's too bad. All your bedding is done for," Grandma said, "but I can make you better quilts out of some old blankets I have. I'll get some good muslin to cover them with, and they will last you for years if you don't let the mice get into them."

"For Christ's sake, Mother, make them longer than those damned old sougans. I had to wear my woolen socks to keep my feet warm."

"I know how long they should be, son. You won't have any trouble with my quilts. But please don't take the name of the good Lord in vain. Son, have you forgotten your religion?"

"Hell, no! I have more respect for religion now than I ever had, but I can also see what a lot of people are doing under the guise of religion."

"I'd like to get in and clean this place up."

"No, Mother, not now. It's too windy to burn that trash, even with little patches of snow on the ground. A prairie fire would burn like hell in this tall dry grass, and the stockmen would run us out of the country if we burned up their pasture. You must always be careful about putting out hot ashes."

"That I will, because I am not wanting to make any enemies with our neighbors, but pray tell me, where are our neighbors?"

"Oh, yes, we have neighbors on both sides of us. Tom Carter's horse ranch is just a mile or so over that hill, and old Major Fields has quite a spread two or three miles over that way."

"How do you know where anything is out here, when there isn't a road or a signpost to guide you?" Grandma asked.

"There are corner stones. Come on, we'll drive over and I'll show you our corner stones."

"I saw a lot of stones as we drove out here, so how would you know which is which?"

"The corner stones are in a big pile, and they have a large N pointing toward the north, S to the south, E on the east side, and W chiseled on the west. This is a section corner, so the stone has been well marked. My land is in Section 28, Township 19, Range 4 East. Will you remember that?"

Grandma was still dubious. "Yes, I can learn that much, but I am not sure that I could find this rock again."

"You will learn the lay of the land like we all do. You see that big butte over there? Don't forget that, because that butte will help you get your bearings if you should get lost. It's higher than the surrounding hills. Why, you can see the lights in Great Falls from that butte. It's called Red Butte because it's red at the far end. That little creek is also on my land."

"Is there any water on my place?"

"No, and that is why it hasn't been taken up before. We will have to carry water from my place to yours until you get it improved. Then we can move your shack down beside mine and have two rooms."

26

"I have to have a shack, too?"

"You sure as hell do, and what's more, you will have to live in it. We can save the ashes from my stove and haul them up to your place, because the inspectors always look around to see how much ashes you have. It gives them an idea how often you built a fire. I'll have to get you a load of coal from Sand Coulee."

"How far is Sand Coulee from here?"

"Only about four miles, over that way."

"That's good, only four miles. I can walk that like nothing," Grandma replied, looking more cheerful.

"I'll pick up an old buckboard and a gentle horse, and you won't need to walk. You can drive me to work if I get on in the mine," Uncle Mike assured her.

"We will have to build a little yard around the house to keep the horses and cows out of my garden, because I'll have to have a garden."

"Yes, Mother, we will have to put up a little fence. I think I'll make it big enough for a pasture for my saddle horse, because a saddle horse is a necessity on a homestead."

"Son, the land is free, but I can see where it will take a lot of money and hard work before we have it in livable shape."

"I know that, Mother. That's why I am so glad that you came out West. I will go as far as I can with the money I have, and then I'll go to work in the mine. With you here to look after the ranch, we will be able to make a go of it, don't you think?"

"Of course we will. I am not doubting that we can make it pay, but it will take time," Grandma answered.

"You bet your bottom dollar we will. That's the way I want to hear you talk, Mother."

As they drove back to town, Uncle Mike made plans to buy horses, a wagon, and even barbed wire, while Grandma made plans to buy a cow or maybe two so they would always have milk and butter and cottage cheese.

"I hope there will be a wee bit of lumber left over after my little house is finished," she said, "to build me a little henhouse. I must have a few hens. There is nothing so profitable as a hen. There's lots of room for them, not like it was in Ireland, where they begrudged the ground to keep a few hens."

Uncle Mike had herded horses for Major Fields for a couple of summers while he was building his homestead shack and supposed to be living in it, and he told Grandma about a time when he was riding Brownie and night herding for Major Fields. He had run the horses into a box canyon to keep them together so he could get a little sleep. But when the horses started into the canyon, all at once they turned and rushed back like they had been shot at.

"Brownie did not stampede along with the other horses. She just stood still, trembling but waiting for me to tell her what I wanted to do. But when I gave her the word, she was off in a flash.

"I wondered what was in there that scared the horses, so the next day I rode over to see. At the entrance of the canyon there was a fair-sized rocky knoll, and it was literally covered with rattlesnakes. I stood and lambasted them with rocks until my arm got tired. I knew I was wasting my time. I may have killed a few and hurt some of them, but after an hour or so of hurling good-sized rocks on them, there seemed to be as many as ever. I had been expecting to see a bear or bear tracks, because horses act like that if they come upon a bear."

Uncle Mike had been out West a long time before any of the rest of his family, and they expected him to be "in the know" about all the ways of the West. But old Brownie had proved that he still had some things to learn.

Another time, the horse herd started to run off their range during a rainstorm, so Uncle Mike hurried to head them off. Just about the time he was riding full speed on old Brownie, they came to a prairie dog town. Of course it was full of holes, and Brownie did her best to keep up speed and still miss the holes. Her dodging almost unseated her amateur rider several times. Finally, she stepped in a hole and went down, throwing Uncle Mike several feet. Brownie was instantly on her feet and ready to go, but Uncle Mike had been knocked out and never knew how long he lay there among the hundreds of prairie dogs, barking furiously to try to scare him out of their town.

When Uncle Mike finally woke up with a big headache, at first he couldn't figure out how he got to such a place. He looked around for his horse, but Brownie had left the dog town, where there is never any grass, and was grazing as best she could with her bridle on. It took him a couple of tries to get on his feet and walk over to her. The horse herd was nowhere in sight. Where had they gone? Maybe Brownie would give him the clue if he let her have her head? Sure enough, she took him straight to the lost horses.

Another surprise Mike got was during a chilly night of rain. He had had a bright idea. He knew where there was a homestead shack not far away, so he headed the horses in that direction where they could graze while it was still daylight. He went in the shack and brushed the cobwebs off the straw-filled bunk, figuring he could at least be out of the wind and rain and maybe get a few winks of sleep. By that time it was too dark to see what condition the shack was in. Its roof didn't leak, but it had no floor, only dirt.

Not being an experienced rider, he was tired out. He soon fell asleep but was awakened by what he said was the damnedest racket. He struck a match to see what it was but saw nothing, so he supposed he must have been dreaming. Again he fell asleep. Again he heard the racket and lit a match. This time he noticed that his spurs and boots had been dragged across the room to a hole dug by packrats, which were fighting over his spurs. Mike got up and hung his spurs out of reach and tried to go back to sleep, but the best he could do was get a little rest out of the rain.

I learned a lot about Montana by listening to Uncle Mike telling Grandma about his experiences. He only stayed on the horse-herding job until he got a few dollars ahead, and then he went to Helena, where there was easier money to be made.

But now that he was homesteading and in need of a good, dependable horse, he went to Major Fields to buy old Brownie from him. He also bought a black gelding to make a team. He rode Brownie and led the gelding, Pete, back to town, where he bought a used Adam Fisher lumber wagon and a set of harness. He lost no time hooking up his team, but to his surprise and consternation, old Brownie wouldn't tighten her tugs. Despite all Uncle Mike's coaxing, urging, and finally cussing and much line slapping, nothing would make Brownie move out of her tracks, although she was trembling with fear and bewilderment. Finally, an old cowboy came to the rescue and said, "What in hell are you trying to do? Can't you see this is an old saddle mare? Put your saddle on her, and I'll guarantee she will pull your damn outfit all over the place, but she won't pull the hat off your head with a harness."

While Uncle Mike listened in amazement, the cowboy continued. "You don't understand these old saddle horses of ours. They have graduated from the best horse colleges in this country. They have won the highest honors of their profession, and they know more than a lot of their riders do. They are disgraced when hooked up to an old lumber wagon. I have spoken for old Brownie because I know she would rather die than live in disgrace."

Uncle Mike learned that the cowboy was right. Old Brownie never did work for anybody in a harness. Uncle Mike used her for a saddle horse and rode her back and forth to work in the mine. He had to buy another horse for his team.

Uncle Mike kept all his old horses until they died.

Uncle Mike advised Mother to save her money while she had a chance so she would have it if she got sick and couldn't work any longer. To guard against giving her money to Hedge, she asked her boss only to give her what she needed at the end of every month so she could save the rest. And not long after that, early in the summer of the following year she was offered a much better paying job at the new Broadwater Hotel in Helena.

She loved the beautiful new hotel and also its picturesque surroundings, but the work was harder, because the dining room was bigger, and there were more parties. She stood it as long as she was able and then asked for a short time off to rest. Meanwhile, Hedge had gone to Sand Coulee to work in the mines, and before he had drawn his first month's pay he was clamoring for Mother to quit her job and come to live with him. Mother wasn't keen on the idea, but she finally told him she would come if he found her a house to live in.

Hedge wasn't fussy about what kind of a house he lived in, and Mother had a rude awakening when she saw her new home. It was a dugout, and not even a good dugout, which has its advantages – cool in summer and warm in winter. This one was just a hole in a hillside, not even walled up, and as dirty as it could be. The only window was a little one in the door, not even glazed. Mother told Uncle Mike not to unload the furniture, just leave it on the wagon until she found a place to live.

When Hedge came in from the mine, he flew into a rage because Mother wouldn't move into the dugout, but for once she didn't weaken. The next day she went looking for a house. All she could find for sale was a boardinghouse, so she bought it.

Grandma was dead against it. She said Mother could never stand the tough grind of a boardinghouse. But although she was pregnant again and in such poor health, Mother did well. The mines were working full blast, and business was brisk; there was money to be made if Mother could stand it. Hedge helped her with the heaviest work. He carried water for the men to wash and change clothes in the lean-to off the kitchen when they came out of the mine so black that you wouldn't know them.

Nothing was modern. Everything had to be carried in and out of the boardinghouse – water, wood, coal, and ashes. Several stoves had to be kept going to keep it heated. Mother had to bake big batches of bread every day to have enough for the lunch buckets and the regular meals, besides dried-apple pies, cakes, and cookies. She had to be up early and late, because the miners worked from six in the morning to six in the evening. Some worked night shift, which called for extra meals and lunch buckets. This is how a little part of the West was won.

Uncle Mike and Hedge had not met since Mike had relieved him of all that gold, but Grandma was worried about Mother, so she asked him to drive her out to Sand Coulee. Mike was reluctant but finally agreed.

Mother looked like a ghost, but her husband was working, and for that she was grateful. It spurred her to keep going, and she told Grandma that she was just tired.

Grandma knew that Mother was expecting again and asked what she would need in new baby clothes so she could start sewing them in her spare time. I can remember when Grandma came later with blue and white outing flannel dresses, belly bands, and barracoats, which were petticoats with a band top about six inches wide that was supposed to support the infant's back. All new baby clothes were made about four times as long as the baby, and I always wondered why.

32

3

Of course, Hedge quit his job in the mines for the usual thousand reasons. The straw boss was a son of a bitch, the barn boss always gave him the worst mules to drive, and so on. He wasn't going to skin mules, he was going to file on the homestead that Mike had told him about.

Mother was much in favor of the homesteading plan. If Hedge got out on a ranch, he might stop gambling. In the meantime, she could keep the boardinghouse going to earn money for a few horses and cattle to get started with and a wagon and harness. Above all, she wanted a warm log house. She made plans with the carpenters who boarded with her, explaining just how she wanted her house built.

"It will be a good place to raise the children," she told Grandma.

"But my child, that all takes money," Grandma warned.

"Yes, but I am making more money than I ever made before. With the mines working steady, we can soon have enough to get started."

Mother and Hedge filed on the land, and she managed to have a good two-story log house built on it. She also bought three nice young mares from Tom Carter, who always ate at her boarding-house when he came to town and gave her advice on ranching. He looked after the mares until she got settled, branded the colts with his brand, and gave her a bill of sale. Mother also bought eight head of good two-year-old heifers at a reasonable price. Mr. Carter branded her heifers for her, too. That made nine head of cattle, counting the old milk cow she had had to buy when she took over the boardinghouse.

She overworked constantly and finally grew so sick that she had to offer the boardinghouse for sale. It was some time before she found a buyer, and then she had to take two yearling colts and an old lumber wagon in part payment. The worst of the deal was that the buyer insisted that she leave him her good cookstove. By the time the sale was completed, Mother collapsed. Uncle Mike came and took her out to his ranch, where she could rest while Grandma took us kids in hand again.

While Mother was trying to get back on her feet, Hedge was supposed to move everything from the boardinghouse and have the ranch house ready for us.

First he rode old Brownie to Carter's ranch to bring back the horses. They were broke horses but not very gentle, and he wanted to drive them a bit before starting for Great Falls, where Mother wanted him to buy her a cookstove.

Horses left alone on the range grow fat and sleek until tough winter weather sets in. Mother's mares looked beautiful when Hedge brought them to Mike's corral. One, named Bess, was a blazed-face black. The heavier of the two bays, Mollie, was to be Bess's teammate. Aggie, the dainty little one, was a bright bay with a star on her forehead. She was too fast for the wagon, so she was to be the saddle mare, although stockmen seldom used mares for saddle horses. They had no time to be bothered with colts. Mares are much worse than geldings for going back to their home range, and they gave night herders no end of trouble on the roundups. But small ranchers often preferred mares because of the colts they raised.

Hedge drove Bess and Mollie one at a time with one of Mike's gentle horses until they quieted down a little. When he was ready to go to Great Falls, Mother gave him money to buy the cookstove and a few other little things she needed. He took me with him, in case a tug came unhooked or something on the wagon broke or got lost, because he wouldn't dare take any chances on relaxing his hold on the lines with that team. They made that old lumber wagon rattle over the rough prairie! I sat in the bottom of the wagon box, and what a jousting I got before Bess and Mollie were winded and calmed down.

34

In Great Falls Hedge drove into the hay market, unhitched the horses, put hackamores on them, and tied them to the wagon wheel. He told me to pick up hay and put it in the wagon box for them but to be careful not to scare them, or they'd break loose.

Bess and Mollie were fresh off the range and didn't care much for the trampled hay I could pick up, but as the day wore on they would take a nibble now and then. I wished I could climb up to the wagon box, but I was afraid of scaring the team, so I sat on the wagon tongue and waited hour after hour until it was dark. All the teams but ours had gone from the market. I knew the horses must need water, because they had been too warm to drink when we pulled in. I wasn't thirsty myself, because I could drink at the horse-watering trough, but I was hungry and wished Hedge would come back and bring me something to eat.

Once a man with a load of hay talked to me when he put his team in the barn. He came back with some doughnuts and an apple and asked me if I didn't want to go to the hotel where it was warm. He would leave a note for my stepfather, telling him where I was. But I was afraid Hedge wouldn't like it. I kept wondering whether Hedge had bought the stove.

He hadn't. He came back without a single thing – except two slices of buttered bread for me. He must have had his supper at the Farmer's Hotel, where food was served family style, and a customer could help himself to as much as he wanted for twenty-five cents.

He led the horses to the horse trough, but they wanted nothing of the city and barely tasted the water. We had quite a time getting them hooked up, and I almost got stepped on several times, trying to hold them by the bit.

Hedge was too smart to go back to Mike's ranch. He drove directly to his own ranch and told me I was to say "I don't know" to anything I was asked about the trip or the stove. He made a fire in the heating stove and tried to fry bacon on it, but the stovepipe took up so much room that there wasn't much space for the pan. Finally, by heating the stove red hot and holding the pan in position, he got the bacon fried. We ate it with soda crackers from Mother's boardinghouse stock.

After breakfast we hitched the team and drove the three miles to Sand Coulee. Going down the big hill at Shacktown, one of Mollie's traces came unhooked and hit her hind leg, and she began to kick and jump. We almost had a runaway, and we did lose the wagon seat. Hedge finally got the mares quieted down. He unhitched them at the bottom of the hill, tied them to the wagon, and walked back for the wagon seat. Then he walked to town, leaving me to watch the mares. I suppose he hoped to make a little money gambling or borrow some money to make up for his losses the day before in Great Falls.

At last, Uncle Mike came along. He had just left the mine, and his face was black from coal dust and smoke from his lamp. If I hadn't seen him black before, I wouldn't have known him.

Like the other miners, he wore a cotton cap with a metal shield in the front to fasten his oil lamp and protect his head from the flame. A miner's lamp looked like a tiny coffeepot, except that the spout was round and started near the bottom of the pot. It had a hook instead of a handle and burned a heavy oil.

Uncle Mike had some of his lunch left, and did it taste good to me in spite of the mine odor!

He wanted to know what I was doing there and whether Hedge got the stove. The only answer I dared make was "I don't know."

"The hell you don't know! You went to Great Falls with him and rode back in the wagon. Was the stove in the wagon?"

I felt too foolish to say "I don't know" again. I shook my head no, and Uncle Mike exploded.

"I'll be damned! I expected as much! Did he get the rest of the stuff?"

I didn't answer at all, just hung my head as though I were the guilty one. Uncle Mike went on talking to himself. "I see, now. You're not supposed to know anything. But you don't need to tell me. I know the whole story. The money is gone without a damned thing to show for it. I had a good notion to tell your mother that when she was giving it to him."

Just then Hedge showed up. "Hello! I was waiting for you," he said to Mike.

"Like hell you were! What do you want from me?"

"I'll need help to get that team hooked and headed up the hill."

Uncle Mike had to swallow his anger and help with the team. Then he took old Brownie out of the corral and rode home, while we went our way. That night we had cheese and crackers for supper with plenty of cold spring water to wash them down.

Hedge waited the next day until Uncle Mike had gone to work, and then he took me with him to Mike's place and told Mother to bundle up her duds and get home. She could look after the babies all right, he said, and he was afraid to have all that grub in the house with nobody to look after it. When Mother asked him whether he had bought the stove, I got scared and went outside.

Grandma tried to persuade Hedge to let Mother stay a few days longer, but he insisted that she leave right away. Grandma could not come with her because she was on a confinement case. She did her own housework early, walked a mile and a half to the neighbor's house, bathed the babies, made the beds, put the house in order, baked bread and prepared whatever food was on hand, then came home to do her own evening chores, bringing the cows along with her as she came, then milking them, feeding the calves and chickens, and preparing supper for Uncle Mike. There was plenty of work at Uncle Mike's, but he and Grandma were happy.

Mother must have been eager to get settled in her own new home that she had looked forward to for so long, because she went readily when Hedge asked her. She was afraid to ride behind the spunky little team, especially with the new baby, but Hedge assured her that he could handle them. She could sit in the wagon box with me, out of danger. I had my own ideas about the danger but kept them to myself.

We had no trouble with the team, but I'll never forget going inside the house with Mother. She cried as though her heart would break. Hedge had dumped everything from the boardinghouse in the middle of the floor. There was no cookstove – and five people to cook for. But she got over her tears while Hedge was watering and picketing the team, and when he came in she was making up the bed to have a clean place to put the babies.

"I'm hungry," said Hedge. "Let's have something to eat."

"Yes," she said bitterly, "you want your supper and I want a stove to cook it on. I've worked myself down to this to make money for a home here. I trusted you with that money to buy the most necessary thing in the house. Now give me the money and I'll go to town and do my own buying. Then I'll know that it will be done."

Hedge stood looking at Mother for a moment as if he couldn't believe she was talking back to him. He walked over to the corner, picked up his saddle and bridle from the floor, threw them over his shoulder, and started for the door.

"Where are you going?"

"Going to town to get my supper."

Hedge stayed away several days. While he was gone, Grandma came over to bring Mother some butter and cottage cheese. She was disgusted to find her trying to cook on the heating stove.

"We will go right over and get that old cookstove I had in my homestead shack," she said. "It's not very good, but it beats this."

She and Mother drove back in the buckboard and somehow got the old stove loaded. They set it up but found they had forgotten the crosspiece that holds up the lids. They couldn't light a fire without

38

it, so I went back with Grandma to get the missing part. I was hurrying home with it when, from the top of the hill, I saw Hedge heading for me at a high lope.

I knew he wouldn't be riding a step out of his way to help me. I had been running along, but now I slowed to a walk, wondering what he was angry about and how I figured in his rage. I soon knew.

"Where have you been?"

"At Uncle Mike's. I had to get this," I said, holding up the crosspiece, "before Mother can make a fire in the stove."

"Didn't I tell you and your mother not to be running over there?" he roared.

I hung my head without trying to answer, which only added to his anger. He jumped off his horse, jerked the crosspiece out of my hand, and threw it on the grass. "Leave it there, and get home and stay there – do you hear?"

With that he shook me and gave me a slap that sent me sprawling and frightened his horse so that she almost pulled the reins out of his hand. For that he jumped on her back and drove in his spurs. "I'll take the scare out of you!" He spurred her till she was racing over the prairie at top speed.

When I got home without the crosspiece, I found Mother crying and cleaning up soot. Hedge had knocked the stovepipe down and dragged Grandma's stove outside.

There was no kindness in Hedge's heart toward his animals, and I think they had none for him. This same little mare, Aggie, got even with him one night when she pulled her picket pin and wandered off. Hedge was furious. He had to walk after her. He took the bridle with him, thinking he could ride her home bareback, but Aggie had other ideas and pitched him higher than he had ever been pitched before. The fall knocked him out. Later he insisted that he lay unconscious for several hours. Aggie managed to lose the bridle before he found her again, and there wasn't much left of the picket rope, either, except a frayed end.

Hedge had left our old cow, Grannie, for us to milk. Mother didn't know how to milk; she'd had the hired girl do the milking at the boardinghouse. Hedge was a good milker when he didn't get into a rage and try to kick the cow's ribs in, which he did once when Grannie hit him in the face with her wet tail. But all I knew about milking was stripping Grandma's gentle old cow after Grandma had finished milking her.

But the cow had to be milked. I led her to water, then tied her to the logs of the unfinished kitchen. Grannie was good-natured, but she knew what to expect of a milker, and she knew Mother's touch wasn't right. She switched her tail and shifted over, and poor Mother was all atremble, not knowing whether she should try again or not.

I said, "Let me try, once."

I did a little better, but both of us together were not good enough for Grannie, which she let us know by banging us with her tail and moving away from us. We managed to get her half-milked, but we knew that we would soon dry her up by milking her that way.

Mother worried about her eight head of heifers and kept after Hedge to round them up. She wanted to give them a little salt and get them used to watering at our spring. This was no easy matter, because they were constantly being scared away from the spring by horses. Our homestead lay between the two big horse ranches, and until we moved in, the horses had come to the spring every day. It became my job to watch for them and set the dog on them when they came close.

Hedge figured out a way to really scare the horses, although by stampeding them, we also scared off the heifers. Our dog was a good heeler. When an old mare with a colt would stop to fight him off, the dog would nip her heels. After he'd been kicked several times,

Hedge decided to put a stop to it before he got killed. He fitted the dog with a little harness to which he attached two tomato cans with pebbles in them. At first the dog hated the arrangement, but when he found out how he could make the horses run from the racket, he would almost ask for the harness.

Mother was afraid her heifers would get picked up by rustlers, who were active around there at the time. Once when Hedge was away, and he didn't come and didn't come, she decided to put the babies to sleep and walk with me to the top of a high hill and see whether she could see them. Climbing the hill overtaxed her strength. She had to sit down and rest many times, and when we got to the top, all we saw was horses.

Hedge came home the next day. Aggie looked as though she had had nothing to eat since he left the ranch. She was so weak that she almost had the blind staggers and gentle enough now that I could lead her to water and picket her. All she wanted was grass and more grass. I had a time keeping her from stepping over the rope as she kept reaching for bites of grass. Finally, I picketed her where the grass was good and left her to feed.

As soon as I got back to the house, Hedge sent me to the spring with a ten-pound and a five-pound lard pail to get him a fresh drink of water. He always slept and slept after he had been away on one of his jaunts, but this time it seemed to take him an unusually long time to get his rest. Aggie was rested long before he was and too frisky for me to lead to water. Mother tried to help, but she was strange to Aggie and scared her worse than I did. Mother was afraid of animals, and they knew it and were the more afraid of her. She never learned how to win an animal's confidence, but she did her best to save Aggie and me from a beating in case Hedge had to be disturbed to water her himself. And she wanted him in a good humor so she could persuade him to go bring the heifers home.

It took a lot of coaxing, but he finally went. He came home with

Bess and Mollie, the mares, but said he couldn't find the heifers. He would take another look around as soon as he had given the team a workout. He had heard about a stove a fellow wanted to sell cheap in Great Falls. I'd have to stay home and milk the cow and water the saddle horse, but he'd hunt up his nephew Pete in Great Falls if he needed help hitching up the team in town.

He came home with an old stove and Pete.

A day or so after Hedge and Pete got back, a fellow by the name of Rasmason drove up to our house in a single buggy, something we seldom saw. I was all eyes and ears to know what was going on and sat on a log at the side of the house while Rasmason told Hedge he wanted to trade the gelding he was driving for the black mare he had seen Hedge driving the day before.

"Why do you want to get rid of the gelding?" Hedge asked.

"I want a mare that will raise a colt and pay for her keep. All the driving I do is for pleasure, and I want to get something back from the money I put into it."

"I don't want to trade. My mares match up well. Same size, same gait."

"A bay and a black ain't a good combination. This gelding's a lot better match for your bay than the black mare is."

After more dickering, Hedge said, "I'd want twenty dollars to boot."

"That's too much. I can buy a horse for twenty-five dollars."

When Hedge looked at the gelding's teeth, he remarked on a strong odor of whiskey. But Rasmason invited him to get in the rig and see how the horse could travel. The horse had lots of go in his, and that was what Hedge liked. Yes, Rasmason explained, he had too much life for the little driving he wanted to do. He'd had to put a kicking strap on him because they were just breaking him to drive single, but he had never offered to kick.

When they pulled up at the house again, Rasmason got out of the rig and offered Hedge a ten-dollar bill. Mother had come out, and she spoke up, opposing the trade. But Hedge had seen that ten-spot, and he wanted it. "Make it fifteen," he said.

"I'll split. I'll make it twelve and a half," and Rasmason handed Hedge the money.

Bess was picketed not far from the house. The men drove over to her, unhitched the gelding, and hitched up Bess. Hedge told Rasmason that Bess wasn't broken to drive single, but Rasmason was in a rush to get away and took the chance. Of course, he was in no danger, not with a good kicking strap, new harness, and buggy.

Mother couldn't believe Bess was gone until she saw Rasmason drive her away. She and I were both sick over it. And of course, with money in his pocket, Hedge couldn't stay on the ranch. He threw his saddle on Aggie and was off for town, leaving Mother to get over the loss of her mare the best she could.

Mother sat up late waiting for him, but he didn't come home. In the morning the cow and Mollie and the gelding all had to be watered and have their pickets changed, and she didn't know how we were going to manage it. She got the babies to sleep while I milked the cow. Then we took the cow to water and picketed her where she could get her fill.

Next we tackled Mollie. She wouldn't let us get near her, so Mother said we would carry the water to her instead of trying to take her to water. I ran home and got the jelly bucket for her to drink out of, but range horses are fussy, and Mollie didn't want water bad enough to drink out of the jelly bucket.

Mother said, "We'll water the other horse first, and then leave the bucket where Mollie can come up and drink if she wants to."

The gelding was jumping around like crazy. When he saw us coming he started to meet us on a high lope, but his picket rope stopped him and threw him off balance. Mother and I were both afraid of him, so we set the bucket down where he could reach it and got out of his way just as he landed upside down on it, smashing it.

Just as that happened, Tom Carter came riding up.

"Keep back," he shouted. "Keep away from that horse. He's locoed. I'll water him and change his picket for you."

I wondered how he was going to do it. He rode up to the picket pin, picked up the rope without getting off his horse, took two half hitches around his saddle horn, pulled up the pin, rolled up the rope, and put a hackamore on Mr. Gelding. The brute sat back on his haunches in true loco fashion, but Carter didn't let that bother him. He kept the gelding backing right to the spring, where he was glad to take time out for a drink.

"Where did you get the loco?" Carter asked Mother.

She explained about the trade and asked, "What makes him so crazy today? He acted fairly good yesterday."

"He may have been doped, for he is sure locoed now," Tom answered. "He is vicious. Keep away from him."

Mother remembered the whiskey odor that Hedge had remarked on and asked whether he could have been doped with that.

"A lot of strong liquor might have calmed him down for the time being. Maybe that's why he is so much worse than any loco I ever saw before. If he were mine, I'd shoot him before he kills somebody."

Locos were numerous on the range. You could always tell them by their peculiar actions and by their manes and tails, which were always thicker and longer than other horses'. They would get so stupid that they didn't know enough to go for water and would die of thirst.

Mother thanked Mr. Carter and asked him if he had seen anything of her eight heifers. "If you do, let me know."

"I would, if that would do you any good," Carter answered and rode away without looking back.

Mother puzzled over his remark. She couldn't make herself be-

44

lieve that Hedge had gambled them away. But she remembered how little concern he had shown when she had worried about them and wanted him to look for them.

When Hedge came home the next day and saw his crazy gelding, he was furious. Tom Carter had left the hackamore on, thinking it might prevent him from breaking the rope, but the horse was too locoed to be careful even when the rope cut into his nose. The hackamore did make it easier for Hedge, who rode up and threw a half hitch around his saddle horn. The loco made a backward lunge, almost throwing Hedge's horse and unseating Hedge, and the battle was on between a man accustomed to beating animals into submission and a crazy locoed horse whose sense had been destroyed by a poison weed.

What Hedge had in mind was to take the gelding to Rasmason's place, where he had Bess picketed, and exchange them while Rasmason was at work in the mines. But he soon found his method of brute force wasn't going to work, because Aggie couldn't drag the gelding. The rope might snap, and the loco would be free on the open range. Still, he managed to get the gelding to follow Aggie, and he did switch the two horses.

Of course, Rasmason was furious when he found Bess was gone. He rushed right up to the ranch on foot and found Hedge thinning out Bess's tail. Rasmason had cut it off square, Canadian Mountie style.

"So you came and took the mare back, like a goddamned Indian," he sneered.

"You gave me a bill of sale stating that your horse was sound."

"He was, when I turned him over to you. You must have hit him over the head or something. I'll take my mare that belongs to me."

"Why didn't you ride your good sound animal over here?" Hedge asked.

"You done something to that horse."

45

"That horse of yours tried to kill my wife. You better go home and kill him before he kills you."

Rasmason wasn't quitting. "I'm demanding my mare, right now," he said, taking a step toward Bess's head. But Hedge's hand went to his gun, and Rasmason weakened.

"I'll have the law on you. You'll see whether I get my mare or not!" he shouted as he walked away.

Hedge stayed around home for a few days, in case Rasmason should come back, then took Bess to Tom Carter's place and turned her loose.

The weather was hot and dry. There were only two unfenced springs in the neighborhood. Ever since we had been putting tin cans on the dog to scare the horses away from our spring, they had had to go to the other, which didn't have enough water for them. And one night the horse herders must have decided to water their horses at our spring, because the dog kept barking all night long, and what a mess our spring was the next morning! Hundreds of horses had trampled around it. Mother was alone with us children and afraid to send the dog out. If any of the buckaroos were still around, they would shoot our dog for sure.

The men must have watched and known when Hedge wasn't home, because this night watering went on for several nights. Mother couldn't sleep when she knew the horses were at the spring, and she waked me to keep her company. We were sitting and straining our ears, listening to the horses milling around the spring, when we heard hoofs close to the house. Mother was terror-stricken.

The men rode up to the front door and pounded on the top panels until they broke, then threw a rock into the room. We thought they were coming in, but they didn't. They rode around the house and broke out the window on the other side.

One fellow said, "Let's set fire to the damn thing."

46

"That's what we're going to do if they don't get the hell out of here," another retorted.

I hid under Mother's bed until I heard the horses leave, then I came out. Mother was sitting on the edge of the bed, trying to quiet the babies, who, frightened by the noise, were crying at the tops of their voices.

I peeped out the window and said, "They're gone." As I spoke, Mother must have fainted and fallen to the floor. I thought a man had jumped through the broken window. I made a dive for my hiding place under the bed, fell over Mother, and struck my nose on the edge of her bed, giving myself a bloody nose and two black eyes. I was so scared I didn't know I was hurt but lay listening and waiting for our dog to make a big fuss over the men breaking into the house.

I was confused when the dog didn't bark at all. I couldn't hear well because the babies were crying, but I was sure no men were walking around the house. When Mother began to groan, I found the courage to crawl out from under the bed. I could hear the dog licking Mother's face, and I whispered, "Are you hurt?" I thought one of the buckaroo's rocks must have struck her, but she soon came to, explained that she had fainted, and asked for a drink of water.

A baby's crying bothers me at any time, but that night my baby sisters' crying almost drove me wild. I wanted to listen for horses coming near the house. The dog would warn us of unusual noises, but if I could hear, I would have a better idea of what was causing the disturbance and whether it was near or far away.

Nobody who has not gone through a night like that knows what a relief daylight is. When Mother saw me in the dim gray dawn, she thought I had been struck by a rock, but I remembered falling against the bed after the riders had gone.

When Hedge came home, and Mother told him about the terrible night we'd had, he said, "We've lived on the ranch long enough. We can prove up. Maybe we'd better move to town for a while."

"What will we do with our cattle and horses? Who will look after them?"

"They'll be all right. We'll turn the horses out. They'll take care of themselves. We'll take the old cow to town with us and put her in the town herd."

"What about the heifers? They'll all be coming fresh in the spring and will need a little hay and shelter during the bad weather. I thought maybe you could get Mike's mower and put up a few loads of hay for them and the milk cow."

"No, I'm not going to ask Mike for his mower. If I can find the damn heifers I'll get somebody to look after them, or I'll trade them off."

Mother was sure, then, that the heifers were gone.

She had spent most of the time in bed since the dreadful night, but she got sicker. Finally, Hedge sent me for Grandma. He went for the doctor, who brought us another baby girl.

Uncle Mike advised Hedge against leaving the ranch when the horse ranchers needed water so badly. They might hire someone to jump the claim. He also reminded him that he had better break the required amount of ground. So Hedge got Pete to come and stay on the ranch with him, and they plowed a small patch by the house. And what a reception they gave the range horses with some specially loaded shells when they tried to come to the spring again!

Mother was making plans to go to work in town for another grubstake, as Hedge called it, as soon as she was able. Our dog used to get lonesome for Mother and me and would trot over to visit us for a while and then go back to the ranch. It was only two miles. The buckaroos must have seen him going back and forth, for one day we found him lying by the roadside, shot.

4

Rasmason made good his threat to bring suit against Hedge for taking back Bess, but long before it came to trial, the locoed gelding was dead, and so was any friendship between Uncle Mike and Hedge. Mother had gone to Belt to work in another boardinghouse, leaving us four children with Grandma, and Uncle Mike had laid off work in the mine to put up some hay. He asked Hedge to help him.

Hedge, who was living on the ranch again, agreed to help Mike put up the hay, but as soon as the work was done, he asked to be paid for it.

"Hasn't my mother been taking care of your family for the last six months?" Mike reminded him.

"Truleen expects to pay for all that," Hedge told him, "and I've got to have money to hire an attorney for that Rasmason business."

Uncle Mike paid him but told him that was the last dealing he would ever have with him. Hedge went to town and hired his attorney, then drove to Belt to get Mother, telling her that he and Pete were tired of batching.

Grandma cried whenever she mentioned that homecoming of Mother's. It was a chilly, rainy day, and Mother was numb with cold, but because Hedge was angry at Uncle Mike, he wouldn't let her get out of the wagon at Grandma's house, not even to warm her hands. We children, who had anticipated Mother's homecoming with great joy, were crushed. I was afraid to speak a word for fear Hedge might not approve, and poor Grandma, who had taken care of us four children for six months, washed for us, sewed and cooked for us, this was the thanks she got. But Hedge was smart. He wasn't giving Mother a chance to offer Grandma any of the money he'd talked about so glibly to Uncle Mike, and more than that, he gave all of us to understand there was to be no visiting back and forth.

We children forgot a lot of the disagreeableness when the wagon was unloaded, and we saw the good things to eat and the yards and yards of calico and outing flannel that Mother had bought to make us new clothes.

But how was Mother to get them made without Grandma's help, I wondered. Mother wasn't good at cutting things out. Grandma always did that. Mother could sew, and she had bought herself a sewing machine. She had bought material for Grandma to make her some new wrappers, skirts, and nightgowns, but how was she going to get the material over to her?

Luck was with her, in a way. Pete saw how things stood and told Mother he would carry the things back and forth while Hedge was in town. If he saw Hedge was at home, he would leave the bundle on the hill until after dark. And in fact, Pete managed to get the sewing back and forth without giving Hedge the slightest reason to suspect a thing.

Besides all the fussing over sewing, Mother had a terrible time with the baby. It didn't know her and wouldn't go to her for several days. Instead, it clung to me night and day, keeping me in the house when I wanted to be outdoors. At that age – about seven – I loved to be outside, riding a stick horse and gathering pretty rocks to build a corral to keep my imaginary horses and cattle in. As I played, I told myself I was not going to be like Hedge. When I got big, I was going to build warm stables for my stock and put up big haystacks so they would have something to eat when the grass was covered with snow, and I would build a fence around my ranch so we wouldn't be bothered with range stock getting in the spring and eating up all the pasture, and I wouldn't be mean to little kids.

Walking over the prairie, I was always picking out nice grassy spots where I was going to build a fence for my horse pasture. As my childhood dragged on, I resolved to get away from Hedge when I was sixteen, a wonderful grown-up age when I would be able to do everything with ease.

Even though Mother had to go out and work for the grub that Pete ate, his being with us made Hedge a little more civilized toward all of us. For this I was thankful. Of course, as soon as Pete saw the eats were getting low, he usually left.

Rasmason's suit must have hung fire for some time until it came up for trial. Mother was so confident of winning as soon as the evidence was presented that she thought the trial wouldn't last any time at all, so she left us children at home alone.

The baby, Rose, was pretty good until bedtime. Then she cried herself to sleep. I went to sleep, too, but she wakened me bright and early and cried more. I did everything I could to quiet her, but the only time she was quiet was when she was asleep. It dawned on me that she might be sick. If she was, she might die before Mother got home. If I could only see Grandma, she might know what to do, but I was forbidden to go near Grandma's. I debated with myself for a long time.

My other half-sisters, Beck and Nora, began to cry, and with all three crying at once, I didn't know what to do but go to Grandma's. I thought maybe I could get back before Hedge came home, and he might not be so angry if he knew the baby was sick and might have died if Grandma hadn't fixed her.

I put coats and hoods on both the little tots. It was a hot day, and the baby didn't want to be bundled up. She cried louder and did her best to pull her blanket off, but after I got going, she quieted down somewhat. I was used to carrying her around the house but soon tired when it came to carrying her any distance. I tried letting her walk, but she fell down so often I saw I would never make the two miles before dark. Beck and Nora were not good travelers, either. They fell down, and cried, and wanted to go back. I told them to hold on to me, and we would soon be there. Grandma would give us lots of nice things to eat, maybe even candy.

I was afraid the baby's crying would attract the attention of wild cattle or horses. I wasn't so anxious about the horses, but the wild cattle gave me plenty of worry. One bunch had a well-known black-necked steer that had chased several men afoot on the prairie.

It wasn't so bad as long as there was light, but when the sun went down I was almost panicky. I thought of leaving the three little tots by the road and running to get Uncle Mike to come and carry the baby the rest of the way. I knew I was headed in the right direction, because I had watched the sun go down, and the sky was still a little lighter where it had set. But I wasn't sure I was on the road, which was used so seldom that the grass wasn't worn off, and leaving my little sisters was too risky. They might wander off, or wolves or coyotes might attack them. No, I must stay with them. How I would protect them hadn't entered my mind.

By this time I was played out, and so were Beck and Nora. They must have been too tired to cry but kept sniffling. But the baby would stop crying for a while and then break out in a wail I was sure could be heard clear to Uncle Mike's. Once a coyote answered her with a weird bark that almost took the last bit of starch out of me.

Uncle Mike's house was down in a coulee. You couldn't see it until you were almost on top of it, but the dogs had heard us and were setting up a frantic barking. Uncle Mike lit his lantern and came to investigate.

The dogs came to meet us, with Uncle Mike following with the lantern. Was I ever glad to see the glimmer of that lantern, and was Uncle Mike horrified when he came close enough to hear the baby crying!

He called, "Is that you, Peggy?"

I couldn't answer. I couldn't get breath enough. I tried, but my voice was so husky he couldn't hear me.

"In God's holy name, what's this? What are you doing here at this time of night?"

Of the four of us, I was the worst off after we were safely in the house. I couldn't stop shaking, and Grandma couldn't find anything to make me stop, although she tried all her favorite remedies. Knowing that I still had to face Hedge and what he would do when he found out I had gone to Grandma's was what kept me shaking. There were no excuses with Hedge. I was in real trouble, and I knew it, and nothing Uncle Mike or Grandma could say would make a difference.

I felt better after a night's sleep, and we had a wonderful time with Grandma and Uncle Mike. One of Uncle Mike's horses was sick, and he had been staying home from work on that account. He spent most of his time playing with us and singing to us between giving the sick horse doses of aconite. But he was just putting the aconite bottle back in the attic when Hedge stepped into the doorway. He was in one of his worst rages and wouldn't let Mother stop for the cup of tea Grandma considered so necessary.

Uncle Mike told Hedge off just the same, and he warned Mother never to leave us alone again, or he'd do more than tell her off. Mother knew it was a terrible thing, but she said nothing because Hedge was already in such a rage.

On the way home I wished the wolves had killed me. Anything would be easier than to take the beating I knew was coming.

Hedge began unhooking the team and told Mother to hurry up and make him something to eat. She sent me out for chips and wood to start the fire.

Hedge couldn't wait to take his anger out on me. As soon as he had finished eating, he told me to go out and get the bellyband off the harness. This was an extra-heavy strap, about two inches wide with no buckles, that he always used to beat me with.

I brought the strap, and he said, "Now pull off your duds, and I'll tan your hide for you."

When I got down to my undershirt, I hesitated, and he jumped up and jerked my shirt off. "So you won't mind what I tell you? Maybe you will after I get through with you this time."

He started beating me from one corner of the room to the other. Mother went into the bedroom with the little girls, who were frightened and crying, but Hedge hollered at her, "You come out here and shut that door."

Mother came. He handed her a little light strap off her valise and said, "Help me give her a good trimming."

I was covered with stripes already. I was tender-skinned, and in many places he had drawn blood. Mother hesitated, but when he roared, "What's the matter with you?" she, too, started beating me – a thing I'll never forget, even though Mother has been dead for many years.

I felt myself getting weak and thought maybe I was going to die. I said, "O God, please let me die."

Mother dropped her strap and choked, "No more," and rushed from the room. Hedge kept on beating me, but it didn't hurt so much now. He ordered me to get up from the floor, but I couldn't, so he picked me up by one arm and one leg and threw me on my bunk, striking my head against the log wall. I lost consciousness and didn't come to until the next day.

Mother was worried and wanted Hedge to go for the doctor. He said it wasn't necessary, but he must have been scared, for he began drilling me in a lie. In his gruffest voice he demanded, "What did Grannie give you to eat last night?"

I was so frightened I could hardly speak, much less remember, but I managed to whisper, "An egg, some cottage cheese, and some potatoes."

"Didn't she give you some bread and butter?"

"Yes."

"What did she put on the bread before she put the butter on?"

I didn't know what to say, because butter was all she had put on it.

Hedge came back at me with a smack across the face. "Why do you try to lie to me? You know she put some of that medicine on that Mike was putting back in the attic when I came. What was Mike doing with them bottles from the attic?"

"Old Brownie was sick, and he gave her some medicine. I think it was the red kind."

"Didn't Grannie put some of that on your bread?"

"I don't think so."

"Listen here, Skin-'em-Alive, I'm going to make you tell the truth about that old woman putting medicine on your bread if I have to give you another licking like the one you got last night."

He grabbed me as if he were going to start beating me again. Mother was afraid he might, too, for she came over and spoke in a soft voice. "Now tell your father all about what you had for supper last night. You never mentioned cake or pie, and Grandma always has something like that for Uncle Mike's lunch pail."

Her sympathetic tone brought on a crying spell, but I did my best to tell her, through my sobs, that we had cake and applesauce with cream on it.

That gave Hedge the opening he wanted. He turned to Mother. "There you are! She won't tell the truth. First she says all she had to eat was eggs and cheese and potatoes. Now she tells you she had cake and applesauce. I had to force the bread and butter answer out of her, and I'll force the answer about the medicine out of her, too. Listen to me, you skinny little trollop, didn't Grannie put some of that red medicine on your bread? Why won't you say yes? You know she did, and that's what you are to tell the doctor if he comes."

"I will, I will," I sobbed.

Mother pulled open my shirt and asked, "How are we going to explain this to a doctor?"

"We'll tell him one of the horses got scared of a rattlesnake, and she got tangled in the rope and dragged before I could catch the horse and carry her home."

He went over the last part several times so I'd know just what to say. Mother shook her head. She was still worried.

"She don't need a doctor!" he insisted. "She's all right! I'm going to take a little nap. I didn't sleep much last night."

"I'm afraid! I worried all night. Don't you know, if anything happened, we'd be in a worse spot if we didn't have a doctor? If you won't go, I'm going to Sand Coulee myself."

She got ready and left. It was seven miles there and back, and she had to walk because she couldn't handle any of our horses, but she went anyway.

I knew from their conversation that I was in a bad way, and I was glad. Whenever I was conscious I prayed that God would let me die. I would go to heaven, where Grandma had told me everybody was kind and good. Thinking about Grandma brought back the lies I was to tell the doctor about her giving me bad medicine. I prayed that God would let me die before the doctor came. Grandma was my best friend, and how could I tell the doctor that she had done something terrible? She had told me God always answered prayers if you prayed for what was good and right, and I thought dying would be a wonderful thing for me.

Mother had set a little pail of cold water beside my bunk, and before she came back I had drunk it all. My prayers weren't getting results. I was feeling better instead of worse. My faith in prayers took an awful tumble that day, and I doubt whether implicit faith ever returned.

Mother had come back without the doctor. He had been out on a case. She had waited in his office as long as she dared, and when she got home she found me better. Luck was with Hedge; if the doctor had seen me, the course of my life might have been changed.

After Hedge won his lawsuit, things went along pretty well until provisions began to get low. Mother urged Hedge to look for a job, and he made several trips to town but came back saying he couldn't find a job of any kind. He insisted that Mother go to town and see if she could do any better. Mother wasn't feeling well and thought for once she would make Hedge go to work, but she thought wrong, for he flew into a rage and threw everything in the house out into the weeds. He sent me for his saddle horse and left.

Mother and I managed to pick up some of the food, the beans and coffee, a little oatmeal, and all the dried prunes. The flour was a total loss. Weed seeds were mixed in it, and we couldn't use it. Mother cooked some beans and prunes for our supper, and I milked the cow, so we had plenty of milk at least. But the next morning we had a rude awakening. The old cow was gone, picket rope, picket pin, and all. Even the axe we used to drive the picket pin was gone.

That night Hedge came home and started giving us fits for letting anybody get away with the cow, although later we learned that the cow had gone the same way as everything else, to pay his gambling debts.

One of the neighbors had given us a half-grown pup when our dog was shot. He was the hungriest dog I ever saw, always begging and whining, and this day he was worse than ever, really hungry. Like the rest of us, he hadn't had much breakfast. His whining annoyed Hedge. He took a bridle rein, fastened it to the pup's neck, and went upstairs with it. Mother and I could not imagine what he was going to do with the dog until we heard it struggling outside the house. Hedge had shoved him out the window, then let the window down on the strap and left him to hang until he strangled to death.

When he saw how horrified and sickened I was, he put the same strap around my neck and threw me over his shoulder. "Come on," he said. "I might as well finish this skinny thing, too" and started for the stairs.

Mother screamed and rushed over and put her fingers under the strap. "Put her down! You're choking her!"

"Damn it, that's what I wanted to do!" He dropped me to the floor as though I were a log. Mother loosened the strap while he looked on and told me what a poor specimen I was compared to his fat little girls.

Hedge's mother lived in Great Falls, and Hedge wanted Mother to leave us kids with her while Mother went to work for another winter's grubstake. Mother knew the old woman couldn't take care of us. She could barely take care of herself, so Mother asked Grandma if Uncle Mike would let us stay with them. Grandma wasn't sure Uncle Mike would consent after all the trouble Hedge had caused, but she promised to ask. I was delighted when she told us that Uncle Mike would let us stay, but I didn't dare say a word – Hedge would have knocked me down.

I don't know how many months we stayed at Uncle Mike's, but they were like heaven. Uncle Mike often went to dances on a Saturday night. Like many old-country Irish, he was good at step dancing and singing, and once he got wound up, he couldn't stop. He'd come home and wake me and sing and dance for me until morning, or until Grandma persuaded him to go to bed. I suppose she wanted to sleep, but I never did as long as Uncle Mike would keep singing and dancing. We were two against one, and Uncle Mike used to laugh at me voting with him.

"Mike, will you whist and go to bed now. It will soon be daylight, and you are keeping the child up all night."

"All right, Mother, you are right. It will soon be daylight, and we'll tumble into bed this minute."

Grandma and Uncle Mike didn't agree on everything, but they

never quarreled. She had certain superstitions that she had a lot of faith in. If the rooster crowed in the doorway, she would exclaim, "Ah, Dick, you are bringing me company!"

If no company came, Uncle Mike would say, "What an old liar you are, Dick," but if someone came, Grandma would say, "I told you! Dick knows when someone is coming."

Mike would often tease her by beating her to the I *told you!*

My little half-sisters were the best children I ever saw. They never cried without reason. One of the first things Mother sent home after she began to work was a baby carriage, and it was my job to wheel the baby back and forth until she fell asleep. The ground in front of the house wasn't level, and Grandma preferred that I do my wheeling indoors, but the baby went to sleep quicker if she was wheeled outside. Grandma was hoeing in the garden one day when I took the carriage out on the side hill. Pushing it uphill was tiresome and slow, and downhill it almost got away from me. I turned it crosswise, and that was worst of all. It turned over one and a half times and terrified the baby. I was too nervous to get the carriage righted before Grandma got there to see what was making the baby cry so hard. She had a skinned forehead, and I got a good scolding.

But all in all, I tended the little sisters faithfully until Grandma's nephew Dennis came to pay her a visit. Dennis was a disillusioned bachelor who had left his sweetheart in the East so long that another man appropriated her. I promptly decided that she must have been both mean and stupid not to wait for such a grand person as Dennis, and I told him I wished she had Hedge for a while.

Irish Dennis was sympathetic and big-hearted and, having no one else to give his affection to, found me receptive. I think he enjoyed me almost as much as I enjoyed him. He took me everywhere with him, mending fences and making repairs. This left Grandma with all the work to do and the baby to tend as well, but I think she was glad to see me so happy.

After he finished the fences, Dennis dug Grandma a root cellar and built her an outhouse. Many of the early-day homesteaders didn't bother with an outhouse but went out in the brush around their cabins. Dennis was shocked at such conditions and told Uncle Mike that an outhouse was a necessity and that he was going to town for lumber to build one. Uncle Mike gave him money for the lumber and said he'd been too busy and also wasn't much of a carpenter.

To haul lumber, Dennis had to take the box off the wagon, leaving only the running gear. Then he asked Grandma if I could go to town with him. She didn't see where I could ride, but he said I would be all right. He would fill a gunnysack with hay for me to sit on.

"Dennis, me boy, a gunnysack full of hay is not what you want. A half a sack will serve the purpose better. How could the child balance on a full sack on her narrow what-do-you-call-it?"

"You are right as you usually are," Dennis agreed. "A half sack will be much better. Will you let her go along?"

Grandma smiled but said neither yes nor no. She went to the stove, lifted the teakettle, and poured hot water into the washbasin on the bench outside the door, and I knew I was in for a scrubbing. That meant I was going with Dennis.

The trail over the prairie was rough, and the wagon made so much noise as the team jogged along that Dennis and I did very little talking on the way to town. Dennis was sitting on the front hounds and I on the rear, so I had lots of time to think. I thought that when I grew up, I would be wise like Grandma, I would sing and dance like Uncle Mike, and I would make things with my hands like Dennis, who was so much better at building than Uncle Mike was. Maybe people were like horses – one was good for the saddle, another for harness. What would I be best for? I was light and quick, more like a saddle horse. But how was I to learn what I must know to be good at all these things? I remembered hearing Uncle Mike say, "I learned a hell of a lot about horses when I worked for old Fields," and Mother would come home with new ways of preparing food and tell Grandma that Mrs. So-and-so had taught her. That was how I must learn, by watching other people and trying to do what they did.

I noticed how differently Dennis did things from the way Hedge did. When we got to town, Dennis first put the team in the livery stable. Then we went to the Farmer's Hotel, washed our hands, and had a nice dinner together. Dennis helped me to everything on the table until I had more than I could eat. This worried me, for I had been taught to clean up my plate. Dennis noticed my distress and told me not to eat any more than I wanted – it was his fault for giving me too much in the first place.

After dinner we went uptown. Dennis took me by the hand, embarrassing me. It had been a long time since anybody walked me along by the hand. He bought fresh meat and thread that Grandma wanted, then went to the lumberyard and loaded the lumber he needed. On the way home, we could sit side by side on the front end of the lumber. I coaxed Dennis to tell me again about his sweetheart and what became of her. I was inwardly satisfied and half glad that she had come West to find gold but had no luck and that the Indians killed the man who stole her away from Dennis.

Dennis ended his story with "Ill-gotten goods never bring happiness." I didn't know what he meant, so he explained that I must never take what wasn't mine, just because there was nobody around to stop me.

He said that he was going to buy himself a saddle horse and ride over to Idaho and Washington to visit old friends as soon as he had things fixed up around the ranch. I told him what a good saddle horse Aggie was and how mean Hedge was to her but that maybe Mother wouldn't sell her. He had never seen Hedge, but I told him a lot, none of it good.

Uncle Mike had sent word to Mother that Dennis was visiting and wanted to see her. She wrote that any time they happened to be in town, she would come back to the ranch with them. This time she didn't let Hedge know so he couldn't spoil her visit, and she did have a peaceful, happy time, with everything to eat and drink, even a glass of whiskey.

We were having a pleasant Sunday afternoon when Hedge came riding up. Uncle Mike went out to meet him, tell him to put his horse in the barn, and introduce him to Dennis.

"Let me take your horse," Dennis offered.

"She's all right. Is my wife here?"

"Yes, she is. Come in and have dinner. We're just through eating."

"No, I'm in a hurry to take my family home."

This remark didn't set well with either Mike or Dennis, but Grandma had Hedge's dinner on the table when he got to the house, and it must have looked too good to pass up, because he sat down and ate a good meal. Dennis put Aggie in the barn and gave her some hay. When he looked her over, he knew I was telling the truth about Hedge being mean to her, and he felt sorry for her.

"What are horses selling for in this part of the country?" he asked Hedge.

"You can get all you want for twenty-five dollars a head," said Hedge.

"Broke horses? Who has good saddle horses at that price?"

"Carter's – up over the hill – has some like the mare I'm riding."

"I'll give you twenty-five dollars for her."

"No, I wouldn't sell her for that. She's fast and surefooted, and she can go all day and all night. And she's only five years old."

"Is she lazy? Why do you use spurs on her until – " Dennis checked himself and didn't finish his question.

"No, she isn't lazy. She's skittish in town – and I'll cure her of that if I have to break her ribs."

"I'd like to try her out tomorrow, if you don't mind. I might pay a little more if she suits me."

"She'll suit you, all right, but the price don't suit me."

"I told you I might go a little higher."

"Well, come over tomorrow and I'll see," Hedge agreed.

The next day Dennis came over to our place, and after riding Aggie and more dickering, he led the beautiful little mare away with him. Eventually, he rode her all over the western states and wrote Mother that she was such a pet, all he had to do was call and she'd come running.

When Dennis first told Mother he was going away, I was brokenhearted, and I was glad when Mother sent me for fresh drinking water, and I could have a good cry all by myself and bid Dennis good-bye without tears. I had heard the grown-ups saying he was probably going to hunt up his long-lost sweetheart, but from the stories he had told me about leaving places where he heard she was staying, I didn't think it was likely.

And now we were back at Hedge's ranch. Dennis was gone, and the bottom had dropped out of my world. All I could do to comfort myself was think what a good time we had had at Grandma's.

The long winter months dragged on. Hedge had to get one of the colts in and break him to ride, so he got Mr. Carter to rope a nice three-year-old gelding that had never been handled, not even halter-broke. Hedge snubbed him to a post, saying, "I'll let him tire himself out, pulling on that post instead of jerking me around, and then I'll see what I can do with him." The colt suddenly threw himself backward with all his strength and fell over on his side. He had broken his neck.

The next colt was not nearly so well built and lacked the life of the first colt, so he wasn't likely to hurt himself, but many an hour of misery he dealt me. He wasn't easily scared, but he was foxy. He would let me lead him to water, but when I started toward the house with him, he would stop and eat grass. If I tried to put a half hitch on his nose so I could lead him, he would stand with his head so high that I couldn't reach it. If he got tired of me bothering him, he would jerk away. Once I tried to hold him when he started after a bunch of horses he used to run with. He dragged me over a big rock, cutting my knee to the bone, and I had to let go. The horses were headed for a spring two miles away, and I followed with my knee bleeding and my elbows skinned.

The spring was in a deep coulee. I couldn't see how many horses were there. If there were wild horses in the bunch, they would run as soon as they saw me, and the colt would run with them. And that was just what happened.

I was left alone at the spring. It was a beautiful place. Chokecherries and wildflowers were blooming on the steep side of the coulee. I climbed up and picked a nice bouquet that I knew I didn't dare take home. Hedge would have said, "That was what you were doing when you should have been catching the colt." I carried the flowers almost all the way, then laid them in the shade of a big rock and went to face whatever he did to me. I was lucky; Hedge had seen the colt get away from me, and he only scolded, "When are you going to learn to stand on your pins and quit falling all over yourself? Look at them knees – the elbows tore out of your dress, too!" and he gave me a slap. "Go wash them knees."

I heard Mother and Hedge talking again about proving up on the ranch and moving to town. I hoped they would, because Hedge didn't have as many opportunities to beat me in town. But we had one more sickening experience to remember from the ranch.

Shortly after Mother came back to the ranch from Belt, she had bought two old milk cows, cheap. When Hedge drove them home, they tried to turn right around and go back, almost before he was off his horse. He told me to bring him the extra picket rope from under the stairs, but he had two cows and only one rope. We looked around and found two short pieces of rope. Hedge tied one piece of rope around the white cow's horns, the other around the muley cow's neck, then tied both to the picket rope.

Tied like this and not being used to picketing, the cows were constantly getting tangled up in the rope. Hedge untangled them several times the first day. At bedtime Mother was worried, but Hedge said the cows were tired and would soon lie down. Mother got up at daybreak to look after them, but she was too late. The muley cow was dead, and the other, tangled and fretted in the rope, had little milk to let down.

Mother was sick over her loss, but Hedge said, "There's no use worrying over a dead cow. The only thing to do now is make beef out of her."

"Oh, Hedge, you wouldn't think of such a thing! That meat isn't fit to eat."

"Why isn't it? The cow wasn't sick, or we wouldn't have bought her. She got killed. So does every cow we eat when we buy beef."

Hedge put me to work carrying water to wash the meat off. He got the hide off in fairly good time, but when it came to the entrails he was in a quandary. The cow was bloated, and he didn't have a tripod to hoist her on so that the weight of the entrails would help to release them. He didn't want to puncture the paunch because he knew the odor would be very bad (he was dainty in that respect and couldn't stand odors), but it was that or give up the job. He punctured the paunch, jumped back until the gases released, then cut handholds so he could pull out the paunch. Even so, he had plenty of difficulty.

He finally got his beef dressed and cut in pieces he could handle, but it would have taken more than water to make that meat look edible. The cow had got the rope in the cleft of her hind hoof. The knot kept the rope from sliding through, and it pulled her head down to her foot. The boss cow with the horns – cows always boss one another – must have hooked her, because her sides showed the marks of the horns. Some had merely scraped hair, but others were deep enough to draw blood. Even the lightest bruises showed up on the meat, so it showed more stripes than the hide did.

I caught the team, and Hedge harnessed them and hitched them to the wagon, although with plenty of objection on their part to coming anywhere near that meat. He drove off toward Sand Coulee where a settlement of foreigners lived, remarking that he could sell them anything if the price was cheap enough.

Mother was apprehensive and kept walking around the house, looking out the windows in the direction of Sand Coulee, but for once Hedge came home promptly with a considerable sum of money. He was in a rare good humor and said he had pulled a good one on the foreign women, peddling that meat all through their part of town. He put me to washing out the wagon box, which was a mess because the meat had not been properly bled.

From this time on, we lived on the ranch in the summer and moved back into Great Falls for the winter. Mother could always get work to earn a grubstake to go back to the ranch in the spring. She made a poor rancher's wife because she was afraid of all animals, and they in turn were afraid of her, but I must have taken after my cowboy father, because I loved animals and got along with them well.

Hedge had always made me lead the horses to water and then picket them. The first few times he went with me to show me how to hold the horses and how to choose a spot where the grass was good and there weren't many rocks. But despite all his warnings, the horses got away from me several times before I learned how to manage them. Hedge would put a half hitch on the horses' lower jaws, and then I had better control, but it was hard for me to take the half hitch off again because I was so small. So most of the time the poor animal was left with that painful half hitch on its lower jaw until it finally worked loose. One time I remember that the rope was so tight that the horse never did get the half hitch off and stood there all night without being able to eat.

We always had to picket our saddle horse because Hedge never put up a fence or anything else on his homestead, not even a load of hay.

Tom Carter, who sometimes rode over to our spring after his horses, would always stop and help me if I happened to be near. I liked Mr. Carter because he praised me for being so capable. When I told him I had to learn to milk the cow because Mother couldn't do it, he said he couldn't see how I managed our old cow's great big teats with my small hands. I told him, "I lock my two hands together until I get some of the milk and her teats are not so full. I have to be careful because my short fingers come right in the middle of her big teats, and my fingernails might hurt her."

5

It was through Tom Carter that I met Charley Russell.

Mother had sent me to the meat market when we were living in town one winter, and as I came close to the market I noticed Mr. Carter standing there, talking to a man who wore a sash instead of a belt.

I saw that both men were looking at me, and I was ashamed of my old coat and badly worn shoes. I hoped to get by without stopping, but Mr. Carter's big smile made me forget my fears as he said, "Why, Peggy! You are not going to pass me up without even saying hello?"

Now I was thoroughly embarrassed for being rude to Mr. Carter, who had been so kind to me, and I said very meekly, "How do you do, Mr. Carter."

"That's a lady. Now come here. Do you know who this gentleman is?"

I shook my head.

"This is my friend Charley Russell. He savvies horses and cows, too. Charley, this little girl lives out near my ranch, and sometimes the horses get away from her, and I have seen her tramping all over the prairie trying to catch them or sometimes looking for their milk cow."

Charley looked surprised and said, "And I thought I got an early start! But tell me, Peggy, how can you manage to take a horse home if you do catch up to him?"

"It's not hard if he has a half hitch on his jaw, but if he hasn't, he will keep running with the other horses, and I never catch up to him. The old cow is easy. She starts home when she sees me coming. Lots of times Mr. Carter catches the horses for me. If he doesn't, my stepfather has to go and get them himself."

I added that I could sometimes catch a horse by offering all the horses a few handfuls of salt. Even the wild horses would sometimes come and get a few licks of salt. They seemed to be starved for it.

As I started to go into the meat market, Charley said, "Let me see if I have any change in my pocket." He pulled out fifty cents and handed it to me.

I said, "Oh! Thank you so much. I can buy a big sack of candy with that much."

Mr. Carter handed me a quarter and said, "Here, that makes seventy-five cents, but don't spend it all for candy. Buy a nickel's worth, and then you will have money left for another time."

I stopped at Regan's and bought a nickel's worth of chocolates, and was I surprised at the small amount I got for my nickel! When I got to the butcher shop I had to be prompted because I had forgotten what Mother told me to get.

A couple of years later we were moving into town for the winter with two milk cows. Hedge had tied them both behind the wagon. The old cow walked along docilely, but the young cow was not broke to lead, and she kept pulling back until she broke the rope. After several breaks and a lot of trouble catching the cow, Hedge said to me as he climbed back in the wagon, "Here, take this club and try and keep her coming."

She was a range cow with a big pair of horns, and she was ready for a showdown. With the cow on the prod and a job I thought was impossible, tears came to my eyes, and a heavy load was on my heart. I knew better than to protest, but Mother tried to convince Hedge that I was tired and not able to cope with such a difficult task.

He replied, "This young cow might follow the old cow for a while. Peggy will be all right with this old broom."

To my surprise, she did follow along pretty good, with just a little urging from me. Sometimes we came to good grass, and she would stop and graze, and several times Hedge had to come back and help me get her started again. Was I ever glad when I saw that we were coming to a fence – it was the fence around the old Calvary cemetery, where the road from the south of Great Falls came into the city until about 1905 or 1906, when the Ayreshire Dairy built another road. Then we called it the Red Road, because of that red rock at the dairy. I did have it easy for a while until we came to where a post was broken off and the fence down to where the cow could jump over the slack wire. I started after her, but she turned to face me, blowing her nose and shaking her head.

I savvied cows enough to know what she meant, and as a last resort I called to Hedge. He came roaring back. But the cow was tired, hungry, and suffering from a very sore head because the rope tied around her horns had pulled so tight while she was being dragged behind the wagon. The rope was hanging down just long enough for her to step on it every so often, which irritated her head and in turn her disposition until she was really on the prod. As soon as Hedge stepped on the fence, she charged him. When he backed out, she started pawing the ground. He said, "Get me some rocks, and I'll take some of the fight out of her."

As I gathered rocks, Hedge pelted her until she took off for the other side of the cemetery. He said, "I think this is the only place the fence is down. I'll stand this post up, and you stay here and throw rocks at her if she tries to come out, but I don't think she will. She's hungry, and she has lots of good grass in there. I'll go on into town and unhook the horses and ride one of them out after her. It's only four miles or so into town."

At first I did not realize what I was up against as I gathered stones to throw at the cow if she came back, but this was in the fall, and it soon started to get dark. I had no company but an unfriendly cow, and soon I could no longer hear the rumble of the heavy wagon as it jostled over rocks and ruts. I looked across the cemetery where several headstones stood up above the tall grass. There must be a lot of dead people out there. Maybe the good ones got wings and went to heaven, but what about the bad ones? If they didn't get wings, they must still be there.

The wind was blowing and kept the tall grass and weeds moving, and my imagination made forms out of those tall weeds until I welcomed the unfriendly cow when she began to graze in my direction. I watched her closely, but she made no signs of seeing anything. I thought that maybe cows couldn't see ghosts. As long as I had kept moving I was plenty warm, but now I was shivering with both fear and cold as some of those headstones seemed to sway and even whisper.

How I wished I had not been so hard on the cow. If we were on good terms, I could stand close by her side and feel much safer, and I could even milk some milk into my mouth. But I did not dare go near the cow, who was still shaking her head from the pain of that tight rope.

Before I could hear or see Hedge coming, the cow looked in the direction of town. She started toward the far end of the cemetery but stopped when she found that the fence was in good shape. On horseback, Hedge drove her out of the cemetery without any trouble.

Our horses were not gentle enough to ride double, so I began the long trek behind Hedge and the cow into town. I needed no coaxing to eat my supper and tumble into bed that night.

The next morning, a beautiful Indian summer day, brought more problems for me because we only had two picket ropes, and they were needed to picket the horses. As soon as the cows were milked, Hedge helped me take them to the public hydrant, where there was an old washtub that everybody in our neighborhood used to water their cows. The young cow had been kept in the woodshed all night with nothing to eat, so she was not in a good humor. Hedge said, "Peg, you will have to herd the cows today. Tomorrow I will see the boy about putting them in the town herd."

In Great Falls we had for many years what was known as the town herd. A big boy would come by in the morning and take all the milk cows out south and bring them back at night for one dollar a month.

Hedge led the horses, and I drove the cows out to the edge of town where the grass was good. Then he said, "You stay on the other side of the cows and don't let them go over the hill. They are hungry, and I don't think they will want to go anywhere until they have had their fill of grass."

Of course, the cows did go to work on the grass, but they must have believed in killing two birds with one stone, because they kept grazing away from town. When I drove one back, the other would be making a little headway toward the ranch. Hedge had said he would be watching, and if they were getting away from me, he would come and drive them back with the horse. I kept looking for him, but I knew he would be sleeping during the day, as he nearly always went out at night. It was not long before the cows were on top of the hill and traveling south. In spite of me with my broomstick, we were soon out of sight of town and still going, across Field's Coulee and climbing Charley Donahue's Hill, now known as Ball's Hill.

Trying to keep ahead of the cows played me out, and finally, they got way ahead. I was following behind, trying to keep them in sight, when I saw a rider coming. I expected it was Hedge, and I knew he would be in a rage over me letting the cows get away. I wiped my eyes with my dress because Hedge would not stand for any sniffling, as he called crying.

As the rider came closer, I knew it was not Hedge, because we didn't have a pinto horse. Then I recognized Charley Russell. He said with a big smile that warmed my heart, "Well, well, if it isn't little Peggy. What are you doing way out here?"

Between sobs I said, "I was herding the cows and they got away from me. I just couldn't head them off."

"Of course you couldn't. Don't you cry anymore. I'll go and bring them back."

Charley was off on a high lope and soon returned with two very disgruntled cows. Then he said, "Come on, climb up." He took his foot out of the stirrup so I could get my knee on his toe and pulled me into the saddle in front of him.

"This good old boy won't mind one bit if we ride double, that is, if we don't ride too far."

He went on to question me about following the cows so far from town and why I didn't run home and tell my father the cows had got away from me.

I explained that when Hedge told me to do something, I dared not say I couldn't or offer any excuses or I would get a spanking. I told him about a lot of times when the horses had gotten away from me and run off with a bunch of wild horses with the picket rope all unraveled and some of it lost from the horses tramping on it, and Charley asked more questions about my home life until he saw that I was reluctant to talk about it.

When we got back to where our horses were picketed, Charley said, "Now you run home and tell your father that I brought the cows back from beyond Donahue's Hill, but you can't stop them if they want to go again."

I said, "I can't do that."

"Why not? Them cows will just take off again. Cows don't like to be moved from their home range."

"Because my father said he wanted no back talk from me, or he would skin me alive. I'll just stay here with the cows."

"Not this time, he won't, because I'll tell him myself."

Charley got off his horse and walked along with me, although I would sooner have stayed with the cows. I began to lag back as we neared the house. By this time Charley was beginning to realize just how scared I was and said, "Come on, don't be afraid. You are not going to get in trouble this time."

Hedge saw us coming, but he pretended he didn't. He was chopping wood at the woodpile. Charley took me by the hand, which made a bad matter worse. Their greetings were anything but cordial. Then Charley said, "Peggy couldn't hold them cows. They got away from her and were way on the other side of Donahue's Hill."

"Thanks for bringing them back. I was just getting ready to go after them. Peg, you go back there and stay with them cows like I told you."

Charley frowned. "That child can't hold them cows. As soon as they get rested up, they will head for home again. Why don't you picket them until they get used to being here?"

"Both ropes are on the horses, and that young cow broke the other rope all to hell when I tried to lead her behind the wagon."

"I see. That sure makes it tough on Peggy."

"Don't worry about her," Hedge advised.

I looked back to see if they would get in a fuss over me, but Charley just waved and said, "Bye-bye."

The cows were lying down, chewing their cuds, when I got back to them. I walked around to their far side and sat down, hoping they were as tired as I was. I sat there for quite a while, watching people coming and going in town. Then I saw Charley Russell riding toward our house at 813 6th Street South, but he didn't stop, he just threw something on the porch. I wondered what it could be. Soon Charley rode out where I was sitting and said, "You won't need to herd the cows tomorrow because I brought you a couple of picket ropes. Now I am going to take a ride out to see your friend Tom Carter, and I'll have to tell him all the trouble you had with them cows. Better luck tomorrow."

"Thanks ever so much for the ropes, but I think we are going to put the cows in the town herd tomorrow. That costs money, and I heard him tell Mother he hasn't got any."

Charley laughed and said, "Neither have I got any money, most of the time. I wish you better luck."

I was happy to think somebody cared about me, although I was afraid that Hedge might resent it. Hedge never wanted me to know anything about myself. I was never even told how old I was or when my birthday was. Still, I wished there was something I could do for Mr. Russell. It has taken a lifetime to tell this little story and show just what kind of a man Charley Russell really was.

I was anxious to see the picket ropes, even though they were just the same type of rope that we all used to picket horses. But one of these ropes was a little different. I'm sure it was Charley's own special picket rope, because it had a swivel spliced in the center of it. It was the first time I had seen a swivel, and I did not realize what a lifesaver it was going to be for me. Nobody will ever know the trouble I had with wet and frozen ropes. When a picket rope gets wet from snow or rain, and a shivering horse keeps walking around and around a picket pin all night to keep warm, that horse's rope gets full of knots and loops that are almost impossible to untangle until the rope dries out. The horse would be cold and nervous and moving while I frantically tried to untangle seventy-five feet of three-quarter-inch rope. As I seldom had mittens, only when Grandma Travers knitted me a pair at Christmastime, my fingers would be so cold that I could hardly move them. But I had to. I had to take that horse to water and then change its picket to where the grass was good and there were no rocks.

I have heard some people say that they would like to relive their childhood. Not me! Going over it now is bad enough.

But the swivel paid off. I always put the swivel rope on the wildest horse.

Years ago I used to visit Sid Willis and Eklund at his upstairs studio at 306 Central in Great Falls. Those two old boys could fill you in on the past history of anybody in Great Falls. Many a happy hour I spent listening to Sid Willis tell about some of Charley Russell's escapades. Here is one:

Charley Russell and two other cowboys were hibernating for the winter in Chinook, a very small town at that time, with very little excitement. There were two trains a day that used to go through Chinook, and the cowboys liked to go and meet the train to see if a tenderfoot got off that they could pull a fast one on.

On their way to the station on this particular day, they picked up some old newspapers, and as soon as the train stopped, they raced up and down the platform, hollering, "Sitting Bill broke out!"

A big fat man from the far end of the train came running as fast as he could and asked Charley, "Where did he break out of?"

"He broke out all over his body, his legs and arms and everything," Charley replied as he jumped off the platform and dashed away on his horse.

Another one Sid told me was about old John Mathison. Mathison was an old-time freighter who had just pulled into Great Falls after a miserable trip from Lewistown. He had taken care of his six horses and was ready to take care of himself when he met Charley in the saloon. Charley was doing a little celebrating while his wife was out of town, so he suggested a drink. Mathison ordered some Hostetter's bitters. Then he added some black pills that he always carried with him and washed them down.

After a couple of drinks, they went to the lunch counter in the saloon and had a big steak with all the trimmings, especially lots of Arbuckle's coffee. Mathison filled his mouth with tobacco and said he was ready to go with Charley to see his new house. So they went to Charley's house, and as soon as Mathison saw it, he sized up the house and then Charley and said, "This is a hell of a fine wickiup for you to be living in! Remember when we thought we were lucky if somebody let us roll out our blankets on the dirt floor of a bunkhouse? Well, well, what changes do come about!"

By this time, after several hours of visiting and drinking, Mathison's black pills began to work on him. He asked Charley, "Where is your horse stable? I need to go out."

Charley showed him to the bathroom, which was all new to John. "I never thought a man would get so low as to shit in his house!" he said.

Charley tried to explain how sanitary and handy the indoor toilet was. He flushed John's chew of tobacco down to show how clean the bowl was. John was surprised but unconvinced.

"Charley," he said, "show me to a regular outhouse – I couldn't go sitting on that thing!"

Another story Sid Willis told was about a mean trick played on Charley.

A lot of cowboys were in town, most of them in the Mint Saloon. After they had been whooping it up for some time, Sid saw that Charley had had enough, so he said, "Charley, I'm hungry. Let's go across the street and get something to eat."

While the rest continued to celebrate, two other fellows joined them, and they went over to the Gerald Cafe. They took one of the closed booths, and Billy Grills, the owner, took their orders. Charley was sitting in the corner, leaning against the wall, and soon he put his arm on the table to rest his head and went to sleep. When the orders came, nobody disturbed him. They cleaned up their own plates and then his, even wiped it clean with their bread. Then they asked Mr. Grills not to take Charley's plate away and to let him sleep. Mr. Grills said, "Okay, until I need the booth."

Finally, the booth was needed, and he woke Charley up. Charley looked around him in surprise. Everybody was gone. Then he looked at his plate. It was slick and clean. He said, "I sure must have had one too many, because I don't remember eating a bite, but from the looks of my plate, I must've done a good job. Did they pay for mine?"

"Oh, sure they did," replied Billy.

The Gerald Cafe was a fine place to eat, with good food and help.

The Mint Saloon and the Silver Dollar Saloon were the meeting places for most people who came to Great Falls. Bill Rance owned the Silver Dollar, which had some special attractions. One was his sidewalk, which had silver dollars imbedded in it, good old Morgan dollars, not those phony-looking Eisenhower dollars. Once when a wool buyer came into his saloon and admired some of Charley's paintings, Bill got word to Charley, who came and made a deal on the spot. Another sale at the Silver Dollar that gave Charley quite a shock was when he timidly asked fifty dollars for a painting, and the buyer gave him a hundred.

Sid Willis's saloon was always popular because it was full of Russell paintings. Poor old Sid hung on to them as long as he could, hoping the state of Montana would purchase them and keep them in Montana. The state made a good start by hiring a lawyer to go out and ask the people of Montana to donate to the cause, which he did, but he also paid himself five hundred dollars a month and expenses. When the people found out how Mr. Lawyer was operating on their money, of course he was finished, and the promoters lost their ambition for another try. So all those wonderful paintings were sold out of Montana. Poor old Sid felt so heartbroken that he passed out as they were removing the paintings from the saloon.

78

Sid was never the same after the paintings were gone. Neither was the Mint. The walls were bare where the paintings had hung for years. I think they were sold for a hundred and fifty thousand dollars. Now one of them alone is worth that.

Sid needed the money, and he was too old and ill to take care of the saloon any longer. But he was a good man while he was able, and he did a lot for Great Falls, whether Great Falls knows it or not.

6

In Great Falls we moved into a little house badly in need of repairs a block from where Hedge's mother lived. Hedge seldom visited his mother, so he didn't know until Pete told him that she was planning to move back to Canada in a few days. Pete worked occasionally and gave the old lady a little money now and then, but she saw she would be in a bad spot when her savings were gone. In Canada her other children would look after her.

When she came to Montana, she had three big black boxes that Hedge had always been curious about. Pete told him she planned to sell some of the stuff in the boxes, and Hedge thought this was his chance not only to find out what was in them but perhaps to buy something cheap from his mother. He told Pete he was going to shave off his moustache, dress up like a woman, and see what bargains he could find. He and Pete had fun fixing him up for the occasion. He put on Mother's long black dress and a black hood that almost covered his face when it was tied under his chin. Mother had a black plush jacket-length cape that completed his disguise, but when he walked across the street, his steps were too long, and his heels whipped his skirt too high around his legs, so he looked anything but feminine.

To avoid the necessity of talking much, he told Pete to say he was a Dutch girl from the riverbank who couldn't speak English.

Pete went ahead of Hedge to tell the old lady that the "Dutch girl" was coming. The poor old soul was hard of hearing, but she seemed to find something familiar about the Dutch girl's voice and would look up with a start when she spoke. Hedge did get a few bargains – potatoes that his mother had raised in her garden, a good lantern, and some carpenter tools that had belonged to his father and that were part of the treasure that had been in the black boxes. There were also some Hudson Bay blankets and a sturdy old rocking chair that Hedge wanted, but his cash was getting low. He had to talk hard to get the blankets at his price. He offered a dollar and a half for the rocking chair, but his mother wanted two fifty and held to her price.

When her head was turned, Hedge asked Pete for his purse. Pete slipped him his buckskin sack, and Mother Wolfe caught a glimpse of it and recognized it.

"That's your purse," she cried to Pete. "So that's where you spend your money and your time, down with the Dutch girls on the river-bank! Take what you've bought and get out," she said, turning to Hedge. "I don't want the likes of you in my house."

The boys could hardly keep their faces straight while they gathered up their purchases – the potatoes they left for Pete to get later. When they told Mother how they had fooled the old lady, they laughed until their sides ached. It was so unusual to see Hedge laugh that I watched him and Pete as they told funny incidents of the bargaining and how Hedge had had to hang his head to keep his mother from getting a good look at his face.

Mother said nothing, but I gathered that she didn't think their stunt was very nice. But I didn't feel sorry for Mrs. Wolfe. She had told Mother, "You work too hard. You won't last long. I'll live to see your coffin walk."

Mother didn't go out to work the first winter we lived in Great Falls because she wasn't well enough, and as a result, we were on short rations. She was worried. She had promised to send me to school, but I needed clothes. When Grandma and Uncle Mike stopped in to see us shortly after we moved, Grandma sensed the situation and bought a few yards of calico to make us children two dresses each. Uncle Mike loaned Hedge twenty dollars to buy groceries.

I started school and went about six weeks. But our cow was going dry from standing tied to the fence all night in the cold with nothing to eat from the time the boy brought the town herd in until he took them out in the morning. Hedge told Mother to send me down to the hay market, where he said I could gather plenty for one cow. That ended my schooling in Great Falls. Every day I took a gunnysack to the hay market, and as soon as I filled it I carried it home and came back for another sackful. That went on every day until the weather got so cold and the roads so drifted that the farmers were not able to haul hay to town.

Mother knew the little girls had to have milk, and to give milk the cow had to eat. She managed to buy a few bales of hay to tide us over until the weather broke and I could go back to the hay market. By then there wasn't much to get. In stormy weather farmers put their teams in the livery stable or used the sheds at the Farmer's Hotel. The only times I could get lots of hay was when a rancher tied his team to the hay rack, and the horses pulled it down as they ate.

Sometimes a rancher would ask me, "What are you doing out in the cold?" and throw me down a forkful of hay. "Put that in your sack and run home!"

If a forkful was too much to go in my sack, I would be back promptly for the rest. Then some boys started rustling hay and chased me home every time they caught me at the hay market. Hedge put the run on them once or twice, but he couldn't watch for them all the time. He told me to go only when the boys were in school, which helped, but of course the cow didn't get as much hay.

We had no such thing as friendly neighbors. Hedge discouraged people from coming to our house. He would meet them at the door and ask what they wanted. If they said they came to see Mother, he would say she had a headache and was lying down. I do not remember him ever letting anyone into the house.

He would come home with the strangest things. One time he brought a light sulky, not the heavy type used to break driving horses but a light little affair like those used in harness races.

Mother was disgusted, but Hedge and Pete found a use for it. They loaded the sulky with their potatoes, Pete pulled, and Hedge pushed the load and did the peddling. They brought home a few groceries with the potato money. A few nights later they disappeared with the sulky and came back with a load of tame ducks. After dressing the fattest, they went peddling the rest and came home bragging to each other how slick they were to sell some of the ducks to the same man they stole them from. They didn't let Mother hear them say this – they told her they had won the ducks in a card game.

Mother had a hard time keeping the house warm that winter. It was harder to heat than our log house on the ranch and didn't stay warm after the fire went down. She never wasted coal, but Hedge complained about the amount she used.

"What's the matter with sending Spindleshanks out to gather wood once in awhile?" he asked. "Get your duds on," he said, turning to me, "and bring in some wood, and after this see that your mother has it on hand."

Wood was not plentiful in town, and I had to do a lot of looking to get the first armful. But I soon found a better way: I went to the stores and business houses and asked for boxes. Everything in those days came in wooden boxes, and the men were very good about helping me out. I was so brow-beaten at home by Hedge that I was never bold or rude, and my appearance was probably wretched enough to make anyone pity me.

Mother was the one who suffered the real hardship. She had been used to taking a nap every day after I got home with my sacks of hay and could take care of the three little girls, but now I went right back out again after wood, and she missed her naps. The next thing she was sick in bed, and I had to stay home to tidy the house and watch the fire.

I hated housework and was never finished with it. It took me all morning to wash the dishes, empty the ashes, sweep Mother's room and the kitchen, and bring in water from the hydrant. I warmed the water and put a basin on a chair by Mother's bed, where she could wash the little girls' hands and faces, comb their hair, and dress them. All this had to be done as quietly as possible, because Hedge would be sleeping.

Mother and I kept up this system of caring for the children and the house for what seemed to me an endless time, but I noticed she grew less strict about my housework. She had always inspected the laundry before she let me hang any of it out, but one day she hardly looked at what I'd washed and said, "I guess they'll do. Hurry and hang them out. I want you to go for the doctor. I was waiting in hopes that your grandmother would come, but I can't wait any longer."

I went straight to the doctor's office, where I had been once before with Mother. I gave him Mother's message, that she was very sick and alone, and she needed him as soon as he could get to her, and the doctor asked me if she had been sick for long.

I answered, "A long time, but she is worse now. She don't care about nothing."

"How do you know that? That she doesn't care about anything?"

"Because she always used to make me wash some of the clothes over again, but today she just said, 'I guess they'll do.'"

The doctor looked at me in surprise. "Do you do the washing?"

"Not all our clothes. I just wash what we need."

"Where is your father?"

"Downtown."

"Where does he work?"

"I don't know." Hedge had warned me about talking to anyone about him or his work.

"All right," the doctor said. "Run home and tell your mother I will be there within an hour."

I dashed to the hay market and filled my gunnysack and then

raced home. I could see the little girls watching out the window for me. "Here she comes, here she comes! We know it's her because she has a sack of hay!"

When Mother asked if I found the doctor, I told her everything he had said.

"Now hurry and straighten up this room before he gets here," she told me.

Mother had let my little sisters play in their bed in their dirty shoes because it kept them off the cold floor and they could watch out the window for me. Now she was ashamed to have the doctor see it so untidy. She told me to go to her trunk and get her good spread and put it on the bed and pick up all the children's playthings. "Don't try to sweep," she said. "I have a choking feeling." I hadn't yet learned to sweep without making plenty of dust.

When the doctor rode up on his bicycle, Mother sent us to the kitchen and told us we must be very quiet, or the doctor might send her away. Even the baby seemed to sense the seriousness of the moment. Then we heard the doctor say, "I will send an ambulance to take you to the hospital." What scared us was Mother beginning to cry. "Oh dear! Oh dear! How can I leave my little children? Who will take care of my poor babies?"

"Send the little girl after your husband," the doctor said.

"She wouldn't be able to find him," Mother said between sobs.

"I'll have somebody look him up. You try to rest until the ambulance comes. Is your husband working?"

"Not unless he found a job since noon."

"Don't worry. We'll find him if he's in town."

As soon as we heard the doctor close the door, we stole into Mother's room and stood by her bed, all of us crying with her. But Mother dried her eyes and began instructing me in the care of the baby – little Rose, only fourteen months old and just able to walk. Mother said if I didn't know what to do to ask a certain neighbor

85

woman who had always tried to be friendly. She told me to manage the housework just as I had while she was in bed, to do a little washing every day so it wouldn't be too much for me, but most of all not to forget the baby and to take her with me whenever I played outside.

I was about eight years old.

The ambulance came, and again she whispered, "What will become of my poor children!" The man lifted the baby so she could kiss Mother, but when he lifted Nora, she was so frightened by the commotion and Mother's crying that she wouldn't kiss her.

We never saw Mother alive again.

After I was grown and long through with Hedge and had come back to Montana, I looked the old doctor up and asked him about Mother. He said he knew she was dying when he walked into her bedroom, but he didn't want her to die in a place like that, with a calf in the coal shed, almost in the kitchen. The calf had hardly been fed after Mother went to bed, and he bawled most of the time.

I also went to see a woman who sat up with Mother the night she died. She told me that Hedge did not come near Mother that night. She knew, because she was with Mother until morning, when she left the hospital to make breakfast for her husband. Mother told her she would be gone before she got back.

When Mother knew she was dying, she asked another friend, a doctor's wife, to see that her children were taken care of, and the woman promised. Mother seemed to relax and passed away.

True to her promise, the doctor's wife came with two other women to see us. They agreed that the orphanage was the only solution and told me to get our clothes together. But while we were busy in the attic, digging out our old clothes, Hedge came home. He was furious and told the women in no uncertain language that he was the boss of his own children, and they were to go home and mind their own business. So the ladies with the good intentions ran into a stone wall.

We wakened early the next morning, as little children do. The house was cold and quiet. Hedge wasn't at home, and so I got up and built the fire, then got back into bed while the fire got started. My little sisters sat in their bed, playing. Two neighbor women were passing by, saw the little girls, and tapped on the window. "Do you know your mother is dead?"

I answered, "No!"

"Yes. She died early this morning," they told us and walked on.

I began to cry, and the three little ones followed suit. Hedge came in just then, and I asked whether it was true that Mother was dead.

He said, "Yes, it's true. Who told you?"

"Mrs. O'Leary."

"How did she find out so quick?"

"She didn't say."

"She's always sticking her nose in other people's business. Now you hurry and get dressed and milk the cow so she'll be ready when the herd goes by."

Some of the other neighbor women came over and gathered up all the dirty clothes, took them home, and washed and ironed them so we would have clean dresses for the funeral. One of the women asked if Grandma had been notified.

Hedge said, "Not yet. Me and the old woman don't get along, so we'll just let her stay where she is."

The woman was not so easily put off. "Her own mother! It's not right!"

We never knew who took Grandma the message, but she said she was not surprised when it came. All that night she had dreamed that Mother was calling her, so plainly that it woke her up.

Grandma and Uncle Mike came to town at once and went to the undertakers to see Mother and learn what funeral arrangements had been made. Hedge had told the county to bury Mother, as he had no money, but Uncle Mike said, "No sister of mine shall be buried in the potter's field," and he paid the undertaker the cost of a decent burial.

Grandma came to our house and moved everything out of Mother's room. She washed the windows and the curtains and scrubbed the furniture and the floors. She and some of the neighbors mended and patched our clothes so we would be presentable for the funeral. Poor Grandma hadn't brought a housedress with her, so she put on one of Mother's. One of my little sisters told her to take it off. She did, but she was deeply hurt, and she cried as though her heart would break.

At the undertaker's, Uncle Mike lifted us each up to kiss Mother good-bye. She wasn't made up as corpses are today. Her lips were very blue, her cheeks pale and sunken, but I knew it was Mother. Until I saw her, I had been doubting she was really dead.

On the day of her funeral, we children were slicked up and dressed, ready to go, when Hedge came in and said, "No, we won't bother taking them. They will be better off at home." So after all the rushing to get us ready, we were not allowed to go to our own mother's funeral.

I knew better than to say a word in protest, but inside I was raging.

Mother, I said to myself, *Grandma says you are in heaven and can see and hear us. I promise I will do the good things you always said I must. But I am going to get away from Hedge. If he beats me to death before I can get away, I will be with you.*

Grandma hated to leave us alone and stayed with us for a few days after the funeral. Hedge told her he had written his brother Zed in Canada, asking if he could bring us children up there so Zed's wife could look after us. Grandma asked him to let her keep me – it would make one less for his sister-in-law to take care of – but Hedge said he was depending on me to be a big help to her, and I gritted my teeth and shut my fists in my determination that someday I would get away from him if I had to die to do it.

I don't know who wrote Hedge's letter for him. He had never gone to school, and he was raising me the same way, although that didn't worry me at the time.

His brother soon came down from Canada, and how different Zed was from Hedge! He was jolly and kind and brought us all kinds of good things to eat. He stayed home with us, did all the cooking, and even washed clothes. Hedge had instructed us to say "I don't know" to any questions Zed might ask. But Zed asked Hedge a few questions, like "Why aren't you working, part-time at least?" and "Will you have enough money to make the trip across the Line?"

Hedge said he had several head of good horses to sell and that he would have plenty of money for the trip. Zed reminded him that it was impossible to make the journey by wagon until late summer, when the rivers were low, but Hedge said he knew that and wasn't planning on leaving until he knew he could ford the rivers.

"How are you going to manage until then, if you don't go to work?"

"I'll dicker around if I can't find work," Hedge answered.

"Dickering around," Zed retorted. "I thought marriage might have changed you, but I guess not."

We children had a heavenly time while Zed was there. Hedge didn't beat me, even once, and Zed bought hay for the cow and calf so I could stay home and mind the baby. I even went over to a neighbor's and played with her little girl until Hedge dragged me home by the ear. I was afraid he would beat me for that after Zed left, but he didn't.

Before Zed went back to Canada he went uptown every day and brought us groceries and meat. We hated to see him go, but now we had something good to look forward to. I wished that fall would hurry up and come, and I think Hedge wished so, too. He was afraid the authorities might make trouble about the way he was providing for us children. Mother's friend, the doctor's wife, came to see us again and asked him if the orphanage wasn't the best place for us until we were a little older, but Hedge told her he had a sister-in-law who would look after us. He didn't tell her or anyone else that we were leaving town. He owed bills, and he wanted to leave before his creditors got wind of his intentions. He gave us girls strict instructions to keep our mouths shut.

After Zed left, Hedge was away from the house almost continually, and we children ran wild, especially me. It was late spring. There was a little pond about a block from our house, and I spent much time playing in the water catching tadpoles until the soles of my feet were so chapped that you could lay a match in the cracks. Every time I took a step the cracks would break open, and blood would trickle down between my toes. I tried to wash my feet, but it hurt so much that I let them go until they were almost black from blood and dirt. Hedge noticed them and made me wash them, but I had only laundry soap, and afterward they were drier than ever. A neighbor saw me the next day as I went to the hydrant to get water. She took me to her house, soaked my feet in warm water, smeared them with Vaseline, and bandaged them. I didn't suffer so much after that, but it took my feet a long time to heal.

I got into more trouble with my feet just before we left for Canada. Boys of the neighborhood were jumping off a coal shed. As soon as they went away, I thought I would climb up and see how far I could jump. There was a pile of old lumber near the shed. None of the boys had jumped as far as that, but I did – and landed on a spike in a two-by-four. A man passing by saw what had happened and carried me into his house. His wife dressed my foot, and they both showed such concern that I was embarrassed. They told me to have my father take me to a doctor, but I knew they were wasting their breath.

During our last month in Great Falls, Hedge was away from home day and night, rounding up horses and getting ready to leave. He traded a couple of young colts and started to break two older ones to make them more salable. He had them fairly well halter-broken when all his horses disappeared overnight from the pasture. Someone must have surmised he was going away and had driven the horses into the mountains to hold until he was gone. It was easy to get away with Hedge's horses, for they all bore Mr. Carter's brand. Carter had hundreds of horses and had sold them all over the country.

The only horse Hedge had left was a light roan gelding he had traded two sucking colts for. He was a boy's saddle pony that had been teased and tormented until he took to biting. Hedge had been using him to round up his other horses. The gelding was fairly good under the saddle, but a team of his sort could never make the long hazardous trip over the Line.

Hedge had to get some kind of a team, but I doubt that he had any money. Maybe he wrote to Zed. In any event, he came home one night with a big chestnut mare, poor and sweenied and wind-broken. She had been a fine animal, with a kind, too-willing disposition, and would have weighed fifteen hundred pounds if she had been fat. I couldn't believe that Hedge was going to hitch her and the gelding together. The gelding couldn't have weighed half as much as the mare.

People were beginning to crowd us for the bills Hedge owed. The milkman (we had been buying milk after Hedge sold the cow) came the morning we were leaving. Hedge insisted that he had paid the driver, but the milkman didn't believe him. They got into an argument, but at last the man left. I was glad, for as Hedge stood arguing, he kept his hand on the handle of a claw hammer lying on the frame of the shed, and I was afraid the milkman might get a blow to the head. After he left, Hedge rushed like mad to get the wagon loaded and get away before word got around that we were pulling out.

Our wagon wasn't new, but it was a good old lumber wagon, with sideboards and a covered top, with bows and a tarpaulin. We loaded a conglomeration of junk on the wagon, old irons, parts of old harnesses, and old cooking utensils, and on top of these went our mattresses and bedding. Anything Hedge didn't want to take, he rendered useless. He took a pick and made holes in two washtubs and a big galvanized tank that Mother had bought when she was running the boardinghouse. Then he threw it all down in the cellar.

We got away before the milkman or anyone else intercepted us, and Hedge pushed his team to their limit to put the miles between us and Great Falls. Jess, the poor old mare, had to do most of the pulling, and her tongue was hanging out most of the time, but we camped that night where the Teton and Marias Rivers come together.

7

The first few days on the road I was at the height of my glory. No housework, no washing – this was the life for me! But one night the rain started. Our tarp was new, and the rain came in, and before morning it had turned to snow. The wind blew so hard that I thought it would tear the tarp off the wagon. The storm was so bad that we couldn't go on. We just sat in the wagon all day, shivering. The poor horses stood on the sheltered side of the wagon, shivering without anything to eat. But after the storm passed all went well. We crossed the Teton and Marias Rivers without trouble, but when we came to the Milk River, it was a different story.

As its name implies, the Milk River is a dirty, milky color, and you can't see below its surface for any depth. The crossing at the Milk River had been obliterated by a herd of cattle that had just been driven across, but Hedge, who had made the trip several times, thought he knew where it was. He missed it by fifty feet, and Jess, the old mare, went down in quicksand. The water was only belly-deep, and yet she was floundering. Hedge knew she couldn't hold out very long, and she was pulling the gelding off balance with her struggles. He would lose the whole outfit if he didn't get help in a hurry.

First he carried my three little half-sisters back to the bank where they would be safe, and then he came back to the wagon and walked out on the tongue to put Jess's picket rope around her neck with a half hitch on her lower jaw. The rope wouldn't reach the bank, but it did reach shallow water. He told me to keep tugging at the rope and talking to Jess to encourage her so she wouldn't give up entirely. If she once stopped struggling, she would go underwater and be drowned.

Hedge left me there and ran to a little fort, the Ten Mile, not far from the crossing but out of sight. I had no idea how long it would take him to make the trip. My little half-sisters watched from the opposite bank. The baby was crying for me at the top of her voice, but my hands were full trying to keep Jess's head out of the water.

Jess jerked me off my feet and sat me down in the water. It was all I could do to hang on to the rope. My hands were almost raw from the rough hemp, and I had the bright idea of wrapping my dress around the rope to protect them. When Jess made a desperate lunge, she jerked me off my feet with such a splash that I thought I was going to drown. The little girls on shore screamed in terror. It was all I could do to hang on to the rope and scramble back to land.

My ducking almost made me forget to talk to poor old Jess or even give her rope an encouraging tug, and then Beck cried, "Here they come!"

First came a lone soldier on a beautiful saddle horse. He rode up and took the rope out of my hands and took a dally on his saddle horn. Then he cautiously rode closer to Jess and took a half hitch with the rope so he could keep her head up.

By this time I could see two more soldiers with six mules coming on a high lope. I had always felt contemptuous of mules, but this time I was glad to see all six of them, with their funny little jerky lope that reminded me of a rocking horse. The soldiers hooked their log chain to the rear axle of the wagon, and the mules pulled the load back until it rested on solid bottom and old Jess was out of the quicksand. The mounted soldier rode in and unhooked the tugs and drove the team across the river a little farther upstream. The mules brought the loaded wagon across.

We were a sorry-looking outfit, especially Jess and I. She was so frightened and weak that she could hardly stand, and she wasn't interested in grass, but the ornery little gelding fell to eating as though nothing had happened.

Hedge pulled the harness off Jess and told me to wash the mud off it. The soldiers looked at him in surprise, and one of them said, "I think that child needs dry clothes, first thing, and I would try that mare on a good feed of oats. If she would eat some oats, she might be all right."

"Oh, she'll be all right as soon as she dries off," Hedge said.

"She might. And then again, she might be dead in the morning. Do you have any oats?"

"No," Hedge said, "but she don't need any."

"I'll go back to Ten Mile and get her a good feed," the soldier said, "or she'll never make it across the Line."

One of the other men pulled handfuls of grass and began giving her a rubdown.

With the cold autumn wind whipping my wet clothes, I was shaking almost as hard as Jess and lost no time getting the mud off the harness so I could put on dry things. I washed out my wet clothes and spread them on rosebushes to dry. Not that you could tell they had been washed, but at least the sand was out of them.

The men with the mules stuck around until the soldier came back with the oats. They were evidently expecting Hedge to offer them a little cash for their trouble, because they started looking over their own outfits and making comments: "I see where we're going to have a nice big job cleaning up our mules and harness."

The average man wouldn't ignore such a hint, but Hedge was no average man. He said, "Much obliged. I don't expect to have any trouble now until we get to the Cypress Hills."

Grandma used to say it was an ill wind that didn't blow somebody good, and so it proved with me and the tough time I endured standing in the river. My foot had been all puffed up where I had run the nail into it. I couldn't stand to put any weight on it, and I had hardly slept at all for several nights. But while I was in the river, I must have opened the abscess, and my jumping around had helped to cleanse it. When I had time to notice it, the throbbing had stopped.

True to Hedge's prediction, nothing much happened until we came to the Cypress Hills in Canada. The trail was steep and ungraded, and the wagon would slew sideways until it almost threw the team off their balance. Wagon, horses, and all would come backing down the hill again. Hedge always made me walk up the hills behind the wagon so I could block a wheel with a rock if the horses got stuck or had to rest, and it's a wonder I wasn't killed, trying to put rocks behind the rushing wheels.

At last the gelding began to balk. When Hedge beat him, he started to kick. He got his hind leg over the tongue and kicked poor Jess until her legs were skinned and bleeding. Finally, Hedge decided to stop and let the horses graze while we had our lunch and then try the hill again. We had fried bacon for lunch, and afterward Hedge poured the bacon grease over a couple of rags. Then he tied the rags on two sticks and gave the gelding the command to move. When he wouldn't, Hedge lit the rags and singed the hair under his belly. You can bet your bottom dollar that horse moved out. I carried the other rag on a stick just in case we needed it, but just a smell of the first one was enough to make that cayuse go for all he was worth. No more balking or kicking after that.

As we came close to the top of the hill, the team dug in and were leaving me behind, so I ran up along the high side of the wagon and finally was able to get hold of the gelding's tug. I thought I was far enough back that Hedge couldn't reach me, but no such luck, he reached around and grabbed me by the shoulders and threw me into a bunch of cactus. I even got thorns in my sore foot, and I didn't get them all out until after we reached our destination.

I think none of us children could have been more happy in heaven than we were that first night at Uncle Zed's. Both Zed and his wife treated us wonderfully, and oh, what a scrubbing she gave us! We girls hardly recognized each other. Zed's wife was concerned over my sore foot and called the men to see how bad it was. I was embarrassed. I wasn't used to having anyone worry over me. She said I must stay in the house and keep off my foot until it was better and added that she had lots of knitting I could help her with.

Perhaps she caught an expression on my face that made her ask, "You do know how to knit?"

"No," I answered, ashamed to disappoint her in the first thing she asked of me.

"I'll start teaching you tomorrow," she said. "In the old country where I came from, girls of eight and even younger can knit."

The prospect didn't appeal to me. I wasn't domestic; I had planned to have a grand time the next day, looking over the ranch and seeing the horses and cattle I had missed so much while we were living in Great Falls, but I didn't let anybody know my disappointment.

Zed's wife was a real domestic, always making something to doll up her home. She had doilies for every piece of furniture in the parlor, and the entire backs of chairs were covered with dark brown crocheted wool covers tied with red ribbons. They gave a homey touch to the big rough log room. The logs were whitewashed inside, and the whitewash kept chipping off, so she was constantly cleaning it up and repainting the broken patches.

Zed was a jolly fellow, and he had a big laugh at Hedge's team. "I don't know how you ever made it with those horses! A good man could push that mare right over. Didn't you feed them any oats?"

"They're all right," Hedge said. "They don't need any oats. I could turn right around and go back to Montana with them."

Hedge always protested that his horses didn't need oats, but I saw him giving them several big feeds whenever he could get the oats for the taking. But his team was the laughingstock of the country, until the jokes got under even good-natured Zed's skin. "If I could spare a team, I'd give Hedge one," he said, "and go out and shoot those poor sons of bitches. That old mare deserves to be put out of her misery."

His wife was kind to me, but I suppose she was curious about us. A day or so after we arrived, while she and I were alone she asked, "So your father had a ranch in Montana?"

"Yes."

"Did you like it on the ranch?"

"No."

"You didn't? Why not?"

I was afraid she would get me to tell something that Hedge didn't want told, and I didn't want him to happen in and catch me talking. But she kept right on asking questions.

"Why didn't you like it?"

"Because sometimes we didn't have anything to eat – sometimes."

"Nothing to eat! Wouldn't your father give you enough to eat?"

"I don't know," I said.

"Well, I suppose you always had bread and potatoes and such, even if you didn't always have pie and cake. Where did your father work when you lived in Great Falls?"

"I don't know."

"What time did he go to work in the morning?"

"I don't know."

This was one too many I don't knows for the lady, and she snapped at me, "I'm sure you do know!"

"No, I really don't. I think he didn't work anywhere. Before she died, Mother sometimes said he was working, if anyone asked."

"Did your mother have nice clothes?"

"Oh, yes! She always bought things when she went out to work."

"Did she go out to work often?"

"Every time we ran out of grub."

98

"She did? And what did your father do when she was working? Stay home and take care of you girls?"

"We stayed at Grandma's most of the time, but one time Grandma lived at our house and minded us."

"Did you like your grandmother?"

"Yes. She used to do everything for us – sew our clothes, and bring us things to eat, and – " But the men came in at this point of the conversation, and I was glad to be let off.

We had been at Zed's home two months or so when the time came to begin preparations for Christmas. When I saw how he and his wife went at it, I thought even Cinderella didn't have anything on us! As usual they sent a big order to the Hudson Bay Company: clothing and groceries for the entire year, luxuries for Christmas (twenty-five pounds of mixed nuts, twenty-five pounds of candy, twenty-five pounds of plug tobacco), and enough yard goods to stock a store. I enjoyed that Christmas more than any in my entire life.

Christmas Eve came cold and dark. We children were worried for fear Santa Claus couldn't find his way in such cold weather. We were all sent to bed early. I had intended not to go to sleep but dropped off in spite of myself. About three o'clock I wakened and saw the lights were burning. Everything was quiet. I listened. I couldn't hear anybody talking. I tiptoed to the door leading from the kitchen, and what I saw I will never forget. The long kitchen table was stacked high with toys of every description.

I rushed back and wakened Beck, my oldest half-sister, and Zed's oldest boy, a little fellow of about five. The two littlest sisters wakened, and they were all up in nothing flat, and all five of us were in the kitchen, picking out which toys were ours. We disagreed on which were which and grew so noisy that we wakened Zed. He hollered at us in his loud, bluffing way, "Get back to bed, every one of you, or I'll take a blacksnake to each of you!" We knew him already and were not scared, but not one of us said a word after he spoke. We went to bed as we were told but took such a supply of nuts and candy with us that the floor of our room was covered with shells and candy wrappers by morning.

We bounced out like so many jack-in-the-boxes the next morning, and Zed had a hard time getting the fires lit and breakfast going. We kept him busy, telling us which toys belonged to each of us and showing us how to work them.

The toys were all on the kitchen table, but we had hung our stockings on the ridgepole. Uncle Zed wore huge German socks of felt, half an inch thick, over his woolen socks. He had hung both of these on the ridgepole, and of course we children thought this was terrible. We were surprised to find them filled – but with nutshells, orange peelings, and rubbish. Uncle Zed took them down and showed them to us. "You see what happens to greedy persons," he said. "I thought if I hung up both my big German socks I would get more than anybody else, but see, I got nothing! Santa doesn't like greedy people."

We all felt sorry for Uncle Zed and offered him a share of everything we had. I have often thought since how nice it was of him to teach us a lesson at his own expense.

Zed was so well liked among his neighbors that they would often congregate at his ranch to celebrate. So it was this Christmas. They came from miles around, and what an occasion it was! There were only four women in the party and innumerable men. The men all wanted to dance, especially after having a drink or two of hot rum. Before daylight the poor women had to go to the bedroom and lie down from pure exhaustion.

This was about two months before my ninth birthday, but the men thought nothing of my lack of years and danced with me and another little girl of my age until we begged them to give us a rest. They did and brought us a nice lunch, but as soon as we finished eating they had us up and at it again. Those were the days when women were really popular, when cowboys would ride miles just to look at a white woman, to say nothing of the privilege of dancing with her. Two of the girls who helped with those Christmas festivities were already married – one at thirteen and one at fifteen. They lived with their husbands till they died, and they didn't die young, either.

There was a big heating stove in the center of the room where we were dancing. The other little girl and I were so light that when our partners swung us around, they lifted us off the floor and bumped our ankles against the stove legs. The next day our legs were so black and blue that everybody was amazed and wondered why we hadn't complained. As a matter of fact, our partners had been too hilarious to pay much attention to our protests, but they were much more careful of us during the remaining days of the celebration.

Everybody danced until daylight. Then after a big breakfast the women and children went to sleep in the beds, while the men made up good fires in both stoves and lay down on the bare floor. Probably they couldn't have slept better in the swankiest hotel.

The hired man and I had to milk and do the chores before I could sleep. I dropped the milk bucket from between my knees several times because I went to sleep milking. One fellow who offered to feed and water the horses lay down in the manger of the calf shed and didn't wake up until he was badly chilled.

The second day the cattle had to be fed, and fifteen men volunteered to do the feeding. It must have surprised the cattle to see how fast the hay came off, load by load.

After the stock was taken care of, the party began all over again and continued through the night, with eating, drinking, and dancing.

Hedge came to none of the parties. No one knew where he was or what he was doing. He would spend a week or two at his brother's, then go again. He was the direct opposite of his brother. Zed was friendly with everybody, but Hedge was friendly with no one.

Zed was a fine man in all respects but one. I am sorry to admit this to myself, but I accept it as it was. He began to send me to do chores around the barns, to sort spuds in the root cellar, to put clean hay in the nests in the chicken house, and all such little jobs when no one was around but him and me. My intuition warned me to be careful, but how could I be? I had to obey. Hedge would have beaten me to death if Zed had complained to him. And then Zed was so wonderful to me otherwise! I didn't dare tell his wife. She might not have believed me, and Zed surely would have denied it.

So shortly after Christmas my perfect heaven changed to a terrible problem that I couldn't do anything about, except duck and dodge whenever I could. Zed was clever about planning situations that were right for him, but most of the time I could get away. If I saw him coming, I would drop my milk pail or whatever I was carrying and run. He couldn't catch me. But the root cellar was a trap with all escape cut off, and that is where my childhood chastity was violated.

The way the root cellar was built made it worse for me. The tool house was over the entrance, and you had to go into the cellar backward down a ladder, with only a lantern for light. I had always dreaded to go to down there, because a rattlesnake lived there. We had run across that snake just before we crossed the Line from Montana, and Hedge had picked it up with two sticks while I held a flour sack for him to drop it in. We brought it with us to Uncle Zed's as a curiosity. When the weather grew cold, Zed put the snake in a barrel in the root cellar to keep it from freezing. There was a screen over the top of the barrel, but I was always afraid the snake would find a way out. I was always wishing it would die. It wouldn't eat the live mice and birds we gave it, and at last it did die. But by that time I had a trouble worse than the snake, and it continued as long as we lived at Uncle Zed's ranch.

There can be no perfection in this world. Neither persons nor places can be perfect. There is always something wrong.

While we were living at Uncle Zed's, I had more time to play than I ever had, but his wife often used to make us children take the baby with us. This hampered my style, for the poor little thing would soon be tired from trying to follow us as we romped over the cowsheds, haystacks, and creek bank. The creek bank was what the baby liked best, but here he required constant watching. I thought if I could put him to sleep I'd be free, but what could I put him in? Looking around, I found a nice cowhide curved over the top pole of the corral where it had been hung to dry. It was just the thing for a cradle.

I pulled it off the fence, turned it curved side down, pried the sides a little farther apart, and laid the baby in it. Rocking it back and forth, I soon had him asleep. I leaned the hide against the fence, wiring it so it wouldn't tip over and frighten him.

That hide was his cradle for a long time before his mother found out. She had wondered why the baby was so good when he was outside with us, but when she saw the cowhide cradle, she was horrified and forbade me ever to put him in that smelly hide again!

We stayed at Uncle Zed's over a year, and I was chore boy until Uncle Zed got a boy from an orphans' home in England. Ranchers could take boys out of the home to work for their board and clothes until they reached a certain age; at least that was what this boy, Hank, told me. It was my business to teach Hank my job so he could take over after I was gone. He was so dumb about ranch work that I had a circus with him. Zed furnished us both with saddle horses, and I had to show Hank how and where to go after the cows and which cows to get. There were hundreds of cattle on the open range, and I tried to teach him the different brands and how to tell a milk cow from a dry cow.

One day a big fat red steer got through the gate in spite of us, and when Hank saw me cutting him out at the corral gate, he asked, "Why don't you milk that big sucker?"

I gave him a nasty look. I didn't see how anybody could be so dumb. Afterward I could understand that a boy cooped up in an orphans home in London wouldn't have a chance to know anything about cattle. But at the time I capitalized on his lack of common ranch knowledge. It was my business to teach him to milk, and at first I really did my best to help him, giving him the easiest cows and telling what I could; but he didn't learn any too fast, and the cows didn't like his slow, awkward way of milking. They would get restless and walk away from him, and then I'd have trouble getting them to stand for me. We didn't have stalls or stanchions, just milked on the open corral in warm weather and in a big cowshed when it was colder. The shed was big enough to hold a hundred head of cattle, and since we were milking only seven cows, they had plenty of room to walk if they didn't like a milker's technique. Sometimes they made their objections more emphatic by kicking over the entire setup, including the milker.

The boy finally got so on my nerves with his inept ways that I took the easiest way out by giving him old Judy to milk. She was a cow with an I-should-worry disposition who would stand all day to be milked, but she was hard to milk, and even a good milker took longer to milk her than any two cows in the corral. I had no more bother; I milked the other six cows while Hank milked Judy.

But Uncle Zed always asked if the new chore boy was improving, and one night he asked how many cows Hank had milked that evening.

I said, "One," with considerable satisfaction, but when Uncle Zed asked, "Which one?" I wished there was a hole in the floor to fall through.

"Judy."

"Well, I'll be damned! You *would* give him Judy, wouldn't you! Hereafter you milk Judy, and I'll see what can be done about improving the lad's milking."

Sure enough, Uncle Zed was on the job the next morning. But after one day, he was more impatient than I had been. He told me to tie up the easiest cow in the corral so she wouldn't walk away and let Hank try to milk one to my two.

Hank became a good milker, but he never could milk one to my two, because I kept stepping up my pace to keep ahead of him.

This was late fall. As the weather turned cold, Uncle Zed sent us out to throw hay to the wet cows whose calves were being weaned. Hank and I marched out to the corral, and I went to look for the hay knife, hoping Hank could handle it better than I could. Meanwhile, he walked over to the haystack and pulled out a few handfuls of hay to throw over the fence to the waiting cows. The cows made a rush to snatch it as the wind whisked it over the ground. After throwing a few handfuls, Hank called to me, "That ought to be enough."

"Are you crazy? It will take both of us from now until dinnertime to feed that many cattle. By the time you're good and hungry, maybe the cattle will have enough hay."

He really could handle the hay knife better than I could. We took turns, and we both peeled off our coats before we had much hay cut. We didn't need any coaxing to eat our dinner or to turn in after eating our supper, either.

We got up at five o'clock, winter and summer, and milked and did the chores before breakfast. In summer we had to go after the cows, and sometimes when the mosquitoes had been bad, the cows would graze facing the wind and wander a long way from their range. They would be hard to find, and it would take a long time to drive them in, because you can't bring milk cows in on a trot, as I had to teach Hank.

Zed cautioned me strictly not to run any races or be up to any nonsense with the horses when Hank and I went after the cows. He didn't want us to spoil the horses or hurt ourselves. I was careful, he knew, but I might be tempted to show off in front of Hank, and Zed said that if he ever caught us in any foolishness we'd have to walk after the cows instead of riding.

I knew what we would be up against if we had to go on foot to cut twenty head of cows out of two or three hundred wild range cattle, especially in the spring, when everyone turned cattle out, so I was careful and impressed on Hank the danger of having to go through wild cattle on foot. He saw how wild they acted when he got off his horse at gates and climbed back pretty fast. The cattle always started to run at the sight of someone on foot but would stop and turn to investigate as soon as their first surprise was over. They didn't look very friendly, standing with their heads raised high. Sometimes an old cow would shake her head and blow through her nose, or an old bull would give a dirty side glance and paw the ground, so the London lad needed no cautioning.

But one evening when we were riding he took a notion to show me how well he could do without even holding the reins. Riding without reins was something I didn't attempt – and neither did he, after that once, when he dropped the reins on the old mare's neck and dug in with his spurs. With one jump she was out from under him, and he hit the ground with a thud and lay without moving. I thought he was killed and went on a high lope to get Uncle Zed. Zed jumped on my horse and tore off, and by the time I got there he had Hank up on his feet and was helping him home. We didn't tell anybody how old Susie happened to throw Hank off.

8

Hedge took up a homestead in Canada, fifteen miles from Zed's, in a spot far from any neighbors. Except for an old bachelor who lived half a mile from our cabin and the section house crew three and a half miles away, we had the whole world to ourselves, and that was the way Hedge wanted it.

He filed on the ranch late in the fall and cut and stacked a little slough grass that had been frozen and was not much good as feed. The cattle he bought were dogies, or orphaned calves (I think Zed must have staked him to them), and they needed good hay and special care the first winter. Hedge built a cowshed of brush with hay stacked around it and a thin layer of hay on top.

An old log shack stood on the place. The old bachelor told me later that Indians had used it for a horse stable. It had a dirt floor. The roof was of small poles covered with hay, then a heavy layer of dirt to keep the cold out. It was warm enough, but sometimes a heavy rain would pour through, and then we had mud above and below.

Zed loaned Hedge the London lad, Hank, to help him put up the hay and then to stay at the shack and look after the cattle while Hedge returned to his brother's home for Christmas. The day after Christmas, Hedge, Beck, and I started for the homestead. Zed had persuaded him to leave the two littlest sisters, Nora and Rose, with him and his wife for the time being.

Hedge had hitched Jess and the gelding to the old lumber wagon. About eight miles from Uncle Zed's, on a steep and icy hill, the gelding started balking again. Hedge went to carve a club out of an old cottonwood limb and told me to get out of the wagon and be ready to put rocks behind the wheels. I stayed well away from the gelding. He would have given me a bite I wouldn't forget, but I knew just what he was thinking and kept back where he couldn't reach me even with his heels. He did kick every once in awhile and made the doubletree ring. Sometimes he missed the doubletree entirely and skinned his leg, until both legs were bleeding. Every time he kicked, Hedge would curse him and promise to take the kick out of him as soon as he had his club carved.

Hedge came back to the wagon, took the lines, and told me to stand ready with my rock to block the wheel every time we made headway. Then he said, "Get up, you son of a bitch," and brought the club down on the gelding. Jess threw herself into the collar, but the gelding jumped forward and then back so fast that he threw Jess on her knees. This made Hedge even angrier. He gave Jess time to get on her feet and again said, "Get up!" Again the gelding jumped back, but this time Hedge was ready for him. He hit him over the head with the heavy club, and down went the gelding. Hedge kept on hitting him after he was down until he realized he was wasting his energy. The ornery little gelding was kicking his last and would never have to worry about icy hills or rivers with quicksand again.

The gelding was out of his troubles, but we were well into ours, eight miles from even the most meager shelter in the bitter cold. But Hedge was not one to change his plans. He said to Beck and me, "You two get busy and carry all the small things in the wagon to the top of the hill, and I'll go back to Zed's and get a horse. Keep moving – no sitting down while I'm gone. I'll expect you to have everything you can carry on top of the hill when I get back."

His orders had a double purpose that I didn't at the time comprehend. We certainly kept ourselves warm climbing that hill with our arms full. But the cold was not our only worry. As soon as the coyotes scented the dead horse, they set up their howling, and every time they howled while we were away from the wagon, we shook with nervousness and fright. I kept assuring myself and Beck that we were in no danger. Uncle Zed had taken me with him on two coyote hunts, and I told Beck that as long as we were near some of the household goods we were safe. A coyote is cautious and seldom ventures close to something strange for fear of being trapped.

We thought it was too far from the wagon to the top of the hill to be safe, so we set a bundle of clothes a short distance from the wagon, a bread pan full of dishes a little farther on, and so on until we had a chain all the way up the hill. Every time a coyote howled, we made a dash for one of these piles. I knew this was a bad thing to do, for a coyote attacks the creature that runs away from him. Also, coyotes attack in numbers, and I knew from their howling that there were a lot of them. But I said nothing to Beck for fear of starting her crying again. If she cried, I couldn't listen for anything that might be sneaking up on us.

Altogether it was a terrible night for us both, and what a relief it was to see Uncle Zed and Hedge riding up on fresh horses. The first thing Zed did was to build a fire and make us a warm meal. Then he gave Hedge the devil for not seeing that we had a fire before he left. Hedge said we were so bundled up he was afraid we might set our clothes on fire if we had one.

Beck and I felt fine around a big fire with a warm meal inside us and could have gone right to sleep; but of course sleep was out of the question, although Uncle Zed had brought along two Hudson Bay blankets and arranged them in the corner of the wagon box where we could keep out of the wind. We stood around the fire while the men dragged the dead horse out of the road, and Uncle Zed sprinkled the icy hill with stock salt. His team was sharp-shod and pulled the wagon without much trouble.

Zed had warned his brother against taking us kids out on such a cold day, and now he told him it was a damned shame to subject children to such hardships. I couldn't help thinking what a good man Zed was to worry about us, in spite of the bad things he had done to me. Those terrible things had faded like a bad dream since Hank had been working with me and Zed no longer had a chance to catch me alone. He had come on his saddle horse, and now he rode back to his ranch, leaving us his fine team to pull our wagon.

We expected to find a warm house when we reached the homestead, but everything was deserted. It was evident that Hank had left the place as soon as Hedge was out of sight. Hedge had left bread to rise for Hank to bake, and now it was frozen solid enough to block wagon wheels with. The surprising part was its dirty blue color. We were taught to eat what was set before us, but even Hedge couldn't eat that.

The unbaked bread was the least of what we found. The hay-banked cowshed was trampled and wrecked, the hay had been eaten, and the shed was more holes than walls. We looked for the little saddle horse that Zed had loaned Hank while he was helping Hedge, but it was gone, with saddle and bridle.

We did no more than we had to inside that first night. Hedge cooked dinner, then he and I went out to rebuild the cowshed. The two cows had not been milked for several days and were almost dry, but we needed the milk so badly that I kept on milking and got about a quart. We went to bed early. The shack was small, ten by twelve feet, with a bed in one corner, a pile of dirt covering the spuds in another, a crude table set under the tiny pane of glass in the door, and a fairly good cookstove. My bed was a pile of antelope skins on the floor. The skins must have been left by the Indians, for I never saw anyone else tan them. They shed constantly and kept everything covered with hair, but they made a good bed for me. I don't think I could have slept on that dirt floor without them.

While Beck did the housework, Hedge and I spent the next two days working on the cowshed. As we were eating dinner on the third day, here came Hank, riding up unconcernedly on Zed's saddle horse. He tied the horse and walked into the shack as though nothing was amiss.

Hedge opened up on him: "You're a fine fellow to leave in charge!"

"Just as good as you are," the boy grinned.

"You're pretty saucy for a kid."

"You're not my boss, so don't think you are."

"I'll show you who's boss."

Beck and I were huddled in the corner, wishing Hank would shut up. We knew what was coming if he didn't. Hedge turned to me and said, "Go get me the old mare's lines."

I did what he told me.

"Now you two go throw hay to the cattle," he said and, turning to Hank, "I'll tend to you."

When Hank came down to help feed cattle, he showed plainly the ordeal he had been through. He had often twitted me for being afraid of Hedge, and I couldn't resist the temptation to say, "Now you know why I'm afraid."

To my surprise, he answered, "You're darned right I do. I bet I have welts all over my body. What made you bring him the lines when you knew what he was going to do?"

"If I hadn't, he'd have given you a licking just the same, and me too."

He was surprised when I told him about the damage the cattle had done to the shed ("They sure raised hell with it, didn't they?"), and I could see that he hadn't realized what would happen when he left. He said he had been so lonesome on Christmas Eve that he couldn't stand it and went looking for a ranch he had heard was about twelve miles from our place.

As usual, we went to bed early. At midnight Hedge got up to keep the fire going and found Hank gone. He went to the shed to see whether Zed's horse was there. It was, so he didn't bother further. He could have gone to the section house and from there notified the Mounties, and they would soon have picked the lad up, but I think Hedge probably thought the Mounties wouldn't have approved of the beating he had given him.

The next morning he rode over to the old bachelor's place. Hank had been there, but the old fellow said he hadn't looked good. He'd questioned him, and when Hank hesitated about answering, the bachelor told him to be off and shut the door in his face. Hank had gone on to the section house, where they gave him a place to sleep and breakfast the next morning. Then they took him on their handcar as far as they were working, and he had started off on foot from there. He had told the section boss that Hedge was his father and had given him a licking for nothing, so he was running away. That was the last we heard of the London lad.

That winter was hard on me and the poor half-starved dogies. Hedge often left us children alone, and I was always in difficulties or getting hurt. Both our pitchforks were big four- or five-tined forks, too heavy and awkward for me. I found a little three-tined fork without a handle and a discarded handle, and I thought I might rig up a nice little fork for myself, but there was a piece of wood in the furl of the fork. I tried burning the wood out, then tried digging it out with a spike, driving the spike in and pulling it out, but finally I drove it in too far and couldn't budge it. I hammered and pulled and jerked, and the spike flew out, hit my mouth, and broke a front tooth. When the cold air struck that broken tooth, it felt as though I'd been shot. After that, I had to keep my mouth shut when I was outside, and I learned not to holler at the horses or cattle until the tooth got over being so sensitive.

Another time when Hedge was away, one of the yearlings fell into the spring and couldn't get out. I didn't know if you could pull an animal out by the head without breaking its neck, but I had to do something. I harnessed old Jess (she stood high, and the harness was heavy, but I finally got it on, bridle and all), and then I got a singletree off the wagon and rode her to the spring. After getting all wet and muddy, I managed to get the rope around the yearling's middle and tied to the singletree. I was ready to hitch it to Jess, but when I looked at the ice around the spring, all jagged with cattle tracks, I thought I might tear the hide off the calf if I dragged him over it. I remembered a hide we had, hanging on the haystack fence, so I ran and brought it back to spread over the ice, but it spooked Jess, and she was off.

Down the brushy slope she went with me and the yearling bouncing behind her. The hide scraping over the ice and then over the brush made such a racket that Jess was too scared even to notice my hold on her bridle. Finally, we lost the calf hide on the brush, and as soon as that noise stopped, Jess stopped and looked around to see what it was all about. I took a look at my legs to see whether the rosebush scratches looked as bad as they felt.

The yearling was covered with black mud and looked as though he was about to die. I led Jess up to the hay corral gate. It was tight even in warm weather and almost impossible for me to open in the cold, but by getting down on my knees and opening the bottom first, I could manage it. I led Jess around to the sunny side of the haystack and unhooked her and left her eating hay, shut the gate to keep the other cattle from getting into the hay, and then rushed back to see if the calf was still alive. He was, but he lay inert, rolling his eyes till only their whites showed. A native range steer would have used his last bit of strength to struggle to his feet, but not a dogie. His spirit had been broken when he was a calf, and it wouldn't take much to finish him off. I rubbed some of the mud off him with dry hay and covered him with more hay, then dashed back to the house to prepare something warm for him to drink, if he would drink it.

I poured about three quarts of hot water into a bucket and threw in several cupfuls of oatmeal and a handful of salt. Beck went with me to help pour it down the calf, but as soon as he got a taste of the warm mixture he showed signs of life and stuck out his tongue to lick it. He tried to raise his head, and with our help, he got his front feet under him. Beck and I braced him up with frozen chunks of cow manure.

After he got his head up, he drank up the oatmeal and water and even licked the thick part on the bottom of the bucket. I picked out some good hay, and he ate that, too. I was happy. I had accomplished a big job and could go home now, take off my frozen, muddy clothes, and have something to eat myself.

I might not have gone to school, but I had to solve more problems than most children. There was nobody to go to for help when Hedge left us alone, and I had to try everything until I found a way that would work. This was my first experience with dogies, and though I felt sorry for the abused animals, I also felt contempt for them because they were such easy quitters. They were like brow-beaten people and had no spunk left in them.

Hedge's ranch was located on a beautiful little creek – Wood Creek – with trees and an abundance of good spring water. In the spring-time, when chokecherries and roses scented the air, it was especially lovely. I didn't mind herding cattle in that season, but in the winter, when I had to graze them on the high spots where snow had blown off to save on hay, I felt sorry for myself. I had to carry my lunch, and most of the time it would be frozen when I came to eat it. To pass the time, I used to dig deep holes in the snowdrifts and crawl down them to sleep. It was quite warm in a deep hole, and several times I slept too long, and the cows went home, letting me in for a good beating.

When spring came, I didn't have to worry about the cows going home, and every day I had a peaceful nap. At times the mosquitoes were bad, especially in the evenings. Cattle will travel miles against the breeze when mosquitoes are bad, and I would have to stay with them until the mosquitoes quit tormenting them, usually about ten o'clock at night. Then the cattle would lie down for the night, and we wouldn't have to go far for them in the morning.

Again my love of sleeping sometimes got me in trouble. There were places where the tall grass arched over deep buffalo trails, and I had all such cozy tunnels spotted. The mosquitoes were not so bad in the trails, and I would crawl very quietly into one and sometimes go to sleep before the cattle lay down. When I would awaken, they might be gone, and it would be dark as pitch and no chance of finding them. Nothing to do but go home and hope for the best. I had no chance of lying about it, for if the cattle lay down, they left their imprint in the tall grass, and if Hedge couldn't see imprints, that was that.

Often I took the mending along while I was range herding in the summer, but one time near the garden I couldn't get any mending done. The garden was unfenced, and if the cattle once got in, it would be ruined. The cattle could smell the garden stuff and kept me busy chasing them. A big steer was the most troublesome. He finally lay down during the heat of the day, and I was busy mending when along came a water snake. I caught it, raveled a string from the flour sack I carried the mending in, and tied the snake to a sagebrush until it was about time for the cattle to go to feeding again. Then I took the snake and tied it to Mr. Steer's tail while he was still lying down. He got up with a bawl that brought the rest of the herd to their feet and jumped and bucked and kicked while I laughed until my sides ached. He soon broke the snake in two, switching his tail and banging it against his sides, but he forgot about the garden for the rest of the day, and I finished my mending.

In the summer, Beck and I milked a lot of cows. Hedge milked, too, when he was home, but we were forty miles from the creamery, and it usually took him four days to make the round trip to town and back. He went once a week with the cream, so for four days out of every week, we children were on our own, with all the work to do.

I thought I was very systematic about managing during the four days Hedge was away. I would milk the cows, feed the calves, and set the milk in the spring for the cream to rise. We used tall cans with a faucet close to the bottom and a glass in the side where we could see when the milk had run out the faucet and the cream was down to the bottom of the can. The skim milk we fed to the calves, and the cream we poured into barrels provided by the creamery. These barrels were wood, lined with tin, with a float to keep the cream from churning on the way to the creamery. They were tough to wash. The creamery sent them back dirty, and I almost had to stand on my head to wash the bottoms.

All this work–except washing the barrels–we children had to do twice a day, whether or no. Weeding the garden and hilling up the potatoes I left for the last two days, just before Hedge was to be home, but sometimes he was a better figurer than I and got his work done and was home before I got mine done. Those were the days I got a terrible beating.

One other thing I was severely punished for, and that was breaking the yearling steers to ride. The actual riding didn't take much flesh off the steers, it was the preliminaries I put them through. I had such a yen for that form of excitement that I got several beatings.

I did my steer riding when I was herding in some out-of-the-way place where Hedge wasn't likely to catch me. I would run the steer around on horseback until he was tired out and glad to stop, and then I would slip my rope over his horns, tie it to my saddle horn, and pull him around until he was ready to let me saddle and bridle him. (Once I pulled my rope off the steer, I always put it on my horse; otherwise he'd run home, and I'd be left afoot with a saddle too heavy to carry far.) I never rode any steer very long. They quieted down in no time, and the fun was over.

We had sixteen yearling steers that first spring, and when I was through with them, they were more gentle than my saddle horse. They were bridle-wise, and they would neck-rein, too, in their slow, stupid way.

Long after the breaking stunt was over, Hedge would accuse me of riding the steers. I was afraid to tell him they were all broken and no fun to ride. One day I took one of my little sisters out with me to show her how gentle the steers were, and of course I wanted her to have a ride. She was afraid to try it, but I urged her until she climbed up. The steer knew she was strange and jumped sideways, throwing her off and skinning her face. I think Hedge must have noticed her face and made her tell how she happened to hurt it–that was how he found out what I had been doing with the steers.

Haying time was something I dreaded. Hedge pitched the hay on the load, and I tramped it down, and after the load got high, I caught each forkful he threw up. He pitched the hay on the stack off the rack, and I scattered it and tramped it. The rose briars and thistles in the bench hay left my bare legs a crisscross of bleeding scratches after I had tramped hay all day long.

Mowing the hay was one of the easiest jobs on the ranch. I did nearly all the mowing that first summer we lived on the ranch, and I even did some for the neighbors. All I had to do was keep the team going at a brisk walk, give the mower a little oil occasionally, and watch the cutting bar to see that it didn't strike the piles of dirt around badger holes or hit any buffalo bones.

A green Scotchman had moved into our part of the country, and his ignorance almost got me into trouble. I was to mow while the Scotchman and Hedge raked and stacked. The Scotchman was to bring his horse to the hayfield to hitch to the mower with Jess. He had his horses harnessed all right, except for a small item he thought wasn't necessary–the martingale. It hung so low that he was afraid the horses might step on it, so he left it home.

When we hitched the team to the mower, I told him we should have the martingale. I had never seen what might happen without it, but I soon found out when the team started down a slight incline. The mower tried to get down first, and the team objected, especially when their collars slid up to their heads and the doubletrees bumped their heels. Dependable old Jess saved me from a runaway by holding the Scotchman's gelding back. Since the mower was in gear, the hay heavy, and the gelding in a hurry, he had to pull more than his share of the load, and by the time we got to the bottom of the hill, Mr. Gelding was almost out of wind. I unhooked him quick before he could take a notion to run again, led Jess up to the mower seat so I could get on her bareback, and took the gelding over to the other field where the men were working. The Scotchman had to go home for his martingale.

We put up a few loads of hay for the people at the section house, too. They only had one cow and calf and one horse, so they didn't need much hay, but we were all tired of haying before the summer was over. Hedge went to town, leaving me to haul in the last few loads to pile around the shed. The shed was on the creek bank, and I knew I would have trouble making the turn with the team and hayrack around the shed on the sidehill. Sure enough, I upset the rack first thing. I could carry the hay to the shed, but I couldn't pull the rack back on the wagon.

Hedge didn't beat me for turning the rack over. I even got a little satisfaction out of the incident. Hedge decided to show me how easy it was to make the turn around the shed. He had Beck and me stand on the upper side of the rack while he drove the team around the corner very carefully. Just as he got to the spot where I had turned over, he called, "Stick on, stick on, she's going over!" and over she went. Beck and I were left high in the air, but Hedge fell out with the hay and didn't have anything more to say about how easy it was to drive around the shed.

That fall we had a prairie fire. I was out washing clothes under the trees when I thought I smelled hay burning and saw what looked almost like clouds rolling overhead. I wasn't positive it was a fire and waited a few minutes before I woke Hedge, who was asleep in the cabin. He took one look and said, "Run and get Dandy," our saddle horse. He collected sacks and wet them while I was getting the horse and then made a dash for the haystack. We had time to burn a fireguard around the stack before the fire got there. Then we went back to the cabin and carried everything we could to the garden, where the fire couldn't reach, then hurried to the hill with wet sacks to try to keep the fire from getting into the brush along our coulee.

We thought it would get into the brush in spite of us, but the section men came running and were able to turn it. By that time the fire was almost to the brush in the coulee next below us, but the men managed to keep it running along the top of the hill. Hedge sent me home to harness the team and collect all the sacks I could find. He put the cream barrels in the wagon, filled them with water, and drove back to the fire.

The men fought the fire until five in the morning, when it began to snow. We all went back to our house, and the men lay down on the floor to get a little rest. The snow was light, and toward dawn the wind came up. The fire must have been smoldering in cow chips, for it started up again. It burned for several days. I heard the men say it had burned out an entire sheep ranch and hundreds of acres of pasture in a strip sixty-five miles long. There is only one good thing about a prairie fire: it can't back up.

After the prairie fire, we had to pasture our cattle on the other side of the creek, and for some reason they didn't like that side and would wander farther than usual. One morning when Hedge was away, we children overslept. The cows must have got up early, because when I went to round them up, I couldn't find them. I kept hunting for them on the side of the creek where the grass wasn't burned off, but they must have crossed the creek and, finding no grass, kept going. I hunted for them for two days before Hedge came home. He was furious because I had let them get away and go unmilked. He told me to get the saddle horse while he got himself something to eat and said that when he got back he'd tend to me.

"I'll give you a tanning you'll never forget," he said, and he was right. He made me take all my clothes off, then he tied my hands together with a rope and tied the rope to the ridgepole of the cabin. He pulled my hands up so high that my feet were just touching the floor.

"I'll tan you till the blood runs down your heels," he said, and he almost made good his threat. He did make the blood run, and my entire body was covered with stripes.

If I had had sense enough to go to the Mounted Police when I was covered with welts, they might have helped me, but instead I made a foolish move. The next day, when Hedge was away, I took the bedding and a few things out of the cabin and set it on fire. I thought if we had no place to live, Hedge would have to take us away from there. I meant to take more things from the cabin, but the fire burned faster than I thought it would.

I thought wrong about Hedge taking us away. Someone had started another cabin not far from ours. Just the logs were in place, no roof, floor, or chinking. We slept in it that night, and the next day we started moving the logs to a beautiful place under the maple trees.

Hedge didn't beat me for burning the shack. He thought it caught fire accidentally. Although my little sisters stood right there and saw me light the fire, they didn't tell on me. They never told on me, except accidentally or when Hedge compelled them to explain something. They were the best little sisters, always doing their share. I planned that when I was grown I'd do something wonderful for them for being so loyal.

The new cabin was better than the old one. Hedge built a bunk all the way across one end of it, making the equivalent of two beds, so I didn't have to sleep on the floor anymore. But we trapped coyotes that winter, and I made the new cabin unlivable by skinning the coyotes inside when Hedge was away. When he was home, he always made me skin them outside. That was hard on my hands and on the coyote hides, too. They would freeze before I could get them off, and I was in danger of tearing or cutting them. But inside, the fleas jumped off and made themselves comfortable in the cabin at our expense.

When Hedge was away, it was my job to check the traps twice a day during cold weather. If a trapped coyote's foot froze, it might break off and let him get away. I had to kill the trapped coyotes by hitting them over the head with a club. If they showed fight, I didn't feel so bad, but usually they didn't, and I had to prime myself by thinking about the dirty work of coyotes, killing little calves and lambs, and how often they scared me when I was alone on the prairie at night. A man might kill a coyote without a qualm, but I dreaded it.

After I learned to shoot a gun I didn't mind killing badgers, rock chucks, prairie dogs, chicken hawks, and rattlesnakes. A rattlesnake was the first thing I learned to kill. I felt sorry for other animals, but never once did I feel sorry for a rattler.

I was never a good enough shot to kill a coyote on the run, which would have seemed different from clubbing one that was helpless in a trap. But no one ever wasted a bullet on a trapped animal because of the cost and also because a bullet made a hole in the hide.

Coyote traps had a spring on each side and were hard for me to set in cold weather. I would jump on the springs to press them down and then try to catch them. It usually took me several tries. Once in my haste I caught my thumb in the trap. For a minute I was panicky. I examined the wire on the trap and saw it was too neat a job to be unwound without a pair of pliers and both hands. I tried to spring it by jumping on it with my knees, but I couldn't get enough force that way and only hurt my throbbing thumb. There was nothing else to do but unwire the trap from the tree before my thumb froze.

It didn't take long. I took off my scarf and wrapped it around my hand and the trap. I knew what happened to a cow's foot if she froze it, and I was three quarters of a mile from the house. I hurried all I could, planning just how I would get the trap open: I would have Beck get two monkey wrenches and open the jaws of the trap wide enough to fit over the springs.

The scheme worked, and what a glorious feeling as we screwed the wrenches down, the trap fell open, and my thumb was free! It hurt worse than ever, but I kept shaking it furiously and running around so I wouldn't feel it so much. Still, it was a sore thumb, badly bruised and slightly frosted.

Hedge rode down to the section house one day, keeping his reasons to himself as usual. The section boss was glad to see him; it had saved him a trip to our place. Fifteen head of cattle had been killed by the train the night before in a cut a mile and a half from the section house.

"It's too cold to burn or bury such a bunch," the section boss told Hedge. "I want you to help me drag the dead ones out of sight from the right of way. I have orders to shoot anything that is badly crippled, and maybe you can help with that, too. My young mare won't stand for shooting a gun around her, and it's dangerous to go near those wild cattle on foot. I went up on the handcar, and they tried to run me off. It's a hell of a mess."

"What's to be done with the carcasses? Are their hides worth anything?" Hedge asked.

"The company told me to take the brands, so I suppose they will pay for them. I don't think anyone would object to your skinning them. The coyotes and wolves will get them if you don't."

Hedge agreed to help and came back home for his team and rifle. After he and the section boss had killed everything that was badly hurt, Hedge started for home dragging two of the carcasses. When his team couldn't drag both, he left one half a mile from the right of way and sent me back for it.

He had told me it was a blue cow, and neither he nor I thought I would have any trouble locating her. But it began to snow as I set out and soon covered Hedge's trail. It took time to find the trail in the snow, and the team was tired and walked slow. I couldn't have made good time anyway, because I was dragging the doubletree by hooking one of the mare's tugs to her singletree and riding the razor-backed little gelding Hedge had bought to replace the one he had knocked in the head.

After riding for a long time, I found the blue cow. I hooked on to her hind legs, seated myself on her hindquarters with her tail for a hold, and thought I could drive the team home. But we were facing into the snow now, and the horses kicked up a lot more. To keep the snow out of my face, I turned my back, thinking that the horses would find their way home. But they didn't like the storm in their faces either and must have turned from it so gradually that I didn't notice.

Hedge had warned me against crossing a big coulee where the snow had drifted and he had gotten stuck. It was time we were coming to that coulee, so I got off the cow and walked ahead, but the coulee was nowhere in sight. The snow was coming down in big flakes, and I could see only a short distance. What puzzled me was that the wind was now in my back. Could it have changed? It didn't seem so. It wasn't any colder, and the snow was falling just as it had. I tried to get my bearings, but it was no use–I couldn't see far enough ahead to locate any landmarks. I knew I couldn't be far out of my way because the team was traveling so slowly, but the question was, Which way were we going?

I hated to admit to myself that I was lost and must make plans for spending the night out. I was a little panicky at first but gave myself a talking-to: You've been wanting to die; maybe this is your chance. But I knew darned well I wasn't going to die. I knew better than to think of resting. I had heard men say a coyote knows by the smell of a horse when he is played out, so I gave my team their heads and let them paw grass, then walked them in a circle by pulling a little on the right rein, never trying to go straight ahead or to the left. I had been lost before and knew how turned around a person can get, but I couldn't go far wrong by keeping always to the right.

I should have thanked God for the abundance of grass on the prairie. When a horse is hungry and there is plenty of grass, he can eat fairly well even with his bit in his mouth. It would have been easier on the horses if I had unhooked them from the cow, but then I would have lost the cow, and Hedge would make it tough for me. Also, I knew the team couldn't get away from me, no matter what happened, as long as they were hooked up to the cow.

I expected the coyotes and possibly the wolves to be hot on our trail all night on account of the cow. Coyotes grow fairly brave when there is a big bunch together, and, as I anticipated, they had a howling good time that night. I kept watching my horses' ears, and when they pricked up, the horses stopped eating, and both looked in the same direction, I knew the coyotes were close. I thought I saw their eyes flash once or twice, but they never came close enough for me to be sure. They were not hungry, with all the dead cattle nearby, but

124

they were curious, and some trappers say coyotes like horse meat better than they do beef. I knew they preferred a young colt to a young calf–anyway, I had lots of time to think about such things that long, cold night.

As the night wore itself out, so did the sacks on my feet. I never wore shoes in the winter, just a pair of Hedge's castoff socks with sacks wrapped over them. It's surprising how warm such footwear is–unless it gets wet. (When Hedge wore the feet off his socks, I sewed the legs across and made stockings for myself, and when I had worn the ends off, I sewed them across again for mittens. They had no thumbs, but they kept my hands warm. The only overcoat I had while I was in Canada was one Uncle Zed bought me. Hedge got hold of a lot of men's second-hand clothes, especially suit coats, and those coats were what I wore, with a strap or belt to hold them close and out of my way while I was working.)

Toward morning it stopped snowing and got a little colder. I kept watching the sky to see whether any one spot was getting a little lighter, and as soon as day appeared dim in the East, old Jess made a beeline for home. The way she lit out made me sure that she had been as lost as I was. I lost no time picking my road, as I usually did, but made a straight shoot for the cabin. I pulled the blue cow along-side the dead steer Hedge had dragged in, drove the team to the hay-stack, unbridled them and looped up the lines, and ran for the house, expecting Hedge to light into me for driving the team all night.

He wasn't home. He had gone somewhere on horseback as soon as he had sent me after the blue cow. But my poor little sisters had been sitting up all night, keeping the fire going for me. They were making hotcakes when I came in. Their eyes were red and swollen. They had heard the coyotes howling worse than usual and thought that they had killed me and the team. They laughed and cried both as they told me about their fears while I ate hotcakes and more hotcakes. I cheered them up by telling them that these were the best hotcakes I ever tasted, and I was telling the truth. Hotcakes never tasted so good.

I was ready for a good sleep, but the cows had to be milked and I had to throw out hay for them, which took several hours. In winter, when all the stock had to be fed, the chores took from five in the morning until noon. Hedge usually put a load of hay on the rack and left it standing in the hay corral, so all I had to do was hook on to the rack, drive it to some sheltered spot, and throw hay off both sides as I drove. But first I had to harness the team. The harness was heavy and the horses too high, but I had to do it, and this is how: I put a handful of salt on the ground, and while the horse had his head down, licking the salt, I slipped the collar on. Sometimes the horse got wise and kept his head up where I couldn't reach it. Then I put the collar on upside down, buckled it loosely, and pushed it up close to the horse's head where I could twist it over. (The horse wasn't keen on that maneuver, either.) I pushed the hames over the horse's neck and fastened the hame strap quick, before the horse could shake the hames off. I brought the breeching, pushed the right-hand side over the horse's back, straightened the harness, slid the breeching over the horse's rump, pulled his tail from under the breeching, snapped the holdback straps to the martingale, and buckled the bellyband. Last, I put on the bridle. This is how I managed: I unbuckled the cheek strap from the left side of the bridle, letting the bit hang free. Usually it took several attempts to get the bridle over the horse's ears. Then I buckled the throat latch. If the weather was very cold, I tried to warm the bit by rubbing it against the horse's cheek so it wouldn't freeze to his tongue. Then I led the team to their places beside the wagon tongue and hooked them up, just like that!

At first I used to feed the cattle by throwing hay over the corral fence and spreading it around so the young or timid stock could get

126

their share. But the stack was on a high, dry spot where the wind could get a good crack at it. Stock do not like wind any more than people do, so I learned to find them a nice sunny spot out of the wind. (Besides, I dropped some hay inside the corral fence, and in reaching for it, the cattle would get the wires to sagging until they could crawl through to the stack. Once cattle learn this trick, it is almost impossible to break them of it.)

The morning after my night on the prairie, I fed the cattle close to the corral. It worried me. It seemed as though I always had worried as long as I had to be around Hedge. Sometimes life seemed one terrible thing after another, until I wished I was dead and thought of ways I might die. But the night in the storm hadn't killed me! I was tired, good and tired, but ten hours of sound sleep was all I needed. I didn't dare be sick.

I was glad to sit down and milk my share of the cows. Milking was restful to me, so restful that I often fell asleep and let my milk pail slip down from my knees. If my cow happened to be a range cow we were breaking to milk, I might get kicked, for the slightest sudden move startled them. But as a rule, the cows and I got along fine.

I always had one cow that was crazy about me. The last pet cow I had in Canada was a big, wild-looking dark red with a black neck and head. She was so anxious to protect me that I had to leave her outside the corral, otherwise she would take a poke at anybody who came near me. Hedge had knocked one of her horns off when she came after him.

Her affection had its drawbacks. Range herding in the summer, I went out with the cattle about seven o'clock in the morning, and they would graze until ten or eleven, then lie down and chew their cuds during the heat of the day. I would hurry to finish whatever mending I had with me so I could sleep. But my pet cow always figured that I needed cleaning up about that time, and she would come over and start licking me. She didn't object to my wearing clothes, but she did object to my having anything tied in my hair. Many a time when I was asleep, she got hold of my braid with those lower teeth of hers, trying to pull the string off. She would pick me up by the hair, and when I hollered, she would *moo-o-o* in the most consoling manner.

To get away from the clean-up job, I would get up and milk her, just enough for my lunch. I milked her right into my mouth. Of course, I didn't drink as much as a calf, but I did pretty well. In fact, I almost lived on milk. When I carried a lunch, the butter tasted terrible after the sun had shone on it all morning, and in the winter, when the butter was all right, the bread was frozen and tasted like wood. Anyway, I wanted to be like the cowboys. They never packed a lunch.

Zed's wife always made me two dark blue dresses for Christmas that had to last me all year. Sun and washing faded them to a pale color. The cattle didn't mind the faded color, but when I put on one of my new dresses, the cattle would run at the sight of me. I had to break in my dresses during the winter when I was wearing a coat.

I hauled nine more head of dead cattle without any trouble. The job of skinning them after they were frozen was impossible until the sun thawed them out on one side. I did a little skinning every day until I got the sunny side skinned. The pigs took over as soon as I left and dirtied up the hide for me. Finally, Hedge had to take over the job himself, for the hair might begin to slip and lessen the value of the hides.

The pigs had plenty of meat. The cattle had been in prime condition when they were killed, big steers and dry cows turned out to rustle for themselves.

9

That spring, Hedge and I went to plant the garden. I took the saddle horse along so I could go look after the cattle every once in a while. We had been working a short time when Hedge went back into the brush that surrounded the garden.

He called to me, "Come here."

I was scared.

I knew he couldn't see anything wrong with the cattle from where he was. The children were at home, and he had warned them not to leave the house. I thought that a cow we were expecting to come fresh might be hiding in the brush, but as soon as I came close enough to see Hedge standing in a nice little grassy spot, my intuition told me the worst had come.

I knew I couldn't outrun him to the house, half a mile away, and if I did, he would give me the beating of my life. I stood terrified, looking straight at him. My eyes told him what my lips didn't dare.

He started toward me. "Come here! Do you hear me? Come here, or I'll drag you over by your hair."

I met him halfway and saved myself additional abuse.

He grabbed me by the back of the neck and pushed me through the narrow path overgrown with rosebushes. I was just tall enough for the bushes to strike me in the face. He rushed me so fast I had no time to push them aside, and he told me to tell the children I got the scratches when I stumbled and fell.

I was a nervous wreck after the ordeal, but we went back to planting the garden. Hedge was making rows with the hoe, and I was dropping the seed, but my hands were shaking so badly I might as well have been broadcasting the seeds. Hedge finally got disgusted with me and sent me to see where the cattle were. When I got back, he had finished with the small seed, and I did better with the peas and beans.

Once Hedge's indignities started, he not only took advantage of me at every daytime opportunity but would get up in the night and carry me from my bed to his. (He didn't dare call me for fear of waking the other children.) When I resisted, he would bump my head against the wall. As a last resort, he would choke me until I had to submit. When I cried, he would hold his hand over my mouth and nose until I almost smothered. Once my nose bled so bad I got blood on the bed and covers.

"Keep your mouth shut," he warned me, "or I'll take you back in the brush, and nobody'll ever see you again or know what happened to you."

Sometimes he hit me in the stomach with his fist, so hard I vomited all over him, and he said I made him so mad with my tricks that someday he'd drag me out in the night and finish me.

I only wished for a quick end.

In the fall the section boss offered Hedge a job – just working extra, now and then. I was delighted when he had to go to work, but he soon quit, saying the work was too hard.

But while he was working, he sent me to the roundup, held not far from our place, to get a little red steer branded 2-B on the right ribs. A new homesteader had recently lost him. I told the cowboys what I was looking for, and they located the red steer, cut him out, and started him on his way for me. As we rode along, one of the cowboys said, "What is your father doing, that he couldn't come and get this steer himself?"

"He was sleeping when I left," I said, "but he works on the section two days a week."

"He is a hell of a man, and you can tell him I said so, to send a little girl to do a man's work while he sleeps. What does your mother say?"

"My mother is dead."

130

"No wonder! Does he treat you good? I can see by your clothes he doesn't spend much money on you."

He asked me about my other relatives, and I told him about my uncle and grandmother in Montana and how Grandma wanted to keep me with her, but Hedge wouldn't let her.

"So he isn't even your own father? That accounts for it. How do you manage, living on his working two days a week?"

"We milk cows. He takes the cream to town, and sometimes he brings back bacon and beans and oatmeal."

"Don't you have bread?"

"Oh yes, I make bread – and I make butter, too."

He looked at me and said, "That stepfather of yours must be a jim-dandy. I'd like to meet him."

He made me feel it wasn't so hard to get to Montana and said if I ever decided to strike out, he'd help me. Just look him up anywhere around Gull Lake – the people there would know where to find him.

"I'll have to get back to the herd now," he said at last, "but remember what I say – if you ever strike out, look me up."

I thought of his face all the rest of the day. The other cowboys called him "The Kid," but he had told me his name was Dave Treu. I wished I had told him more, but I was ashamed to tell him of my worst trouble, and I didn't know what words to use. I knew how to speak about livestock, but those words didn't seem right. No, I would forget the idea of telling anybody. I would try to run away to Montana and forget the whole terrible nightmare.

All that fall and winter I made plans to run away. Each time Hedge outraged me or beat me, it strengthened my determination. I knew I must wait for warm weather, for there might be long distances between stopping places, and I might have to sleep out. I planned to follow the railroad track instead of the wagon road. The railroad had bridges to cross rivers and creeks. There was no danger of getting lost, and probably I could make it from one section house to another in a day's walking.

When I told my half-sister Beck of my plans, she listened with her eyes wide and said, "I'm going, too."

"I'm going to start right now. I'm positive Hedge went to town, because he took the cream, and that gives me four days before he gets back."

"Where are you going?"

"To Uncle Mike's in Montana. A cowboy told me I could make it in a month."

"I'm going with you. I'm not going to stay here and do all the work and then get beat up for it."

"He wouldn't beat you like he does me."

"He might, if I was the oldest. I'm going with you anyway."

"Then we'll have to take the little girls down to the section house. They would be scared, alone, and might wander off."

The little sisters were picking Juneberries somewhere in the brush while Beck and I were washing the milk things. I told Beck to get them and clean them up. They weren't keen on going, but we explained that we had to look for a cow that had strayed, and we might be gone a long time. I made bacon and bread sandwiches for Beck and me, and we took some oatmeal – we often ate oatmeal when we came in hungry and couldn't wait for the fire to cook something.

We took the two little girls part of the way to the section house, close enough that I was sure they wouldn't get lost if they stayed on the trail and that no wild cattle were in the neighborhood. The girls wouldn't know how to scare wild cattle away or might be too frightened to try.

(It is easy to scare wild cattle. I used to squat down and let the cattle come fairly close, then jump up and yell. They would run off like a herd of antelope. It was harder to scare the bulls. They were not so wild, because they were kept around the ranch most of the time and fed in the winter, so they were used to people. When I saw or heard a bull in a herd of cattle, I did my best to go around. But once I was running along the trail to the section house when I saw quite a big herd of cattle, about a mile from the trail on a high sidehill that overlooked a lot of country. I didn't think they noticed me, and I don't know what started them running after me, but they did; and because the wind was in my face, I didn't hear them until they were almost on top of me. There was a small, deep coulee off the trail to my right, and I dived into the chokecherry brush while the herd pounded across the head of the coulee. I watched as they went tearing past me. They had a mile or more of level country ahead of them, with no deep coulees or creeks to pile up in, so they could keep running until they were out of wind.)

Cattle were in a bad mood that year, because wolves had killed a lot of young calves in the spring. My little sisters knew nothing about handling them, and I was glad there was not a hoof in sight when we left them.

Beck and I took a shortcut to the railroad. Before we had gone five miles, it began to rain, enough to get us soaking wet but not enough to make us turn back. We made better time after we got to the railroad track. The ties were easier on my bare feet than the prairie. Beck's feet always toughened up quickly, but mine never seemed to, and I was always picking my steps.

That night at sundown we got to Carmichael, seventeen miles from our place. There were only men at the section house, all of them Gallicians who could hardly speak English. They looked puzzled when they saw us, but they gave us supper, and two of them gave up their bed for us. The next morning they gave us breakfast, and we started for Gull Lake.

We had gone only a short distance when we met a man on horseback. He recognized me before I did him and exclaimed, "Well, I'll be a son of a gun! What are you doing out here on foot?"

It was Dave Treu.

"I'm going to Montana."

When Dave found that we really meant it, he said, "I'll give you a horse. I don't know whether he'll let you kids ride him, especially double, but you wait here while I get him, and we'll see how he acts."

"Who is he?" asked Beck as Dave rode away.

"You remember I told you about a cowboy helping me with that 2-B steer? Well, that was Dave Treu. He said he'd help me get to Montana."

We could see Dave coming over the hill, leading a white horse. He had only the one saddle and bridle, but he said, "I'll give you the bridle, and I'll try to get along with a half hitch on old Baldy's jaw. Snow, here, bucks once in awhile, so I'll ride him around first and knock some of the hell out of him. Maybe that will trim him down till you kids can ride him."

He rode Snow around until the horse was out of wind and ready to calm down, then told us to go to his head and pet him on the nose. But Snow wouldn't let either of us near him. Our dresses were flapping in the wind, and he wasn't used to skirts. Dave took Beck up in his arms and made Snow smell her dress, and when he snorted and pulled back, Dave used his quirt on him. Finally, he said, "I think he is all right. Climb on, but don't hold your reins too tight, or he will throw you for sure – he is very tender-mouthed."

Dave told us that he didn't think the Canadian Customs officials would let us take the horse across the Line into Montana. "Go to my boss's wife at Gull Lake," he said. "Her name is Mrs. Holden. She will know what to do. I hope you make it to your grandmother's."

He stood a few moments looking at the ground, saying nothing,

134

slapping his chaps with his quirt. Finally, he asked, "Peggy, how old are you?"

"I don't know for sure," I said. "My stepfather won't tell me. But I know I was eight when my mother died, and I was at Uncle Zed's on my ninth birthday, and I've had three birthdays since, so I must be twelve and a half."

"You'll soon be a young lady – what are you going to do when you grow up?"

"I'll have a nice ranch, all fixed up, with a house and a big barn where I can put all the stock when it is cold," I began, all my dreams bursting into words.

"You'll have to marry a big rancher to get all that."

"Oh no I won't!" I said but kept myself from finishing, *because I think men are terrible.* I was thinking about my plans and not giving Dave's questions much consideration.

"Tell Mrs. Holden I'll be in tonight if I can get the cattle all gathered up. I'll help you kids on Snow now, and then I'll get back on the job."

He boosted me on first. I was not afraid of the horse for myself, but I worried about Beck. It was eight miles to Gull Lake, and if Snow threw us and one or both of us were seriously hurt, there would be no one to go to. And anyway, I didn't want to go to Gull Lake at all. I had had enough of backtracking, and the fine horse Dave had loaned me was not what I wanted. For the first time in my life I wanted an old plug. But I had made my break, and I must take whatever happened.

Dave lifted Beck on, and as soon as she had her arms around me, he let go of Snow's bridle. The horse lit out like a streak of lightning. He neck-reined at a touch, so I headed him for Gull Lake and hung on.

He didn't slacken his pace for over a mile, then he slowed a little. I knew by this time he was surefooted. I wasn't a good bareback rider, but I did my best to keep the horse thinking I was in control. Poor Beck hung on and didn't say a word.

In sight of the buildings, I began to figure the best way for us to get off. If Beck got off first and landed near Snow's hind feet, she might get kicked. I told her we would get off together. Snow tried to jump away from us when we hit the ground, but I hung on to the reins and led him through the gate toward some children we saw playing there. One of them dashed away to the house to tell their mother.

The woman seemed astonished to see children alone, but she asked us to dinner, then sent us to the Holdens' house. One of the boys knew the horse and wanted to know how we happened to be riding him. I explained that Dave had loaned us Snow.

"You must be good riders," he said. "Dave's horses are all crackerjacks. I'll bet he has to let me ride Snow, now that he's let you girls ride him. Where did you come from?"

I said, "We are going back to Montana."

"Do all the kids in Montana know how to ride like you?"

Mrs. Holden saw us coming and met us at the door. She must not have roughed it much herself, because she could hardly keep from crying as she talked to us and looked at our clothes. I looked worse than Beck because I always tore my skirt off the waist in front from climbing on horses bareback and on hay racks. I always sewed the skirt and waist together again, but the front kept getting shorter and shorter till it looked as though I was wearing a train. Sometimes when I was off my horse, walking, when the sun was low and made my shadow long on the grass, I was ashamed to see how the tail of my dress dipped.

Mrs. Holden asked whether I did the sewing, and I said, "Yes." She asked me why my legs were scratched when Beck's weren't. I told her I had to tramp hay, and Beck didn't.

She said we must take a bath, and she'd try to find some of her daughter's clothes that would fit us. I thought all her suggestions were a waste of the precious time I needed to put distance between myself and Hedge, and I told her we had to be going, if we could get one of the men to help us back on our horse.

"Do you mean to tell me you two little girls want to ride that horse from here to the Montana Line? It's the most foolish thing I ever heard of! Why do you want to go to Montana?"

"My stepfather beats me," and I pulled open the neck of my dress to show her the black-and-blue stripes.

"I'll see that there is a stop put to *that*! That's shameful! Go scrub your feet while I try to locate one of the Mounties."

We could hear a telegraph instrument tapping away in another room. When Mrs. Holden went into the little room, I thought that must be the way she was going to locate the Mountie.

Our first clean-up didn't satisfy Mrs. Holden, especially our hair washing, but she finally got us clean enough to meet with her approval. At the marks all over my body, she exclaimed, "I don't blame you for running away from such abuse!"

I wanted to tell her there was something worse than this, but how was I going to say it? I thought of telling her that Hedge was like a bull, always chasing me, but what if she asked, "What for?" What I endured seemed too shameful to tell a nice lady like Mrs. Holden, and anyway, it didn't seem necessary to make her any more shocked than she was.

Mrs. Holden must have suspected I might try to run away and told me to stay upstairs. Beck had good eyesight, and I tried her patience, calling her to come look out of the window and see if she could see Dave anywhere. Dave knew how Hedge made me work and how he beat me, and I hoped he would come and side with me. Beck didn't want to keep looking for Dave; she wanted to play dolls with Mrs. Holden's little girl. I was too worried to play; anyway, I never cared for dolls. Pets of any kind interested me more. I made pets out of all kinds of animals – prairie dogs, badgers, coyotes, porcupines, even a baby skunk. I tried to tame birds, too, and had good luck with wild ducks and geese but none with prairie chickens. I had a crow once. He had a lot in common with my coyote, tricky and never to be trusted.

The Mountie arrived before Dave did. He questioned and cross-questioned Beck and me in such a kindly way that he gained our confidence, and my black-and-blue marks explained how Hedge got so much work out of me. After the Mountie was through questioning us, we were sent back upstairs. Mrs. Holden served us supper on her daughter's little table. Her father had made the table and the little chairs to go with it, and I thought to myself, "Some kids have all the luck! Hedge wouldn't fix a pitchfork for me."

I saw Dave coming while we were eating supper and wished I could get to him and tell him how all my plans had gone askew, but we were upstairs, and I didn't dare call to him. I did hear him saying to the Mountie, "You don't know that son of a – excuse me, Mrs. Holden – he worked his wife to death, he works his horses to death, and he's doing his damnedest to work that little girl to death. I've seen her all over the range, sometimes on foot, looking for cattle. Why doesn't he do his own riding? No, he lies at home and sleeps until she brings in the lost stock. Those kids do the milking, they make the bread, they churn!"

"I know that," replied the Mountie quietly. "I have been questioning the girls."

"Maybe you do know that, but I bet you don't know what he does with the money he gets for his cream. He gambles it away instead of buying food for those poor little kids. I know. I've seen him. If you Mounties can't throw a scare into that lazy son of a so-and-so, I know a bunch of cowhands who can."

138

"Calm down, Dave. Why didn't some of you fellows report this long ago?"

"I'm the kid of the outfit," Dave said. "I did tell some of the older men, and I thought they'd do something."

Just then, from the upstairs window, Beck saw a rider coming. Soon she recognized Hedge on his old cayuse, jogging along. We knew the horse must be tired out, or Hedge would have come in on a high lope. I was tense with fear. Hedge wouldn't dare beat me while we were here, but if the Mountie made me go back with him, I was sure he would kill me.

We heard Mrs. Holden let Hedge in. She asked him how he knew his little girls were here, and he said that the section men had spread the word from one section to another until he heard about it in town.

From there on, the Mountie took him over and gave him such a raking over the coals as he never had in his life. To my surprise, Hedge didn't attempt a word in his own defense or fly into a rage, as was his custom. He was polite and agreed to do just as the Mountie told him.

"Now I'm going to call the children down and see how they feel about going home with you."

Dave had been silent up to this time. Now he said, "When are those girls going to have any chance at school? There isn't a school within fifty miles of his place."

"Yes," said the Mountie, "you must make some arrangements about sending them to school."

"I will, as soon as I prove up on my homestead."

"When are you going to prove up?"

"Next year."

The Mountie called me downstairs and pulled down my collar, exposing the black-and-blue marks. "Did you do that?"

Hedge made no answer, and the Mountie went on, "We will tolerate no more of such abuse." He called Dave to see the bruises, and Mrs. Holden told them I had such marks all over my body.

"I'm going to let you take these children home on one condition: that you stay home and look after them. If there is any more of this, I'll see that the girl is taken away from you. I understand she is not your own daughter?"

"No, she is not."

"I'll drop around and see how things are when I'm in the vicinity."

Hedge seemed anxious to get away. "Come on, get your duds on, and we'll go," he said to us.

"You're not going tonight? Your horse is tired. How are you going to manage with one horse and three people?"

"We'll take turns riding."

I knew that was a lie. He would not think of letting me ride while he walked.

And I was right – I walked every step of the way. I got home before he and Beck did, because Hedge's horse played out entirely, and I wasn't even very tired.

This was Nora's story after Hedge brought them home from the section house: "When it started to rain, we didn't keep on to the section house, we came home, but we got all wet anyway. When night came, we were so scared, we didn't know what to do. The pig kept pushing the salt barrel away from the door and coming into the house. She got into the sack of oatmeal and spilled it. When Pa came home that night, I thought he was the pig and told him to get out. After he lit the lamp, he asked where you were, and we told him you went to look for a cow a long time ago. When he went down to the spring, he found that the pig had been in the spring, too, and upset all the milk cans. When he went to the section house, the men told him his girls had gone to Gull Lake. He said he would go after you and bring you back, and he did."

They seemed to be glad that Hedge had brought us back. I told them, "Your father can't beat me anymore. If he does, the Mounted Police are going to take me."

I didn't get another beating as long as we stayed on the homestead. If I had only had sense enough to tell Mrs. Holden what my worst trouble was, I would not have had to be tortured anymore. As it was, that part went on as before.

The talk with the Mountie did seem to rouse Hedge to some effort to feed and clothe us better. He went to his brother and persuaded him to send part of his sheep to our place to pasture. Zed sent the herder with them, but Hedge got a cut anyway. Zed came over and brought us clothing and a big grubstake. He even brought candy, but the fruit was what we enjoyed most. We never had fruit, except such wild fruit as grew along the creek – gooseberries, currants, Juneberries, chokecherries, and a few wild raspberries, delicious but scarce.

Zed started to build a bridge across the creek so we could cross with a wagon without getting stuck, and he built a shed and corral for the sheep. He was using old railroad ties, which Hedge and I were hauling, for the shed. Hedge was driving Zed's team, and I was driving our old nags and not doing a very good job, either. We had to go along a sidehill with only a cow trail for a road. Both horses wanted to walk in the one cow trail, and I wasn't driver enough to keep the upper wheel on the trail. The wagon turned over, and all the ties rolled downhill. Hedge had to unhook his team, come back up the hill, put my wagon back on its wheels, and load the ties again.

The next day the ties stayed on, but I didn't. Zed had dug the edge of the creek bank straight down, about eighteen inches deep, so he could set the pilings for his bridge. We came with a load of ties before he had the temporary poles in place, and we had to cross just at that spot. Hedge had taken the precaution of putting a rope around my load. I noticed his load lost a few ties as it dropped down into the creek, but he didn't signal for me to stop, and I followed right behind him.

I was sitting on the jockey box in front of the wagon bed, my toes barely touching the doubletrees. My seat wasn't secure, and I had no way of bracing myself when the wagon dropped down into the creek. The ties came forward and pushed me off the wagon, down behind the horses into the creek. The front wheel of the wagon went over my head, pressing it down into the mud. I had a sore head for days. Otherwise, I was okay, but I was a terrible sight. The hair was scraped off on one side of my head and took a long time to grow out.

After Zed went home, Hedge cooked for all of us, including Zed's sheepherder. The herder didn't like beans and sowbelly as often as Hedge gave it to him, so he quit his job as soon as Zed came back. He was the stupidest man I ever knew, but I was sorry to see him leave, because Hedge had to behave while he was around.

Zed got another man, and by the time he was ready to quit, the lambing was over, the close pasture was fed off, and the sheep had to be moved.

I didn't like sheep, but I could tolerate anything that helped keep Hedge from outraging me. He was worse than ever the rest of that summer and the following winter, until I decided a life like mine was not worth living.

One morning, after he had tortured me all night, he left, telling me to pick up the coyote bait we had put out. Someone had told him that if the poison was rained on, it might wash off the bones on the grass and poison the cattle.

There had been lots of coyotes around. The carcasses of the cattle hit by the train had attracted them, until it seemed as though all the coyotes in the country had come to our neighborhood. We weren't doing any good with traps, so Hedge had tried poison. He would saw a hole in the ribs of a carcass so he could get at the liver and the big clots of blood. We would make an X in this bait with a shovel and sprinkle a little strychnine on it. We didn't touch the bait with our hands. I would fasten a wire around the liver, tie it behind the sulky, and drag it so the coyotes would follow it from one carcass to the next. The liver would wear out by the time I had made my rounds, but it left a mark on the snow that I could follow the next day when I went out to gather up dead coyotes.

We found the clotted blood made good bait. It would always be gone by morning, and the first few days, I found dead coyotes lying all over. I was glad to see them killed off. They had caused me many a night of misery, and even after they were dead they made me suffer. They had fleas. When I piled the sulky full of dead coyotes, the fleas jumped off the coyotes on me and almost drove me wild. I was glad when spring came and the hides were no good, so I didn't have to pick up dead coyotes.

I had heard that coyotes would eat coyote flesh, so when I hauled out the carcasses, I stacked them up in such a way that I would know if anything touched them, but nothing but mice ever came near. I could tell by the tracks in the snow.

When I gathered up the bait that particular morning, I felt at the end of my endurance. I knew that the strychnine that killed the coyotes was one sure way of putting an end to my intolerable life. I told Beck, "I'm going to take poison. Your father always does nasty things to me and won't let me sleep at night, and I can't stand it any longer."

"I know he does," she said. "I heard him last night. I was so scared I couldn't move."

"When I'm dead, and he comes home, tell him he made me do it. Maybe I'll be with Mother after I die."

"I'll die, too, if you do. Wouldn't it be nice to have a mother like that little Holden girl has?"

"I was so happy at the Holdens'; everything was nice, and I didn't have to worry about your father – that was the best part of it. I can't get away from here any way but dying. If I take a lot of poison, I'll die quick, like the coyotes do. But I don't want you to take poison. You are all right. Your father doesn't make life miserable for you like he does for me."

Beck began to cry as if her heart would break and said she wanted to go with me to Mother.

I got the strychnine, wet my finger, dipped it in, and put my finger in my mouth. The strychnine was very bitter. I took a drink of water to wash it down and waited a few minutes to see whether I felt any effects.

Beck asked whether I felt bad, and I said no. She dipped her finger into the poison, tasted it, and reached for the water quick. After drinking she said, "It's terrible bitter, isn't it?"

I knew it would be bitter. It left my hands bitter even after washing them when I gathered up the cattle bones. (We wired the bones to a tree, and by spring the coyotes had eaten the meat, and the bones were all that was left.)

Soon Beck said she was very sick and asked what I could do to help her. I told her to drink some milk. That was what we gave the dog when he was poisoned. She asked me whether I felt sick, and I said, "Not a bit."

I wet my finger and took a second helping. As I looked out of the door I saw a cow going toward the haystack. "Bluey is going to the stack," I said to Beck. "I'll go head her off."

Beck started to follow me but had gone only a short distance when she said, "I can't go any farther." I turned back to her, but she fell in a spasm before I could reach her.

As soon as she could get up I took her hand, but in a moment she

144

fell again. I was frightened. When she could get on her feet again, we started for the house. "Oh, I wish I hadn't taken that bitter stuff," she cried. "I feel awfully sick. Do you?"

"No, just a little, not bad like you. I'll go get somebody to come and do something for you."

"Don't go," she pleaded, but I felt I must get help for her and left on the run.

I took the shortest way, which meant crossing the creek. It was high, with a thin film of ice from the night before. I waded in, afraid I might have a spasm and drown before I could get across, but I made it without stumbling into a hole and ran until I came to the creek again in front of the bachelor's cabin. By that time I was getting dizzy but not sick. The creek crossing at the old bachelor's was boggy and full of holes. I swayed through the water, slush, and mud like a drunk.

I expected the old man to be concerned and rush to Beck's aid, but he was cool as a cucumber and said he couldn't walk that far. I was aghast but rushed to the next cabin, where the green Scotchman lived. I had no faith in him, since the time he left the martingales off his team and almost caused me to have a runaway, but I thought he would stay with Beck while I went to the section house. The people there would be sure to know what to do.

I asked him to go quick, because Beck was awful sick. He said, "You're a little bit excited. She'll be all right."

"No," I said. "Go quick!"

"Where are you going?" he asked me.

"To the section house."

I found it hard to climb the hill from the Scotchman's cabin. My legs were numb, I supposed from crossing the creek and my cold, wet dress flapping against them. I thought I would warm up after I got to the level bench, but I was disappointed in the slow progress I made even on the downhill stretches. When I came to the creek crossing again, I lay down on my stomach to drink but almost fell headlong into the water. I had difficulty steadying myself after I got on my feet, and it was with genuine fear that I waded into the deepest crossing of the three.

But I made it across and up the hill on the other side. The rest of the way was downhill, and I needed the encouragement that knowledge gave me, for my head was dizzy, and my legs were getting even more numb. I had no pain whatever, though, and I had expected terrible pain from the strychnine.

The section boss happened to be at home. I had more confidence in him than in anybody else in the neighborhood.

I told him Beck was terribly sick, that she had spasms like a coyote had when it was poisoned.

"She may be poisoned," he said. "Your father keeps strychnine around, doesn't he?"

"Yes."

"I'll go right over and see what I can do."

I hung my head as his wife looked me over. I was a sight to behold. I had been traveling with my back to the sun, so the back of my dress was wet and the front frozen, with the front at my knees and the wet tail dangling down behind. I was covered with black mud. She must have felt sorry for me, because she asked me to stay and not try to go back right away, but I was expecting the strychnine to end my troubles any moment, and I wanted to be alone. I started up the small hill. My legs seemed tangled up, and I stumbled and fell twice. The last time I fell, it felt so good to lie down that I stayed where I was, hoping everything would be over before anyone from the section house saw me.

As I lay there, I began to wonder why the strychnine took effect on Beck so quickly, when I didn't feel bad enough to die yet. I hadn't even had a spasm, and I had taken twice as much as she had. I would

146

have taken more right then if I'd had it. I was going to try to get up and get back to Beck when I saw a man coming toward me, and I lay my head on my arm, where it felt better . . .

Later, lying in a warm, comfortable bed, I was haunted by the thought that Beck might die, and I would live to be sorry for the rest of my life. Why did I tell her what I was going to do? Why? Why? I couldn't remember just what happened to me or what they had done after they put me to bed, but I learned afterward that they had telegraphed for Hedge and a doctor. I do not remember the doctor's coming, but the next day I was able to get up. They asked me if I wanted to see Beck, and that I remember only too well.

She lay in a rough, homemade box hardly big enough for her; in fact, she seemed to be pressed into it. She looked as though she had suffered. Her hair was combed back slick and seemed to be wet. She wore an old white nightgown belonging to one of the section house ladies. There she lay, a child who wanted to live, and I, who didn't want to, lived on. I hoped she was in heaven with our mother. This was the only consoling thought I had.

It was a cold, miserable day when they took poor little Beck away in an old lumber wagon, back to Hedge's ranch to bury her on the hill in front of his cabin. Three of the section men went with Hedge to bury her. There was no fence around her grave.

A day or so later the Mounted Police came to question me and the two little sisters. Beck had told no one what had happened, but they suspected poison, because I had said Beck was having spasms. The Mountie asked me whether I had handled poison lately, and I told him I had brought in poisoned bait the day before, because my step-father had directed me to pick up all I could find. He asked where I had put it, and I said I had scraped it off my hand into a box nailed on the door. He took me to the ranch to show him the box, but to my surprise the poison was gone. Perhaps the mice carried it away – that was the only explanation I could think of.

We kept the milk cans standing behind the door, directly under the box shelf, and the Mountie thought that some of the poison might have fallen into the milk. I didn't think so. It was so greasy it would have floated and been easy to see. The Mountie fed some of the milk to the cats, but they didn't get sick.

The Mountie took us all to the barracks. I thought they might put me in jail, but anything would be better than living with Hedge, subject to indignities and abuse. I wouldn't have to dread the night.

In the barracks I was taken to a room where a man sat at a desk, writing. He turned when I came in, told me to sit down, and began questioning me.

He called in the section boss's sister-in-law, and she told a fantastic tale. She said I had told her that Zed's wife had promised me a team of horses if I would poison my stepfather. The man asked me if this was true, and I said I had never heard of such a thing. The sister-in-law was just a green German girl. If she had had any sense, she would have known I wasn't interested in a team of horses. I was crazy for a good saddle horse. But she made up that silly story, and when she had told it, she began to cry.

Next Zed's wife came in. She was crying, too. "It's all your fault that I am here!" she said to me.

The men asked her whether she had said anything to me about a team of horses. "No," she cried. "She must be crazy to tell such a thing on me – and when I've been so good to her, too!"

"Maybe she is," the man answered. "She says she didn't tell any such a thing, because you never said it. You can go."

She left, crying. I didn't understand what they were all crying about, but one of the Canadians told me they were crying because they were all foreigners and scared to death of the law. None of the native Canadians did any crying.

148

Hedge was called in. To my surprise, he told nothing but the truth, without even exaggerating.

They examined all the people who had had any contact with us, including the section boss, who was with Beck when she died. When they asked him whether she had told him anything, he said no, but that one of the little girls, when he told her Beck was dead, answered, "Well, we've got the best one left, anyway."

The man turned to me and asked whether we children liked each other, and I said we sure did.

They let Hedge take me home with him, and that was the worst deal I could have got. All the way home I went over and over the time I had spent on Hedge's homestead, and it all seemed bad, and now I was bad too. Poor little Beck had to die because I wanted to die, and maybe God wouldn't let me see my mother now even if I died, because I had done so many terrible things.

The days that followed were the blackest of my miserable childhood. I condemned myself as everybody else did, although the Mounties had been as kind and considerate as they could be under the circumstances. Now I would have no more contact with them. I wished I could meet a friendly cowboy. The cowboys were always kind to me, but it was too early in the spring to hope to meet any of them riding. I could hope for no spark of human kindness in those dark hours of remorse and despair.

I milked my cows first and then started on Beck's. Each one of hers reopened that chapter of sorrow, and my tears often fell into the milk. It was a relief when I began to feed the hungry calves that jostled around and gave me no time to think of anything but them. I washed the milk things and went out with the cattle. My pet cow was happy to have me with her. We kept going until we came to good grass, and then I leaned my head against her and cried. She was too busy getting me cleaned up to let me lean quietly against her, but at last she started to eat grass. I went along by her head and

149

picked handfuls of grass to feed her. We developed a rhythm - she would take two bites, then reach over and get my handful of grass.

When my hand got tired, I sat down and looked over the peaceful cattle and asked myself why God was better even to a herd of cattle than he was to me. God is all goodness, yet he took my mother away and left me to live in misery with nothing that cared for me but that cow - and the cow couldn't understand what happened to poor Beck even if I told her. I looked up at the blue sky and thought, That is where heaven is. Beck must be happy up there now, away from nasty men like her father.

I had Hedge's heavy dark blue shirt and his socks to patch, so I sat with my back to the wind and made one sock out of two. By that time the cattle were some distance away, so I put my mending back in the flour sack and walked along toward them with my pet cow. I sat down on the far side of them so they wouldn't go any farther from home and took up my mending again.

Days like that were repeated over and over again. I had time to think of Dave Treu, and how disappointed I had been not to have a chance to talk to him before we left Gull Lake. Dave knew the Indian sign language fairly well, but I didn't know enough to answer. He had tried to tell me something as we were leaving, but all I got was, "I will see you."

10

Hedge was late coming home one night. The next morning he told Rose, Nora, and me that he was going to put us in school. I was delighted but asked no questions – anything was better than living on the homestead with Hedge.

He sold part of our cattle to a new homesteader. The people at the section house bought my pet cow and came with a fat mare to lead her home. Hedge made me put the rope on her, and I felt like a lowdown traitor, betraying the animal that had always befriended me. I gritted my teeth to keep from crying, but she broke down all my resistance when she started licking me.

The section man was deeply touched and told me they would take good care of her, but I doubted whether she would give them any cooperation. She wasn't broke to lead, and, being a range cow, she didn't submit without a struggle. I heard afterward she came near killing both horse and rider, who hadn't known better than to tie her to the horn of his saddle. He had seen cowboys do this, but they knew how to do it, and so did their horses. They never could gentle her and finally had to trade her off for a more tractable cow.

I had hoped a rancher would get her. She was a fine, big range cow, and she raised calves just like herself. She was a good rustler, the kind that takes to the high ridges where the wind has swept the snow off the grass and stays there in spite of the cold until she's had enough to eat. When she had fed, she would go to the shelter of a coulee or brush – just the opposite of a poor little dogie that humps up in a sheltered place, waiting to be fed, growing weak from hunger and cold, and lying down to die without a struggle.

While I was putting the rope on my cow, the rest of the cattle were hurrying down the road to the bench where the grass was good. I caught up with them but saw our bull a quarter of a mile beyond them heading straight for a big bunch of strange cattle.

I knew it would be hard to turn him, but I meant to try before he got into the strange herd. When he saw me coming he started to run, but a heavy bull can't run fast. I overtook him, but there were strange bulls challenging him from the herd, and I was having a hard time turning him. When I was prepared to go after bulls, I would put a fine popper of wire on my cattle whip, but now all I could do was strike him over the eyes with my quirt, and I couldn't get my horse close enough to hit him very often. The horse had been gored and knew the danger.

I was on the losing end until a cowboy came riding toward me. It was Dave Treu.

While two other cowboys ran the strange bulls back into the herd, Dave tackled our bull. He had a horse that would lean against an animal, giving his rider a chance to use his quirt to advantage. A few well-placed lashes under the belly (the only place where a bull's hide is thin), and the bull headed for home. Dave rode along with me to make sure I had no more trouble.

"My stepfather says he is going to put us in school," I told him.

"Where?"

I didn't know.

"When are you leaving?"

"Now."

"I'm sorry," he said.

I was so surprised that anyone should be the least bit interested in me that I asked, "Why?"

"You told me you wanted to have a cattle ranch with a nice house and a big barn. I've started working on that already. I'm taking most of my wages out in cattle this year. I'll be ready by the time you're grown up. There are hundreds of ranches in this country. Where would you like best?"

"Maiden Creek, where there are lots of trees and good spring water. I don't like well water," I answered, as though everything was settled.

"I'll take a look at Maiden Creek, but I think all the good land there has been taken up. I'll find a place just as good. As soon as you get where you're going, let me know where you are."

We had loaded all our belongings on the wagon the night before and left the homestead in the morning. I was horseback, driving the cattle. Hedge drove the team. We spent that night at Uncle Zed's, and Hedge left the cattle there – I didn't know whether he had sold them to Zed or just left them. The next morning, early, we started for Montana.

It was a nice day, the wind in the southwest. We made good time, but by noon the next day the wind had changed to the north, and it began to snow, a blizzardy snow that made visibility poor and the horses hard to handle. They wanted to get to shelter. So did we, as the snow blew into our wagon, making it wet and disagreeable. Hedge turned back and got into town late that night. He told us to cover up and get some sleep, while he tried to find a nephew of his who would take the horses and the entire outfit back to Zed's.

We tried to sleep, but the snow kept blowing in our faces. And sooner than we expected, Hedge came back, calling, "There she is! Hurry up! Come on, now, the train only stops for a few minutes!"

This was our first inkling of what he meant to do, and we were delighted at the thought of a train ride, out of the storm. We didn't know where we were going, but we didn't care, just so we stayed on the train.

We got off at Lethbridge. Hedge left us in the depot while he found a house to rent, then came back for us. On the way to the house he bought a loaf of bread, some cheese, and a can of tomatoes. He opened the can with his pocket knife and cut the bread and cheese with the same knife, the one he used for castrating the calves and pigs. I never saw him wash it, just wipe it off and drop it in his pocket. He wasn't dirty, he was fussy about his food, and probably he didn't think what he had been using the knife for. I did, because I always helped him at these operations.

The tomatoes were not very good without salt, but we dipped our bread into them and made out our supper.

To our delight and surprise, Hedge took us shopping for furniture for the house and clothes for ourselves, with nice new bedding for the two beds. We girls enrolled in school, and Hedge went to work driving mules in the mine.

I never liked housework. Nora did most of it and was exceptionally good at it for her years. I did the cooking, made the bread, and did the washing and ironing. Bread making and washing were old stuff to me, but ironing and going to school were new. Ironing I soon got the knack of, but school! I was anything but good in school. I was past twelve years old and had to stand up with the little tots, and I couldn't do as well as they. I was almost speechless with embarrassment and would often say, "No, Ma'am," when the teacher asked me a question, whether I knew the answer or not.

We needed a clock. Up to this time we had been getting up at the same time we did on the ranch, which gave us plenty of time. Hedge went to work when he saw the other miners going. But finally he got tired of guesswork, and one evening we went out to buy a clock.

At the jeweler's, Hedge picked out a nice eight-day timepiece. As the man was wrapping it, he told Hedge that I was badly in need of glasses. He knew, because I put everything right up to my face before I could see it. Hedge said, "She's always been like that. Her eyes are all right."

"No, I beg your pardon, her eyes are not all right," the jeweler said. "If you will wait just a minute, I'll prove to you how bad they are, and it will not cost you a cent." He fitted me as well as he could with glasses out of the case. But he had none on hand strong enough for me and persuaded Hedge to order the proper glasses because I needed them so badly.

I was never so surprised in my life as when I looked through that pair of glasses. I saw a different world, a brighter, cleaner-looking world. Things that had been just a blur stood out in definite shapes and colors. The jeweler said he would lend me a pair of glasses until mine came, and I walked out on the street wearing them. That was when the fun began for me. I could hardly take a step without falling over something. The glasses brought things closer. I would try to set my foot on a step when I was still too far away and just reach it with the tip of my toe. My foot would slip, and I'd almost fall. But I soon became used to the glasses, and my difficulties disappeared.

I was anxious to get my own glasses, because the jeweler said they would be even better than these. He said it would take ten days or so before they came. But before the ten days were up, Hedge got tired of his job and quit. He said the mine was too wet to work in, and the mule kept splashing mud on him. So the next day we began selling the furniture and kept selling it until everything was gone but the cookstove, which Hedge wanted to take with us.

The night before we left, we went downtown to see whether my glasses had come. They hadn't. We left the next morning, waiting at the Salvation Army headquarters until train time. The Salvation Army officer advised Hedge to go to Frank, a new mining camp just starting up, but after we got on the train, a man who had been there told him there were no houses to rent in Frank, and it was not a place to take little children. So we went to Fernie, British Columbia, instead.

We children stayed at the hotel in Fernie while Hedge went to Coal Creek, five miles from town. The mine was between two high mountains, steep and covered with shale. The shale caused slides every so often, and yet quite a few houses perched on the precarious mountainsides. Hedge rented one, a double house with fireplaces, the first I had ever seen.

We found that fireplaces didn't heat a house as well as the heating stoves we were used to. Hedge slept downstairs, and I spread our blankets upstairs in front of the fireplace. The next morning I had a cold and felt terrible, but since I was never sick, I thought I'd be all right as soon as I got out into the air.

I couldn't cook over a fireplace, and neither could Hedge, so we had a bad time. If it hadn't been so cold, we might have gone outside and built a campfire. We might have blackened all the pots and pans, but we would have had well-cooked food. Our stove soon arrived from Lethbridge, and I was able to cook again, but my cold didn't get better, it got worse.

Hedge went to work in the mine, and we children started school again. We had a man teacher. He was exceptionally nice to the girls but strict with the boys, punishing them for things the girls were really to blame for. If the girls didn't actually take part in the mischievous stunts themselves, they dared the boys to.

For instance, the teacher had to pass under the mine tipple on his way to school. The girls dared the boys to hide behind the big cable spools and knock off the teacher's hat as he came by. The snow was three feet deep, and when the teacher came walking along the path, waist-deep snow on both sides, wham! Snowballs began coming fast and accurate. The derby hat went into the deep snow, and as the teacher stooped to recover it, another flight of snowballs landed on a spot well protected by his heavy overcoat. The man's dignity must have been hurt. As he straightened up, he exclaimed, "Of all the ungentlemanly acts I've seen committed, this is the worst! Boys, you are going to be punished for this!"

He kept his word. He lined up the boys he suspected, made each hold out his hand as he marched past, and brought his pointer down with two cracks on each palm that made me flinch as I sat safe in my seat.

Coasting was the main sport for the children in camp. The mine foreman's daughter asked me to go with her, because she was afraid of the boys and their tricks. They would wait until the girls had pulled their sleds up the long hill, then take the sleds away from them and coast down themselves, making the girls trudge down after them.

The best place for coasting was the road from Fernie, cut into the mountainside, which sloped gradually as it approached the mine. You could ride a mile or more at a speed more thrilling than safe. The excitement was much to my liking, and I planned to learn to steer a sled as well as any boy. For me, there was no separate standard for boys and girls, and it had never occurred to me that it would be unladylike to use my fists on a boy if he did something I objected to. This lack of sophistication and my Irish fighting blood got me in bad at the camp and eventually cheated me out of my coasting fun.

The foreman's daughter and I had just reached the top of the hill when a big bully, showing off by walking at the very edge of the grade, demanded our sled. The other girl knew all the angles and pretended not to hear him, but I gave him a dirty look and got ready. As he swung around to throw a snowball down the mountain and watch it land, I caught him off-balance and gave him a push that sent him rolling down the steep slope. There wasn't a tree or boulder to stop him.

I laughed with satisfaction to see him roll clear to the railroad tracks. He couldn't climb back the way he went down, and I felt safe; but the other girl recovered her voice and cried, "Oh, I feel sorry for you! Run home quick before you get killed. He'll follow the track and come back up here and throw you down a worse place – don't ever come here where he can catch you!" I realized she might be right and hopped on the sled for my last thrilling ride at Coal Creek.

To get even with me, the boy began calling me "Hayseed" at school. I didn't think it was a bad name, in fact, I was rather proud of my ability in a hay field, but when the kids roared with laughter, I was embarrassed. The boys who called me that were too big for me. It is surprising that I didn't take them on anyway, I was so dumb and reckless. But one day when the bell rang for us to fall in line, a smaller boy just ahead of me turned and said, "I won't stand by no hayseed."

Before I realized what I was doing, I doubled up my fist and struck him squarely in the mouth. He made no attempt to defend himself but put both hands to his mouth. I threw him flat on his back and got in two good cracks to his face before one of the big boys picked me up bodily. The kid was too much of a coward to hit me even when the big boy held my arms and told him, "Give her a couple of pokes."

The pupils had broken ranks and rushed to see the excitement. The teacher, who had been standing in the doorway, walked out and marched us into the schoolroom without a word. When we were seated, he stood with his back to the door and demanded to know what Andy was crying about. Between sobs, Andy told him that that terrible girl had hit him in the mouth and made it bleed, and he showed his hands, all bloody.

Then and there I got a stern lecture on what constituted ladylike conduct and for the first time in my life realized that a lady doesn't use her fists to put boys in their place. I was too bashful to ask what a lady did do in such circumstances.

I suppose the teacher was too surprised at the fracas to inquire what started it until he got done lecturing me. Then he asked, "What made you hit Andrew?"

"Because he said he wouldn't stand in line next to a hayseed."

"Did you say that, Andrew?"

"The big boys all call her that," said the cowardly little tattletale.

The teacher reached for his powerful persuader, the pointer, and repeated his question: "Did you call this young lady a hayseed?"

"Yes, sir."

"I'll let you go this time, but if I hear of you, or anybody else, calling this young lady such an unbecoming name, I'll deal with you as I do with all second offenders."

I had lost my precious glasses in the scuffle and was afraid to tell the teacher. But after thinking it over, I got up enough courage to ask if I might go out and look for them. The teacher said, "No. You couldn't find them if you did look." He sent the big boys out and gave them five minutes to find them.

I had been suffering from a cold ever since the night we slept in front of the fireplace. The night after my fight I slept very little and got up feeling worse. Nevertheless, I went on as usual, made breakfast, and went to school. On my way home I coughed so violently that a lady stopped me and asked whether I was taking anything for my cold. She didn't know me except from seeing me pass her house on the way to school, but she said, "Come into my house, and I will fix you up," and she did. She rubbed my chest with goose grease and put a flannel cloth on it.

"You have a little fever," she said. "If your father will let you stay with me for a few days, I'll put you to bed and have you all right in no time."

It embarrassed me to have anyone fuss over me, but it surely felt good to be in a warm room without having to make a fire and get supper. The lady gave Rose and Nora a drink of light tea and some homemade cookies, and they went home to start supper for Hedge.

Hedge didn't even wait for supper but came right down to bring me home. He told me to get up and dress and assured the lady that he would see that I followed all her instructions. When we reached home, he said, "Pack up all our duds, and we'll get out of this place. The gas in the mine gives me a headache all the time, and I can't stand it."

We had to hurry to catch the night train to Fernie and took only what we could carry to the depot shack. I never learned what Hedge did with all the things we had in the house; maybe he sold them or told the bachelors living in the other part to sell them for him. We waited in the Fernie depot until after midnight for the train to Spokane, and the next day the papers carried the news of the terrible Fernie mine explosion, the very mine where Hedge had been working.

We must have come into Montana, for Hedge inquired about putting us in a sisters' school in Missoula. Then he heard about a cheaper school in Spokane. In Spokane the sisters told him about a little school near Colville, very reasonable in rates, so we went to what is now Ward, Washington. The rates must have satisfied Hedge, because he left us there.

My coughing had been so bad that everyone on the train and in the hotels complained about it. In Spokane the man in the room next to ours had come in as soon as Hedge left and asked me whether I had any medicine for my cold. When I said no, he brought me two bottles. When Hedge came back, the proprietor called him to the door and told him either to send me to the hospital or get out of the hotel.

"That's just what I'm going to do," Hedge told him, "so don't get yourself excited over nothing."

One thing that had made my cold so bad was that in Missoula we slept in a private house in a room the family weren't using because it couldn't be heated. With no heat and sleeping on the floor with hardly any covers over or under me had almost finished me off. In the morning the lady had asked Hedge if I was sick, and he told her, no, I just had a cold. The lady asked him what he was going to do with us children, and he said, "Put them in school. I'm going to the Klondike."

This was news to me, and I felt good over it in spite of my tight chest. We got on the train for the last lap of our journey, a short ride of eighty-five miles or so north of Spokane. I was happy when the train stopped at the little three-sided shelter that served as a waiting room for passengers coming and going.

From the first, the little white Convent of the Sacred Heart gave me a feeling of security. The footpath from the station shed to the convent was a lane between tall trees, with rosebushes lining the way. This was winter, and the spot was not in its summer loveliness, but still, it was a beautiful picture in the deep snow.

Hedge rang the bell. A sister with a serene, gentle face came to the door. She invited us in and made us comfortable in a neat little sitting room.

"Would you like to see the sister superior?" she asked.

"Yes, if she is the person in charge."

Hedge's voice brought me back to a world I wanted to forget. In a few minutes another sister entered. She had a more business-like air than the first sister.

"How do you do?" she greeted us. "What can I do for you?"

"I want to put these girls in school. What is it going to cost me?"

"That depends on their instruction. The regular school course costs fourteen dollars a month for each child. If you want them to take music lessons or drawing, that will be more."

"Teach them to read and write and figure. That will be enough," Hedge answered.

"Do you want them to begin school now?"

"Yes. I want to leave them here now. I want to catch the next train back to Spokane. When does it go by here?"

"At half past two."

"I'll have to hurry."

The sister and Hedge exchanged a few words about our clothes and other matters, and then Hedge hurried away to flag the train.

The sister superior took us upstairs to the sister in charge, who showed us where to hang our coats and hats and then took us downstairs to the little girls' classroom. Still another teacher assigned us to our seats. She questioned me about our schooling, then put away the books she had supposed I would need and got out another set like those she had for Nora and Rose. We all started in the first reader. I had been happy until now, but the sight of the books gave me the jitters, and the warm room seemed close to me and made me sick. I wanted to lay my head down on my desk, but I was too bashful until I began to feel so dizzy that I had to. The sister came quietly to my desk and put her hand on my forehead, asking me if I was sick.

"I've had a cold for a long time," I answered, "and maybe I got too warm here, so close to the stove. I'll be all right if I can go outside."

"No," she said gently. "I will take you upstairs to the infirmary."

She had a quiet little conference that I couldn't hear with the infirmary sister and then went back to her classroom. The new sister put me to bed and asked me how long I had had a cold. When I explained that I had been more or less sick ever since I slept in front of the fireplace in Fernie, a long time before, she said, as if to herself, "I thought so."

Once I gave up and went to bed, my sickness took full possession of me. I was delirious. When I came out of the delirium, I had a terrible swell of loneliness. I didn't say anything to the sisters about it; it seemed so silly to say I was lonesome when I was in the best place I had known since I left my grandmother. The sisters had a few old cows, and every time I heard one of them bawling, it brought tears to my eyes as I thought of my pet cow and knew she had done a lot of bawling for me. I was anxious to get up and out and have a look at a cow or horse, but I was disappointed when I did, for the horses were old plugs, and the cows all old and poor, except one, and she was no prize.

On Christmas Day I was still in bed, but when everyone went to Mass, I was feeling so good that I tried to get up and was surprised to find I couldn't stand. I was glad to get back on the pillow that felt extra good to my dizzy head, and I didn't pester the sisters to let me out of bed until they said I could. That was my treat for New Year's Day.

The first letter from Hedge came from Dawson City, Alaska. He wrote that he was worried about me, he had dreamed that he saw me dressed all in white going up a big hill close to the convent, and he thought that I had died. I was astonished that he should be worrying about me but more than satisfied to be with the sisters instead of him; but his own little girls were so happy over the letter that they cried and had the sister read it over and over to them. The letter was hard to make out. Hedge had never gone to school and was a poor writer. He wrote that a man could make big wages if he could stand the climate, but he intended to go prospecting for himself as soon as the weather permitted. He said he had walked a hundred miles carrying his bread and bacon on his back, only to have a bear eat the bacon and scatter the flour all over the snow. He had been camping in a cave and built a fire that drove the bear out.

For six months after I had pneumonia, I felt sick most of the time. The sisters took me to their hospital in Spokane, where the doctor said it would take time, but I would be all right.

By the time I was able to go back to school, my little sisters were way ahead of me. That embarrassed me more than ever. Luckily for me, a big girl, just over from Ireland, enrolled. She and I became a pair. We studied together, spending all our spare time at our books. She mastered her lessons better than I did, but I managed to keep up with her. Our teacher was a sweet little French sister who helped us after school, so we were able to finish the first and second readers in the last half of the term. I finished, in spite of having another serious sickness before the term was over.

The sisters must have thought my sickness more serious than I did. They explained to me the benefits of religion and the need for baptism, telling me that one who died unbaptized could never see the face of God. That didn't make as great an impression on me as they expected. I hadn't forgotten all my prayers that had not been answered, that God had taken away my mother and left me to Hedge and his tortures. I possessed little of that sweet resignation to the will of God that made the sisters accept all their problems without resentment, but I figured their problems were mild compared to mine. When God took my mother, he forced me to take her place at eight years of age. At every move, even in play, I had had to carry my baby sister on my back. I washed clothes, baked bread, and cleaned house while other children played with their dolls. And I had worse problems. All these things came back to my mind when the sisters tried to impress me with God's great love and wisdom.

My thoughts must have showed in my face, for the sisters stopped preaching to me for a time. Instead they sent me Donna, the sweetest girl I ever knew, with the type of beauty I admired – big brown eyes that sparkled when she was happy and long braids of dark hair. She was planning to become a sister when she finished school. It was her secret, but she said she had to tell someone or she would burst with joy. I felt privileged to share her secret.

She explained how religion would restore my health, if it was the dear Lord's will. She asked me what I wanted to do when I finished school. I said I wouldn't live long enough to finish school, but as soon as I was sixteen I was going back to the country, to the wide open spaces with horses and cattle. Just one week on horseback would cure all this sickness without God's help.

She was horrified and told me it was wrong to belittle God's importance in our lives. "Do you know what I wished you would say you were planning to do?" she asked. "To join me as a sister as soon as you could."

I told her I thought she was born good. "Take animals, for instance. They don't know anything about God, but some are born good, and others are hell on four legs."

I had shocked her by my language. I knew she wanted to say more but was too modest to force her opinions on me. The supper bell rang, and she went to bring me something to eat. I, who had always had a good appetite, wanted no food of any kind now. I was like a wild animal – I couldn't thrive in captivity.

I was hoping to be up soon, now that the weather was growing warm, and get out into the beautiful orchards, now in full bloom. I could see green hills from my window but no cows with calves playing at their sides. What I wouldn't have given for a ride on a good cowpony! This comfortable bed and the pills the good sisters so carefully prescribed for me were not what I needed. I was acting like a dogie, not like range stock that never quit as long as a breath of life remained. Right there I made up my mind to get out of that bed and stay out. I opened the window wide and sat by it until Donna popped in with my supper.

"Oh my goodness!" she exclaimed. "You mustn't sit in the draft! Did Sister open the window for you?"

"No, I opened it myself. I need fresh air."

"Of course you need fresh air, but not a draft! I'll open the window for you, but not while you are eating."

I ate the fruit and the small portion of ham that was my supper.

Donna had brought me milk, supposing that because I was from the country, milk would be what I liked best. But it was skim milk, and I was no skim-milker, so I didn't drink it.

My open window brought bad results that night. My temperature went up. The sister who stayed with me at night grew worried and called the sister superior. She must have been worried, too, for they redoubled their attentions with flannels, camphorated oil, hot water bottles, hot drinks, and capsules – quinine, I think – until I was ashamed and disgusted with myself for causing them so much anxiety and bother. I felt their stir was all unnecessary, but by morning I was sick enough to be satisfied to lie quietly, with nothing but an occasional sip of water.

The sisters must have telephoned for a doctor, for one came from a neighboring town. He told the sisters to keep up their procedures and to give me some pills that he left. The sister who had made such effort to help me with my lessons came to see me before she went to her classroom and in her kind, sweet way suggested that if I were baptized it would be pleasing to God and might restore me to health. For her sake, and not because I expected beneficial results, I said if I didn't feel better by noon, I might take her advice.

Donna stayed out of school to take care of me, although the sister superior was in the room most of the time. I knew Donna wanted to ask me if I had decided to be baptized, but nothing was said until the sister came to take my temperature. As I held the thermometer tightly in my lips, my nose started to bleed. In spite of all the sister could do to stop it, the nosebleed continued. The sight of so much blood must have scared poor Donna. She began to plead, "Sister, please let me go get the priest!"

"No, not now," Sister Superior told her, "but have Sister Mary come. I want her to telephone the doctor about this."

The sisters spoke in French, so I didn't know what they were saying, but the doctor must have told them to put icepacks on the back

166

of my neck, because icepacks came next. Either the icepacks stopped the nosebleed, or it stopped of its own accord. I listened to the girls marching down to the dining room and knew it must be noon and that I must make up my mind what answer to give my teacher about my baptism. I was sorrier for Donna than myself and finally told her that to make her happy, I would be baptized.

I had said the wrong thing again.

"No, no, that would be a terrible sin," she remonstrated, "to be baptized for someone else's sake. Baptism and all the Holy Sacraments must be accepted for God's sake, because you want to fulfill his holy will."

"All right, I'll do it for God's sake, then," I said, but even that answer didn't make her happy.

"I thought you understood religion better than you do," she said, "and it is my fault that you don't. I should have explained more to you, and I will, as soon as you feel better."

By this time the sisters were back in my room, and we said no more about baptism until my teacher came in.

"You are feeling better," she said. "I offered many little prayers for you since I was here this morning. Do you remember your little promise?"

"Yes, Sister. I am ready to be baptized if you think it is best for me."

That was all I remembered of that day and the following night, but the next morning when I awakened, I had a brand-new godmother who was to look after my religious education.

11

I knew Donna's new office made her very happy. She was deeply religious and sincere to a fault. She and all the sisters believed that my baptism saved my life. I wished I could have such implicit faith, but I didn't; in the first place, I hadn't thought that I was sick enough to die. I said no more about my doubts after I was baptized but did my best to get well so I could go outdoors. My zealous little godmother mapped out a program of religious training for me that began as soon as I was halfway able to study.

As soon as I was able to walk out on the porch, I stayed outside as much as possible. Outdoor air was my religion, and I believed in mine as they did in theirs. As I grew stronger I walked up and down that porch for hours. Donna often walked with me and helped me with my schoolwork or catechism.

I was glad Hedge couldn't see me. I was nothing but bones. He used to call me Spindleshanks and Skin-'em-Alive, and I didn't know what he might compare me to now. Thinking of him made me appreciate my present situation all the more. Everyone was nice to me, and nobody ridiculed me. Some of the girls complained that the sisters were too strict and resented the work they gave us to do. Four girls would be assigned to certain work each month, such as sweeping and dusting the recreation room, and then given other tasks the next month. Such light work was almost play to me.

After school was out and most of the girls had gone home for the summer, we who were left had a grand time. We were given many privileges – picnics in the timber, swimming in the river. None of us could swim, but we had fun wading and catching crawfish. I loved the long walks, romping over the hills and picking flowers. We helped gather fruit and had all we wanted to eat, although it took me some time to learn to like muskmelons and other unfamiliar fruits I had never tasted before.

Our "swimming" suits were high-necked, long-sleeved dresses of heavy ticking with full, gathered skirts that came down around our ankles. Usually Sister Isaac came down to the river with us when we played there. She knew the river, how swift the current was, and where some of the deep holes were, and probably she would have stopped us if we had started to do anything dangerous. But one day Sister Joanna went with us. She was young and sweet and timid and no doubt thought we knew more than she did.

Six of the girls got into a boat that was moored at the riverbank. Since they had no oars, they asked Tenino and me to tow the boat up the river and give them a ride. Tenino was an Indian girl, half white, and she and I were the tallest girls at the river that day.

We decided to tow the boat across the river, but the water was deeper and swifter than we thought, and our heavy dresses held water and put so much pressure against our legs that we could hardly keep our feet. We were being carried downstream toward the rapids. Indian-like, Tenino said not a word when she realized our danger, but she grew so pale that her face was the strangest color.

When we came into the deepest water, close to the far bank, I had to throw back my head to keep my mouth and nose out of the water. Fortunately, a growth of red willows loomed over the bank, and by holding on to the branches we managed to tow the boat into shallow water.

When we got back to the riverbank, Tenino and I were exhausted and stretched out on the sand to rest, though we said we were just trying to get warm. We hadn't given a sign that we understood our danger for fear of throwing the other girls into a panic. We knew we couldn't hold another ounce of pressure, and if they began to move or rock the boat, we were lost. We never told the sister of our experience, for fear Sister Superior might put a stop to our river expeditions. I felt sick for several days afterward, but Tenino and I kept our own counsel.

She and I had another little adventure the next spring. Two sisters took fifteen of us older girls out to pick wild strawberries. It was fun to hunt for the wild berries, and we rushed from one clearing in the timber to the next, paying no attention to where we were going. The sisters were carrying our lunch and trying to keep up. When they began to tire and asked us not to go any farther, we dashed back to show them our baskets, almost full, and begged them to let us look for just one more patch.

They reluctantly agreed, and off we scampered, deeper into the timber. We found a beautiful big clearing, thick with strawberries, where we filled our baskets and the sisters served us our picnic lunch. One of the sisters had promised to tell us a choice story if we filled our baskets, so as soon as the dishes were washed and packed in their hampers, she began. She was very good at telling stories, and everyone became so absorbed, and time passed so quickly, that no one noticed how late it was until we began to grow chilly.

The sister suggested that we had better start for home and promised to finish the story later. But when we were ready to start, nobody knew for sure which way to go. All we could see were trees and more trees. We wandered for a while until the girls and the sisters, too, became frightened. The sisters said it would be better not to go any farther and asked us to gather wood for a bonfire to keep the cougars away and show rescuers where we were.

As soon as the fire was going well, the sisters asked us all to kneel down and pray for guidance. I went through the motions with everybody else, but I wasn't satisfied to settle down for a night of prayer. It wasn't quite dark yet. Looking at the sky, I could tell where the sun had set, and I remembered that we had faced the sun when we came into the timber. So to get home, we must keep our backs toward the place where the sun went down. I surveyed the lay of the land and decided that I, for one, wasn't lost, and I was almost positive I could go straight home once I made my way through the brush.

I finally found courage to tell one of the sisters that I knew the way home and would go for help before dark if she gave me permission. Before she could answer, Tenino said, "Let me go, too. I can find the way out."

Tenino's confidence helped the sister decide, and she said, "All right, I'll let you both go – with this understanding: we will sing hymns while you are gone, and you must not go farther than you can hear us singing, unless you reach the road before you are out of hearing distance."

She repeated these instructions twice, although we understood the first time. It was growing darker, and we were anxious to get started. She instructed us to pray, but we both realized we had to compare notes and make plans for getting through the thick brush and crossing the little creek we had come to several times on our way into the timber.

After half a mile of hard going, Tenino and I were out on the open road that led straight to the convent. Our clothes were a sad-looking sight from our struggle through the underbrush, but the sisters, worrying and praying in the chapel, looked three shades brighter when they saw us come in. They were afraid we had been attacked by a cougar. When we assured them that we were all right, Sister Superior said she would summon the hired men to bring lanterns and go back with us, but she lost time asking how it all happened and exclaiming over our scratches, which the sisters wanted to doctor before we started back.

Tenino and I were impatient to start. The hired men were not keen on leaving their comfortable beds to crawl through thick underbrush, and they were skeptical about our ability to lead them, but at last we were on our way, with the two men carrying lanterns and the sisters back to their praying.

After walking a mile and a half, we caught snatches of the singing and left the road to head straight through the timber. It was no fun, forcing our way through the brush, but we finally reached the grateful party.

The big question was how to find a way out that so big a party could travel, especially the sisters in their habits. One of the men finally volunteered to go ahead and pick a trail, although Tenino and I had to do a lot of prompting before we reached the road. We were glad to crawl into bed that early morning. Tenino and I knew we were given more praise and credit than we deserved. Aside from briar scratches, we hadn't suffered, and nothing about this adventure had been half as terrifying as our river experience.

Tenino and I had much in common. We each longed to be out with our saddle horses again. We would sit together for hours, building air castles about our big ranches, fine horses, and the cattle we would have someday. Donna didn't approve of our daydreams, but she was too kind to voice any objections.

Donna was delighted when the sister told her she should begin to prepare me for my First Communion, a serious occasion in the Catholic discipline that required much religious instruction. In her zeal, she kept me busy every spare moment. I was slow at books, but I did my best to master my catechism, feeling that I mustn't fail Donna. Tenino and I missed our range dreams. She would sit and look across the room at us as Donna heard my lessons, devoting most of her own study periods to me. Donna was so smart that she needed little time to prepare her own lessons.

Finally, the day of my First Communion came. I felt an inward happiness that I had never known before and asked myself why I could not be content with this serene way of living, which was paradise compared to what I had known before. I determined to make myself like it. No more daydreaming about going back to the range, no more thoughts of horses and the open sky.

I kept that promise to myself for some time, until a new girl came to school. Her name, Gladys Treue, stirred memories in me, until I felt so restless and dissatisfied that I asked her whether she had ever known Dave Treu. She had not, but Tenino heard me ask, and then I had to tell her all about Dave, and how he had told me he was going to provide the kind of ranch I wanted.

Tenino kept teasing me to tell her more about my stay in Canada and whether I intended to go back. To that I didn't know the answer. I kept many of my experiences to myself, wishing I could forget them altogether.

About once a month the sisters used to instruct some of the girls about personal hygiene, but only the older ones. This let me out, and I was glad, because at that time I had a foolish sense of modesty about my body and its functions.

I knew that some of the girls who enjoyed our swims in the river sometimes sat on the bank and wouldn't join us in the water, no matter how much we urged or teased. They would say they had a cold or a headache or give some other excuse that sounded silly to me. Finally, one of the girls said, "You'll be sitting out here on the bank with me one of these fine days."

Neither of us guessed how soon her prophecy would come true. The following Saturday I discovered I was in no condition to go into the river, but I was determined to keep the matter to myself and do as I had always done.

Everything went well for an hour or so. Then I began to have cramps. The pain slowed me, and I felt colder and colder but was too self-conscious and stubborn to leave the water until the sister called, "All out!"

All that evening I had chills. The sister noticed that I was wearing my sweater, though the evening was warm, and asked me if I was feeling sick again. I told her I was just a little chilly, but I was glad to go to bed that night as soon as confession was over.

The next morning we expected to go to Communion in the chapel. I had had chills and cramps all night but said nothing. We all wore our white dresses, as required for Communion, and we waited and waited in the chapel, but the priest didn't come. At last the sister gave us the signal to rise and turn and told us we would have to go to the church, half a mile away, since the priest evidently expected us there.

Since we had dressed for the chapel, we had worn no coats, and we hurried out without them. The early morning air was chill and damp. There was no fire in the church, and I thought I would freeze to death before Mass was over. By the time I reached home, I was sick enough to admit it and asked the sister if I might go and lie down.

She sent me to the infirmary and soon came to take my temperature, telling me to undress and get into bed while she prepared hot water bottles and a dose of castor oil. That castor oil was wasted. By the time she came back, I was so choked up I couldn't even speak but pointed to my throat and tried to whisper. She hurried to bring turpentine and put a few drops on a lump of sugar. I took that slowly, and it gave me a little relief, but I was still having great difficulty breathing.

The sister superior telephoned the doctor, but he was out on a call. She tried the next town, and that doctor promised to come immediately. To her surprise, both doctors arrived at the same time. They looked me over, and their verdict must not have been good, for the sister telephoned the priest to come at once.

The priest told me I must have confession, though he knew I had been to confession only the night before. I couldn't speak, so he asked me questions, and I nodded or shook my head, yes or no. The windows in the infirmary had been open, but now the sister closed them, because the draft was making the priest's candles flicker. I felt suffocated. She saw my distress and gave me more sugar and turpentine. This helped a little, but the candles smoked, and the priest's garments smelled of incense and tobacco, and the holy oil anointing my nose and mouth was smothering me.

The priest continued to administer the last rites while I drew on all my staying powers to hold out until he had finished and the windows were opened again. Then he startled me by saying, "Dear child, do you realize you will soon be in Eternity? Ask our dear Lord, who himself passed through the agonies of death, to help you in your hour of need."

I took his advice. I prayed with faith and hope, but in the back of my mind was this certainty: *I'll have to be a lot sicker than this before I die.*

Was this heaven? Gradually, I saw that the light was the ostensorium, bright with candles. I stared at the shining ostensorium, trying to decide where I was, until I gradually made out some of the sisters and a few girls, kneeling around my bed and praying for me. I felt relieved, but I still stared at the ostensorium, which I had never before seen out of the chapel. I had to smile, thinking how silly it had been of me to suppose I was in heaven.

My smile filled my devoted friends with hope, but Donna mistook it for a smile of farewell. She rose and, putting her warm hands over mine, said with grave sincerity, "Keep your faith. Our Lord is with you."

I smiled and nodded my head. Sister Superior finished the prayer I had interrupted, then dismissed everybody from the infirmary. "You may go to the chapel to pray now, if you wish," she told them.

This sickness was the third attack of pneumonia I had had within a year and the most severe. The physician said it was bronchial pneumonia. It got me down physically but not mentally; on the contrary, I had time to dream up beautiful, well-stocked ranches, with spirited saddle horses that I could ride from morning to night. I wondered whether Dave had selected his ranch yet and what it was like. I imagined a good piece of rangeland, well watered with springs and creeks, with meadows for hay and timber to shelter the stock and give that touch of beauty that I considered so important. I knew that such ranches were still to be had.

These thoughts comforted me during my recovery. I learned to darn while I was still in bed, and Sister even taught me fancywork. After I had practiced on a few small doilies, she gave me a large tablecloth to work on. It had a strawberry pattern, and I loved it. I tried to do my best work on it, because the sisters raffled off such things and used the money for little improvements in our recreation room. I was happy to do anything I could to partially repay them for all the trouble I had been, and besides, I doubted whether Hedge had been faithful about paying for our support.

Early in the spring we received a letter from Hedge, enclosing tickets for us to come to Coal Creek, British Columbia. His writing was so illegible that the sister read it to us. Nora and Rose were happy, but I exclaimed, "I am not going back. I won't go back to that kind of life for anything!"

"Why not? Most girls are glad to go home!"

I felt the blood rush to my face but didn't know how to put my secret reason into words. "Please don't ask me, Sister," I stammered. "I'll never go back to him. If I can't stay here, I'll go somewhere else, but I'll never go back."

The sisters began packing Nora's and Rose's clothing. One sister walked with me to Meyers Falls to see whether the depot agent would let me go as far as Nelson, British Columbia, with my little sisters, then come back on the ticket Hedge had sent. She seemed pleased when he said I could, and if she was pleased, I was delighted. I felt we had won the first round.

We started on our trip the next day. All went well until we reached North Port, where we learned that there were snowslides between us and Nelson. Most of the passengers decided to remain in North Port, but we children had no extra money for stopovers, so with a few others, we stayed on the train and went on. Later I heard a man say that it had taken us five hours to go fifteen miles. The conductor was wonderfully kind to us and made us as comfortable as he could, but nobody could sleep much, with the train constantly starting and stopping and starting as the extra gang cleared the track.

When we reached Nelson, twenty-four hours late, the conductor asked me whether I knew how to put my little sisters on the ferry that carried passengers from Nelson to Kootenai. When I told him I had no idea, he said he would take care of them. "Come on, little girls," he said and, turning to me, "Wait here until I come back."

Returning, he asked, "Do you want to go to the ferry and tell your little sisters good-bye?"

"Were they crying when you left them?"

"No, they were all right."

I swallowed before I could answer. "If they were all right, I better not go, for they will surely cry."

That is how I left my little sisters, thinking at the time that it was the best thing to do, knowing that I couldn't keep from crying, and surely they couldn't either. I did not ask myself whether they might at some time blame me for such a silent parting.

I went back to the sisters, safe and happy to be under their protection. But my happiness was short-lived. In a few days, Hedge arrived, trying to appear agreeable, trying to coax me into going back with him. He even resorted to tears, which surprised me so much that I stood staring at him until he said in a pleading voice, "Come on, let's all be together again in our happy home!"

At that, my surprise turned to contempt. The sister superior urged me to explain exactly why I refused to go with him, but all I could say was that he knew why, and it was too terrible to talk about. This must have alarmed Hedge. He left, and I hoped he would be afraid to come back.

Not long after my trip to North Port, Donna came rushing to me. "I have the most heavenly news to tell you," she cried.

I knew it must be something pertaining to religion, for her eyes sparkled, and her whole face glowed. "I'm so thrilled I can hardly talk," she continued. "I'm going to be a sister. I just got the letter admitting me to the novitiate."

I was glad to see her so happy but saddened that she was leaving me. "When are you going?" I asked, soberly.

"In June, after I graduate. I think it was grand of Mother Provincial to accept me," she said in perfect humility.

"If they wouldn't accept you, nobody would be acceptable," I said. "I think they're lucky to get you."

"You are always trying to persuade me that I am good, but really I am not! I have always gone to confession as other sinners must, but from now on I must be better."

Sister gave Donna special books to study, mostly prayers that the sisters must know in both French and Latin. Donna grew less and less chummy as her mind centered on heavenly things, but she was always ready to talk to me about joining her in the novitiate. She was so sincere and enthusiastic that I almost made up my mind to ask for admission.

Why not? I asked myself. *It's a sweet, clean life. No Hedge.* I knew the sisters were afraid he would come back and cause trouble, and I

178

made Donna happy by promising to pray and asking her to pray for my intention.

"I have always been praying that you might become a sister," she answered softly, "and I know you will, someday, if it is our Lord's will."

Tenino laughed at the idea of me becoming a sister. She told me I was too much like an Indian – I would die in confinement. I was afraid she was right but thought that I could grow accustomed to being cooped up.

The next time I went to confession, I asked Father Meaghan what he thought of me seeking admission to the novitiate. To my great surprise, he was not wholly in favor of it. He explained his hesitancy. In the first place, the life was too confining for someone accustomed to the outdoors, as I had been. Then he asked me what had made me consider entering the novitiate.

I told him that the sisters and I were afraid my stepfather might come for me again. I was determined never to go near him, but I couldn't remain here and keep the sisters in suspense. Also, Donna's happiness had greatly impressed me.

The priest explained that he believed every human being would be happy if he found his rightful place in life, but too many persons rushed blindly into the wrong choices and were miserably unhappy. "Wait a month," he advised me. "Wait a month before asking for admission to the novitiate, and I will give you a recommendation."

I knew I was not a first-class prospect for a sister. My lack of education and my poor health were against me. And perhaps I depended too much on horse sense and determination to see me though instead of blind faith in God. The sisters, for instance, claimed that God had guided our footsteps the night Tenino and I found our way out of the timber. Maybe so, but I had gotten out of lots of other tight places by using common sense and staying qualities.

I was always less embarrassed talking to men than to women. I hadn't found it too hard to ask Father about entering the novitiate, but I couldn't find courage to talk it over with Sister Mary. She was the finest kind of person, clever, refined, and highly educated, and I admired her greatly. She couldn't have been better to me if she had been my mother. She had wisdom and understanding, was partial to no one, and did as much for the poor girls as she did for the girls whose parents had money.

But with all my admiration and affection for her, the thought of approaching her with my secret desire threw me into a panic. How many times that week I planned little maneuvers to meet Sister Mary alone, and how many times my courage failed me! I knew her quick little step on the stairs and along the hallway, and I would sit close to the door, apparently buried in a book, intending to slip out into the hall and speak with her. But I couldn't move. As she drew nearer and nearer, my hands grew tense, my breath came fast, my knees grew weak. I could not force myself to speak to her until a graver trouble swept away my diffidence.

I had been reflecting so eagerly about entering the novitiate that I almost stopped worrying about whether Hedge would come back for me, but suddenly, he reappeared. He tried the same coaxing and tears he had used the first time, but when he saw he was making no impression on me, he jumped up, caught me by the hand, and dragged me from the sisters' sitting room before either they or I realized what he intended.

One of the sisters ran to the telephone, while Hedge kept jerking me from side to side until he had me out on the porch. Another sister called to the hired man working in the garden, for by this time Hedge was dragging me away from the convent while she hung on, but the man pretended not to hear and went on with his hoeing. Sister cried frantically, "Run to the boys' school and tell Father to come at once – we are in trouble!"

At that, the man started on a run.

Sister Mary had come to help us when she heard the commotion on the porch. By jerking at me, Hedge made headway against all our efforts. He was almost pulling my arms out of their sockets. I couldn't understand where he was taking me – it wasn't train time – until I saw the team and buggy and driver behind the little three-sided shed of a depot.

Sister Mary glanced back. Father Meaghan was coming on a run. Hedge redoubled his efforts to thrust me into the buggy and make his getaway before the priest could reach us, but the commotion frightened the horses, and they bolted before the driver could stop them. Hedge pushed the sisters away and broke their hold on my arm. I was on my own now and almost played out.

Hedge shouted to the driver to back up the team. He picked me up and threw me into the back of the buggy; but as the horses felt the jar they leaped ahead, and Hedge and I both fell to the ground.

The driver wheeled the team. Hedge tried to throw me into the buggy, but again the team crowded back, and I landed on the axle, between the wheel and the body of the buggy. My skirt was caught between the axle and the hub. Hedge jumped over me into the buggy and tried to pull me in after him, but with my skirt wrapped around the axle, he couldn't budge me. He snarled at the driver to whip up the team, but the driver retorted, "I don't want to see her killed!" The team pranced a few steps, my skirt was unwound, and I fell under the buggy. At that moment, Father Meaghan arrived.

"What are you trying to do here?"

"That's none of your damned business!"

"I've called an officer, and he'll be here to take care of you," answered Father.

"Who the hell are you to be telephoning for an officer when you don't know what this is all about?"

"I am a priest, and it is my duty to intervene in such violence."

Hedge jumped from the buggy and started menacingly toward Father, but Father did not step back. He was a big, fine-looking fellow, and his fearless attitude must have shaken Hedge's confidence.

"For half a cent I'd knock your damned nose off," he cried, "so you wouldn't be sticking it into anybody else's business for a while!"

"My nose is right here, sir," answered Father.

At that moment, two riders came in sight from the river road, riding at top speed. Hedge wheeled and jumped into the buggy. "Let's get out of here, quick," he said to the driver.

His hat lay on the ground where he and I had fallen. No one picked it up.

The two riders who had come into sight at the opportune moment were young fellows riding for fun and dropping in on the mission where they had gone to school a few years earlier. They got off their horses and walked up to the mission with Father, while the sisters and I turned toward the convent. None of us realized how badly shaken we were until we had sat down for a while and then tried to get up.

I knew the poor sisters were badly shaken, but they said no word about themselves; instead, they explained to Sister Superior about the rough handling I had been through, even before the wheel battered my shoulder and elbow black and blue. My skirt was torn and ruined with axle grease. My shirtwaist was in shreds. My undershirt had stood the ordeal, and my stout corset cover held out on one shoulder. Sister Superior dressed my shoulder, bruised by the wheel when I hung over the axle with my head almost against the horses' hocks. I still felt hot with the shame and embarrassment I had felt as Hedge and the driver made off and I had stood for those few minutes on the road, half-undressed before Father, the horseback riders, and all the rest.

Hedge's hat lay in the road day after day, reminding me of the hideous experience.

I knew now that I had no choice – I must leave this beautiful spot that had been a haven for me. Hedge might come back at any time. Fear of him haunted everything I did. I dared not go with the other girls on walks or picnics – Hedge might be watching for just such an opportunity to drag me off into the brush. He might kill me the next time. I knew the sisters felt the same anxiety, and I made up my mind to ask Sister Mary whether she thought I should write asking for admission to the novitiate.

I stuttered and stammered when I finally found a chance to talk to her, but her goodness and sympathy put me at ease. She explained that my decision was being forced by present necessity, and she was not in favor of my entering the novitiate to solve a difficulty. She would discuss my desire with Sister Superior and talk with me again. In the meantime, she and Sister Superior would make a novena for my intention. She suggested that I ask Father's advice and was quite surprised when I told her I already had talked with him. I told her the truth, that he had not been enthusiastic either.

"Maybe the life of a religious is not for you," she answered quietly, "but I feel that God has important work for you. He spared your life when you were so very ill and has protected you in danger. We will pray, and I am sure our dear Lord will make known his will."

Waiting for Sister Mary's decision on my applying for admission to the novitiate, I spent many hours in the quiet little chapel in prayer and meditation. There was a volume of beautiful religious poems in the chapel, so inspiring that I spent happy hours reading them and always felt comfort and reassurance.

Two days after my talk with Sister Mary, she took me to Sister Superior, who questioned me about my reasons for wanting to become a sister and advised me to examine my conscience to be sure I was not seeking the holy habit to hide me from my stepfather's menace. She did give me permission to write a letter of application to the mother provincial.

I wrote in pencil for Sister Mary to look over:

Dear Reverend Mother:

In compliance with the advice of Father Meaghan, I write to ask if you will please admit me to the novitiate.

I have been at school here for nearly three years. I am sixteen years old, an orphan, and entirely dependent on the sisters for support. Ever since my little sisters went to live with their father, I have been expecting a letter from them, but I have never heard. I have nothing but the wish and will to consecrate myself to God and do all that is required of me.

It is my fervent prayer that my request may meet with your approval.

Very respectfully,

Margaret Olson

After my letter had been mailed, Sister gave me a book of Latin prayers that all sisters must learn and books to study to prepare myself for the life of a religious. I was delightfully happy, as happy as any girl making preparations for her wedding, although I was anxious that I might not be accepted. I was overjoyed when I received the following letter from Mother Provincial:

My dear child,

In reply to your letter of May 10, in which you so fervently beg for admission to the novitiate, I can but say, "Come." Between now and the date of your entrance, which should be no later than August next, pray with all your heart that you may correspond exactly to God's holy will in your regard. Ask our dear Blessed Mother to prepare you herself to be a worthy spouse of her Divine Son.

Recommending you and your holy intention to the Sacred Heart, I am, my dear child, most cordially yours,

Mother——

Provincial Supervisor

I carried the letter around with me and read it over and over. If the paper had been flimsy, it would have been worn out. I wrote to Donna, and she was even more thrilled than I and wrote me an ardent letter full of counsel and encouragement.

Father Meaghan congratulated me and asked me to do him a favor if I took the final vow. "When you take your new name, take a woman's name, not a man's. I cannot understand why so many of the sisters take men's names. It is distasteful to me to address a 'Sister Peter,' 'Sister Paul,' 'Sister Samuel.'"

I told him I would take a woman's name if I had anything to say about it, but I thought novices were assigned their names. Blind obedience, I whispered to myself. The order numbered sixteen thousand, and I might not find a woman's name not already given out.

12

The Mother House was located at Vancouver, Washington. Sister Mary and Sister Agnes Marie were going there for their annual retreat. Two of us were to go with them and begin our first training. We arrived the last Saturday in July and were admitted to the novitiate the following day.

The ceremony was impressive. My throat throbbed with ecstasy as I knelt in the little chapel, wearing my holy habit and giving thanks to God for the privilege.

This was the attire of a postulant: lightweight, two-piece underwear, long sleeved and ankle length; corset; long-sleeved chemise of unbleached muslin tied close at the neck and falling below the knee. The sleeves reached well over the hand, to be turned back and pinned close as cuffs. Those wearing the chemise dispensed with the fitted corset cover of heavy ticking.

Over the chemise, long slit-panel pockets of ticking hung at either side from a belt buttoned around the waist to carry our belongings – rosary, prayer book, numerous keys, sewing kit, and so on. Next came the underskirt, the upper part made of ticking and the lower part of thick black serge, with a wide binding to protect it from wear. The outer dress was of finest black French serge, with a tight bodice lined with ticking and a box-pleated skirt of instep length.

The foundation of a postulant's headdress was a small, close-fitting cap, often of figured calico, that tied under the chin. To this was pinned the white linen garniture with its three little hollow squares of pleating. Over these, a fitted black cap concealed the neckline.

Our indoor dress was completed with a cape that fell below the elbows in front and was long enough in back to conceal the waist-line. For street dress we wore, in addition, a long, heavy cape.

The day after I entered the novitiate, Sister Nastoria took me to Portland to consult a specialist about my eyes, which had always troubled me, perhaps from the times I had herded cattle in dazzling snow and been almost snow-blinded. Sister had many errands all over Portland, soliciting money for the convent and shopping. I carried her accumulating packages for her as she strode from place to place, and I really suffered from the heat that August day. I had recently changed from light summer clothing to the heavy habit, and as I followed her I thought I would faint; but I had been schooled against complaining, so I said not a word.

When Sister had finished her shopping, she took me to St. Vincent Hospital. I marveled at the way she climbed the hill to the hospital, for it seemed almost more than I could manage. She left me there, and I remained three weeks, having my eyes treated.

When I returned to Vancouver, I was sent to help in the boys' school. Sister Teresa and her co-adjuditrix, Sister Bower, had been in charge of the little boys for some time, but Sister Teresa became sick and nearly died and could not come back to work, and now Sister Bower needed an assistant. I liked the boys, and they liked me. Sister Bower and I took turns staying with the boys at night, but she usually spent the evening mending while I told stories to the boys. On Sundays I would take them for a romp in the woods, where we would have what the sisters called a *congé* – in plain English, a picnic. Once I took the boys to the sisters' farm, where they sorted potatoes while I told them stories.

Sister Bower could get more work done in one hour than I could in two, but my stories were what the boys wanted, and they put up such a howl when it was my turn to have recreation with the other sisters that I soon found myself staying with them every evening. The long hours began to tell on me. Sister Assistant Provincial noticed and told me, "I am going to ask Sister Superior if I may take you to the farm once in awhile. We cannot find a good man to manage the farm, and all the little calves are sick. Maybe you'd know what to do for them – we've tried all kinds of medicine."

"I'd be glad to help," I said, "but the way we raised calves on the range, they never got sick."

When I saw how the sisters' calves were crowded into a small pen inside a big shed, I saw at once that they were scoured. As soon as I turned them into the pasture in the sunshine, their scours cleared up, and they were all right in a week.

There were many little things around the ranch that needed changing, and the sisters gave me too much credit for such simple advice. The big event came later.

We were using a heavy old spring wagon to take a load of milk from the farm to the Provincial House. Four of us rode on the back seat while a man drove. The horse was a nice young animal, just broken to drive, but he was soft, and the load was heavy. By the time we reached the city limits, he was tired. He kept slowing down to a walk, and finally the driver struck him with the ends of the lines just as the wagon wheels struck the cement crossing. Startled, the horse gave a jump that broke the singletree and let the shafts down. The harness was new, and the holdback straps on the shafts kept him attached to the wagon, but the shafts were bumping him on the legs, and he kept jumping and trying to run.

Somebody needed to get to his head, quick. I was sitting on the right-hand side of the wagon, and when the horse made a right turn at a corner, I saw my chance and jumped out. I tucked my long cape under my arm and made for his head, grabbing him by the bit and bringing him to a stop within fifty feet. I knew I had taken a chance on being jabbed by a shaft, but I would have let go the bit if I'd seen a shaft coming at me. The driver got down and unsnapped the holdbacks, and all the trouble was over.

The poor sisters were so scared, they could hardly get down from the wagon after the horse was unhitched. Knowing nothing about driving, they thought I had done something wonderful.

I began to apologize to Sister Assistant for taking over while she was in full charge. The sister who is oldest by entrance into the order gives all permissions, and I, the youngest in the group, had used my own judgment without consulting my superiors. I had never seen the rule of seniority broken, and I was a little worried about what might happen to me. But I didn't have time to worry long. As soon as Sister Assistant was on the ground and I began to stammer apologies, she put her trembling arm around my shoulders and said, "My dear Sister, you have saved all our lives. Thank God for sending you out with us today! Our dear Lord has been merciful to us. We will go to the chapel and give thanks to him as soon as we get home."

Sister Assistant was French – sentimental, demonstrative, and most lovable. Her prayers and good wishes went with me always. That evening she came to summon me to the sisters' community, and I was struck with dismay, but I remembered blind obedience and went without a word. All the sisters who could be spared from work were gathered to meet me. Entering the community would have been less disconcerting if I could have met them at the door; but I had to walk to the farther end of the long room where Mother Provincial, Sister Superior, and all the head sisters were seated and be presented to them. Sister Assistant Provincial made a beautiful little speech of introduction, elaborating on what to me had been a simple matter.

By the time I was shaking hands with the sisters nearest the door, my embarrassment had subsided somewhat, although I was glad none of my range friends were there to see me saluted as a heroine for stopping a horse! I hoped I could return immediately to the novitiate, but Sister Assistant's sweet voice interrupted me: "Many of the sisters would like to have you explain how you had the courage to jump from the moving wagon and take hold of that frightened horse."

My voice trembled as I began my story, but now I was on familiar ground. I knew my horses. "I am very grateful for all this appreciation," I began, "but stopping that horse was only common sense for a person raised on a ranch. The horse was not mean. He was frightened and getting more terrified every moment. I knew if I could get to his head and talk to him, I could reassure him and make him understand that he wasn't going to be hurt if he stood still until we could unhitch him. Once a horse runs away, he isn't worth much. He will try it again and again. He will make opportunities to run. He will be what we call a spoiled horse. Your horse is a good animal, and I didn't want to see him spoiled."

I was more at ease after I had finished explaining, but the voluble little French sisters loaded me with praise and such thanks that I hardly knew how to answer and was glad when I was safely back in the postulate.

Contact with farm life was good for me, but it was costing me the instruction and training that I must have to make profession. Another anxiety kept me awake nights. Two of us were doing the work of three sisters in the boys' school, and the hours were too long for us. We couldn't find sisters who had any aptitude for handling a hundred and fifty noisy boys, and some who tried caused more confusion than they corrected. Once, when I had gone to eat my supper, leaving a young sister in charge, I heard an unseemly racket and hurried back.

The sister had ordered several of the larger boys to go to the dormitory and fold the bedspreads. This was a nightly chore, for the spreads were not left on the beds at night; but the boys took turns at the work and were objecting to doing it out of turn. The room was in an uproar. Sister had tried to enforce her demands with a broom, and the boys had grabbed the broom and were jerking her around while she held on.

As I opened the door, the noise subsided, and the boys looked sheepish, for I had promised to finish a story I was telling them if they behaved themselves while I was gone.

"Well, boys, I see you didn't want to hear the rest of the story to-night."

"We do, we do," they clamored, "but this sister spoiled every-thing! Weren't we good all day? Didn't we do everything you asked us to?"

I agreed that they had been good all day but that they weren't being good when I came in, and they had treated the sister badly. One boy retorted, "We were good most of the day, weren't we?" and when I said yes, he came back with, "Then you have to tell us most of the story."

We compromised. A few of the boys folded the spreads, and I told the story.

The small boys worried me, too. Two of them habitually wet their beds in spite of all the precautions I tried to take. The routine pun-ishment for bed-wetting – getting them up at four-thirty, ducking them into a cold bath, and making them wash out their wet bed-ding – upset me. It was more painful when they were given a beat-ing. Sister Teresa, whose sickness had left us short-handed, beat them more than once, and I, who had had so many beatings myself, could hardly stand it when they screamed under the blows. She for-bade their drinking anything at suppertime, and they suffered cru-elly from thirst on hot nights. Her punishments weren't doing any good – the small boy was growing ugly and defiant, and the older boy was shame-faced and embarrassed, and he began to slink away by himself and take any abuse without the spirit to fight back.

To help them avoid accidents, I used to set my alarm clock at eleven o'clock at night and again at two in the morning to get them up and to the bathroom. When we went through the entire night, they were as proud and happy as I was.

In the smaller boys' dormitory there were forty little fellows, most of them so young that they couldn't dress themselves. The sister who slept in the dormitory with them had her hands full in the morning. The youngest was only eighteen months old. For almost a week I heard him crying every morning and wondered what was the trouble, since he had seldom cried before. This sister and I took turns going to church with the big boys on Sunday mornings and staying home to dress and feed the smaller ones. When it was my turn to stay with the youngsters, I started to dress the little chap, and he began to scream.

He was all right in my arms, but when I tried to stand him on his bed, he wouldn't stand. I took him on my knee and had no trouble dressing him until I came to his shoes and stockings, when he almost went into hysterics. I hugged him and tried to soothe him. "What's the matter, Baby? Tell Sister what hurts you," and rocked him back and forth. He picked up his little foot with both hands, and there, under his toenail, was a sliver so big, the toe so festered and swollen, it would seem impossible to force a shoe on his foot. And yet he had had his shoes on every day that week.

That sister was a good, hard-working woman (they had to have someone with the little boys who could turn out a lot of work), but she was just like a machine; she never stopped to figure out why the baby was crying. After I had dressed and fed everyone else, I took care of the baby's toe and saved the sliver and the pus to show Sister so she'd know he hadn't been crying for nothing.

The boys wore suits or short pants and blouses in their classrooms, but they wore overalls when they were playing or working. They liked to go for walks in the woods, and so did I. Sister Bona, who decided what I could or could not do, did most of the mending for the boys – and there was plenty, great baskets of long stockings every week. She didn't like to have the boys playing in the woods because it was so hard on their clothes. But sometimes when she had a headache or was tired of their noise, she would suggest that I take them out for a few hours while she put the smaller boys to bed and enjoyed a little quiet and the chance to get her work done. Outdoors, the boys romped and played while I sat in the grass and mended stockings.

My health was fairly good as long as the weather was pleasant, but when fall brought cloudy, wet weather, I didn't feel so well. We postulants seldom complained about illness, because we knew that health was our prime requisite, but the postulant mistress watched over us like a mother and probably noticed my condition before I did.

She was kind but firm, and she never forgot. If she made a correction, she expected her first order to be final. Most of us had bad habits of long standing. I, for instance, had a habit of walking with my fists clenched, the way I used to walk away from Hedge after he had beaten me. Another girl used to throw her head back when she walked. We were told to correct these faults, but sometimes we forgot, and then we had to say extra prayers and kiss the floor.

I had been avoiding the postulant mistress for fear she might notice that I was feeling under the weather, but I took a sudden desire to write to my grandmother, and to do this I had to have the postulant mistress's permission. I was afraid she might object, since I had made no mention of my family up till now, but she gave her permission without asking a question.

I didn't know whether Grandma was still living on the ranch or whether she was living at all, but I wrote to the old address and waited for a reply. It came promptly. Grandma and Uncle Mike were both well and living in the old spot. They were overjoyed to hear from me. Grandma asked a dozen questions about my being on the

West Coast when she had supposed I was in Canada, and she wanted to know about my little sisters.

When I answered her letter, I inquired about my father, whom I hardly knew. Her answer to that question was the most important part of her next letter. Uncle Mike had enclosed an address that he thought would reach my father, so I wrote him. I thought, *If he writes to me, my happiness will be complete.*

Perhaps because I had something to look forward to, my health was better while I was waiting for these important letters. My father's reply came without delay: he was glad to hear from me, but, not being a Catholic, he disliked the idea of a convent and especially disapproved of my intention of becoming a sister. He enclosed thirty-five dollars and asked me to visit him in Great Falls.

After I had read his letter, the postulant mistress called me into her private office and asked me if I would like to go to Montana to visit my father, grandmother, and uncle. She added, "The change to a drier climate may be just what you need."

Her allusion to my health took away all desire I might have had to visit my relatives. "No, Sister," I said, "not if the visit means leaving the novitiate."

"Say nothing about this to anyone," she instructed me. "I will talk it over with my superiors tonight, and we will all pray for you."

I didn't sleep much that night. The postulant mistress called me to her office again the next day. "It has been decided that your health comes first. A change of climate may improve your condition in a short time and make it possible for you to return to the novitiate. We will welcome you back. Sister Assistant has spent many hours in prayer and tears, hoping for your improvement. Your work in the boys' school is the marvel of the school, but you know you have not the strength to continue the work much longer. We discussed Sister Assistant's suggestion that you be sent to a hospital, but the close confinement of a hospital is not what you need. You must have open air. You were reared in an outdoor life. I am not saying this to discourage you in your avowed intention, but I firmly believe you cannot be healthy in any other kind of environment. Go to your grandmother's ranch. Live out of doors as much as possible. I am sure that within a year you will be in perfect health again. Take my advice. Will you?"

I made no answer. I was too heartsick.

The postulant mistress took me to the storeroom to select a secular wardrobe for my trip. There were many lovely outfits in the storeroom, worn by wealthy girls only once, when they exchanged them for the holy habit, and they were never needed again because their happy owners made profession. The postulant mistress took time to select and fit a trunkful of clothes for me, choosing each garment with care. She even exchanged my trunk for a nicer one and did most of my packing. I appreciated her efforts and thanked her warmly for her kindness, but all my dreams and hopes and air castles had come shattering down around me, and my spirit was too nearly crushed for me to feel interest even in a nicer wardrobe than I had ever hoped to own.

The postulant mistress knew what I was going through. She asked me gently how I felt. I answered that nothing mattered anymore; the meaning had dropped out of everything.

She took me to Sister Nastoria, whose duty it was to solicit money and other donations for the convent. Sister Nastoria greeted me, "Yes, I'll take you to the depot in Portland, but I'll expect you to pay my expenses."

Such expenses were the ferry charge from Vancouver to Portland (twenty-five cents) and our lunch at a little room close to the depot, good food and abundant, served by a middle-aged woman with an extremely large goiter. Sister Nastoria apparently knew this woman, who tipped her off to the prosperous spots where she might beg successfully. When they had finished their conversation, Sister Nastoria took me to the depot, told me to stay where I was until I heard them call my train, and left.

The long wait for the late-night train did nothing to lighten my downheartedness. What did help was that Sister Nastoria had got my Irish up by escorting me to the depot and charging me for it, and I forgot my troubles every time I thought of her and how I'd lugged parcels for her that hot day in Portland before I went to St. Vincent's Hospital.

13

The trip was uneventful. When daylight came, I enjoyed the miles and miles of magnificent mountain scenery. A freight wreck in the Flathead country disrupted our schedule, so that instead of making connections for Great Falls at Shelby, I had to go on to Havre and spend the night there. The sisters had wired my father that I was coming, and he waited all night in the Great Falls depot.

My father knew me at once, possibly because I looked so unsophisticated, but partly because I looked so much like him. I liked his looks immediately. He was neatness itself, and blond, not too tall or the least bit fat, just trim and poised as I had always wanted to be. At his city manners, I felt as awkward as a colt hooked up for the first time. What I marveled at most was the whiteness of his small hands, which were much more delicate than mine.

He had a nice room for me at the hotel. He went to clean up a bit before taking me to breakfast. I did a little freshening up also and was ready and waiting when he came. He wanted to know how and where I had lived since my mother died and we left Great Falls, and I told him briefly of our journey to Canada, my stay at Uncle Zed's, and life on Hedge's homestead.

As we talked, I kept glancing at the clock until he noticed and asked me why. I said I was going to church – it was Sunday morning – and asked him to show me where the nearest Catholic church was. I longed for the inside of a church, comforting and familiar.

I am sure my father thought it wasn't necessary for me to run to church as soon as I got to town, but he made no objection. "I'll get a little sleep," he said, "and you better do the same when you get back from church. I'll take you to dinner whenever you say – about five o'clock? Restaurant food is best about that time."

I enjoyed that morning's Mass more than any I could remember.

The church, with its prayers and the hymns I knew so well, was a haven to me. I was sorry when the service was over.

We went to a very nice place to eat and sat in a booth where we could visit. My father began questioning me again, about Uncle Zed's, about the homestead, about our neighbors, and how we lived and what we did. His questions began to come too close to things I didn't know how to tell. As I answered, I thought, *Why didn't you find out then, when Hedge was abusing me? Why didn't you put a stop to it then, instead of asking me now?*

He must have sensed my resentment, for he said quickly, "Now it's your turn! Ask me anything you like."

"Do you live in town all the time?"

"No, I have a homestead where I have to spend part of my time."

I looked at his fine clothes and had a suspicion the homestead hadn't bought them. I didn't know what to think of my father. I loved his carefree ways, though. I had never been carefree. "Tell me about cowpunching," I said.

He laughed. "Those were the happiest days of my life. I'll tell you about my last trip to Cheyenne, in 1884. The buffalo were about gone, but the longhorns were still coming up from Texas. They sent me to bring some longhorns from Cheyenne to Miles City.

"Cheyenne was a wild town, and I liked it. As soon as we fellows hit Cheyenne we made a beeline for the Cheyenne Club, where you'd see more excitement in a day than you would in a month anywhere else. They served champagne for breakfast! There were all classes there, rich men, college men, English noblemen from the big cattle syndicates. Money rolled over the gambling tables – faro was the big game. Dancing was almost continuous.

"We cowpunchers told the Englishmen fantastic tales and got a laugh at their ignorance of real conditions. Many of them were re-mittance men – young chaps out of bounds in the old country, sent over here and set up in the cattle country to save the family name.

They brought their thoroughbreds with them, so horse racing was a big sport. You could see some of the best horseflesh of old England running at Cheyenne.

"The town was full of Texas cowboys, and I enjoyed swapping yarns with them. They were pretty much like us fellows, except that where we spoke some French picked up from the half-breeds, they used a Spanish lingo. They were good riders and ropers – they had to be, to handle those longhorns they started north with. By the time we took over, the cattle were trail-broke. But one thing I noticed, the cowboys' morale was slipping, especially the fellows who worked for the big syndicates. They didn't respect their bosses, and the bosses didn't respect them or know who was doing a good job and who wasn't. We Montana boys were proud of our reputation for defending a brand entrusted to us."

Recalling the past touched his emotions. He lowered his eyes, took his watch from his pocket, wound it, and toyed with it. "How would you like to take a drive around town?"

"Fine!" I answered. "That would be nice."

"Do you mind if we go back to the hotel and invite Mrs. Steadly? She gets out so seldom, and she enjoys a drive."

"Of course I wouldn't mind."

Mrs. Steadly was the woman who ran the hotel. She and her daughter seemed pleased to go with us. Father came with a beautiful surrey and a good driving team from the livery barn. He was an expert horseman. He and I sat on the front seat, and Mrs. Steadly and her daughter sat in the back, but Mrs. Steadly did most of the talking, calling my father by his first name and tapping him on the shoulder to draw his attention.

The drive was a treat for me. Father had a good singing voice, and every now and then he would sing one of the old songs I had learned from Mother. He drove on the Red Road south of town, then turned back to the hotel. I was surprised when we stepped from the surrey to have Mrs. Steadly put her arm around my waist and walk with me into the hotel.

She invited us to her apartment that evening and made such a fuss over me that she embarrassed me. Her daughter resented it, and I couldn't blame her; I was not the kind of company a girl could show off to her friends. However, I learned something about myself that evening that I had never dreamed of. While Mrs. Steadly and Lila were showing other guests to their rooms, several baseball players came in. We chattered without constraint, I at ease with them and they with me. When Mrs. Steadly and Lila appeared to show them to their rooms, one of the boys took a red rose from his buttonhole and tossed it into my lap. Lila frowned.

Boys could like me. That was what I had learned.

The second morning, my father asked me if I would mind eating breakfast alone and laid a dollar on my dresser. He dropped into a chair and asked, "What do the sisters ever do for a little fun?"

I described a congé we had had at the sisters' farm in Vancouver. They had sent the hired man to bring a gentle horse for us to ride, thinking it would be a great treat for me, and were puzzled when I helped all the other sisters on and off the poor old mare and took no ride myself. While the sisters who had never been on a horse were having great fun riding back and forth, Sister Assistant, always watchful of my interests, asked, "My dear Sister, why do you not take a ride yourself?"

Not wanting to hurt her feelings, I answered, "Many of the other sisters want a ride, and the poor old mare is getting tired. She is not a saddle horse, she is a work horse and not built for running."

"Would you not like to take one little ride?"

"No, Sister, I would not enjoy riding a work horse, especially a tired work horse."

Father looked up alertly as I finished the story. "Do you like to ride?"

"I surely do."

"Tomorrow we'll get two good saddle horses, and you and I will ride together."

After lunch the next day, a beautiful bright day, we went together to the livery stable. Father knew the men, and they knew what kind of horses to offer him. I was given Socks, a black horse with white feet. Father's horse was a bay with a blaze face, a well-put-up horse, better than mine.

I was at home in the saddle. Usually it would take me a little time to get in step with a strange horse, but Socks and I were in perfect step before we were out of town. He had plenty of life and action, the kind of horse I loved, one to be ridden with a tight rein. Never would I forget that ride, I told myself.

At first Father rode rather close to me, not knowing how much experience I had had with horses. Finally, he remarked, "You handle your horse like an old hand. Where did you get your riding experience?"

"I rode all the time I was in Canada. I range-herded cattle and rode the roundups looking for stock that had drifted off the home range."

"Why didn't Hedge tend to that kind of work himself?"

"I don't know. He always took over after I brought the strays back to the ranch."

"Sure he would – the sly, lazy son of a bitch!"

My face turned red. This was the first time I had heard my father curse. Of course, I had been accustomed to rough language before I went to the sisters' school, but now it sounded terrible to me. Father saw that he had embarrassed me and apologized.

He suggested that we ride to Giant Springs, five miles out of town. We rode at a good clip until the horses were satisfied to slow down, and we could visit. Father told me I must have taken my love of riding from him, because my mother was so timid around horses that she made them nervous. He told me how he used to set me on a horse and leave me there before I was two years old, and he described women who were expert rodeo riders.

"I'm not in that class," I said, "but I can bring the cattle in, when I can locate them, with my horse and cattle in good shape. That's more than some cowpunchers can do, when they get in too big a hurry with the cattle."

We sat on the hill above the springs and let our horses cool off before watering them. Father said, "I saw a herd of buffalo come down here one day. I suppose somebody had been chasing them, for they were excited and thirsty – just a small herd, there were no big herds by that time.

"Buffalo are a marvelous animal, with great tenacity of life. I have seen buffalo shot to hell, with blood pouring from their mouths, still running, trying to keep up with the herd. When loss of blood slows a buffalo to a walk, then to a stop, he spreads his four legs wide to keep from toppling over. His big form sways, and he is forced to lower his shaggy head and go down on his knees. He sinks down but remains lying with his knees under him, resting his chin on the ground. Not until his lifeblood is gone does he roll over on his side and give up. There were buffalo bones and buffalo chips everywhere when I first came to this country. It is a shame that so many of these fine animals have been so wantonly destroyed."

"We used to burn buffalo chips around the cow corral for smudges to keep off the mosquitoes," I said. "They're good for holding a branding fire, too, when you don't need much heat."

"The last time I came up the Texas trail, a nester let us hold our herd on his land overnight, just so he could have the buffalo chips, as they still called the cow dung. They had nothing else to burn – and it was a good thing for us they hadn't, for by that time the homesteaders had the trail so fenced off there wasn't much place to stay except on their land. The big free-range days were about over."

"I never knew they burned buffalo chips in the cookstove. We always had plenty of wood."

"We burned plenty of them along the trail. Buffalo bones and buffalo chips, and a cowboy's grave almost any place you happened to look – shot or drowned or their necks broken – and buried under the stars. Sometimes buffalo chips were the only fuel the camp cook had. A campfire of buffalo chips and a dutch oven – maybe that was why the camp cooks were so ornery. They fed any stragglers that showed up, but it was to the tune of 'Don't eat if you can't wash dishes.'"

We fell silent, and the wind brought the scent of sage. I was happy almost to tears.

We rode home in happy unity, acquainted now – my horse and my father and I. But were we? Had I found a real companion? I admired my father. He pleased me, with his clothes and good manners. But did I really know him? I thought of Mrs. Steadly and her air of intimacy, almost connivance, but I forgot her in the creak of my saddle, the smell of horse and leather, and a sudden memory of the sisters' old plug. At a rise of ground near town, I looked south toward Red Butte, the direction of Grandma's and Uncle Mike's ranch, and felt a tug at my heart. They were the ones I wanted.

"Your face is sunburned!" My father's chuckle broke in on my reverie.

"I know it. But that isn't what's worrying me. Look at Lila's jacket!"

Lila had lent me her divided skirt and jacket to wear on the ride. Her clothes had been apparently unused, in perfect condition, and I wanted to return them in the same condition.

"Don't worry about the jacket. I'll have it dry-cleaned before you give it back to her. What do you think of Socks by this time?"

I raved so about the horse that when we got to the barn, my father asked the barn boss what he would take for him.

"Not for sale," the man answered. "He's no rent hack. He belongs to my wife, but once in awhile we let a good rider take him out to keep him from getting too frisky."

At the hotel my father brought me a bottle of lotion for my fire red face and excused himself. Mrs. Steadly and Lila didn't ask me to dinner with them, so I asked the chambermaid to get me a sandwich and a glass of milk to eat in my room. I was hungry after my long ride.

The chambermaid who brought my sandwich was little and quick and had pretty blond hair. She was always laughing. When she saw my face, she ran to bring her own jar of cold cream, which she said would be better for my sunburn than the barber's lotion my father had left me. While she was gone, an older maid came in to ask if there was anything she could do for me.

I didn't like her looks as well as I did the younger girl's. She had sharp black eyes too close together, but she was pleasant to me. She and the younger girl called each other Sadie and Mame and stayed in my room to talk and visit, but they kept an eye out that nobody should catch them at it. They asked me all manner of questions about myself and joked together about boys, especially Fred Steadly, who, Sadie explained to me, had never yet found a girl who would go steady with him. Tonight she laughed as she went out and put her head back in to say, "Look out! Mama Steadly is going to marry Fred off this time if it takes a leg!"

No one came to my room until almost noon the next day, and then it was Lila with a box of her white face powder. I wasn't nearly so red as I had been the day before, but Lila put powder on my face so thick that I looked like a ghost until we thinned it out. She bustled around, poking through my closet to select a dress she liked and fussing with my hair until she made me uncomfortable. I wondered if she thought I didn't know how to dress right. When she had me looking to suit her, she said, "Now I want you to come downstairs and meet my brothers – your father is downstairs," she added as an afterthought.

In the parlor as we entered were Mrs. Steadly, my father, and Lila's brothers, Fred and Will. The boys seemed like nice fellows but nothing for looks. Their hair was lighter than mine, and they were almost as badly sunburned as I was. They were very polite to me, but when they began to talk, they sounded more like kids than men and told such ridiculous stories about horses and stock that I thought at first they were having fun with me to see whether I'd believe them. Father looked at me uneasily once or twice, as if he were afraid I might say something I shouldn't; and when Will finished telling how Fred had roped a wild bull by the horns and dragged him twenty miles, Father rose and suggested that he and I go to lunch.

While we were eating, I told him I wanted to go to my grandmother's for a visit. The idea didn't please him, and he asked me to postpone the visit for a while.

After lunch Mrs. Steadly could hardly wait to get me alone to ask what I thought of her sons. I said they seemed like nice fellows. She watched me intently, waiting for me to say more. When I didn't, she told me they were her parents' only grandchildren and would inherit everything her parents had when they died. Her parents had already given Mrs. Steadly the hotel, so the grandsons would get the ranch, the stock, and everything but whatever money her parents had in the bank. "With the ranch and stock and all, they'll be well fixed," she said.

"They surely will," I said before I thought. "That's what I've always wanted, a good ranch."

She came back at me quick: "I was just thinking what a good farmer's wife you would make!"

"Oh, no, Mrs. Steadly, I'm not going to be anybody's wife. As soon as I'm strong and healthy again I'm going back to Vancouver to be a sister."

"You dear, dear child," she said with sympathy, "your father would never want you to bury yourself in such a life. Wait till you get out with the young folks and see what fun you're missing!"

"My father doesn't understand," I answered. *Mrs. Steadly doesn't either,* I thought. In fact, talking with her only made me more lonesome for the sisters and the novitiate. After she left, I wrote two letters, one to Sister Assistant Provincial and one to my dear godmother, Donna.

Father must have lost no time telling Mrs. Steadly of my intention to visit my grandmother, for she came back to my room just as I was starting downstairs with my letters.

"I'll mail them for you," she said, reaching for them. She insisted on taking them, even though I didn't want her to and stood holding them as she talked.

"My dear girl, you don't know how much we all like you and how nice it is to have such a fine, lovely girl in the hotel. Some of the girls – tch, tch – " she shook her head from side to side, "they're just not the kinds of girl I would ever want my sons to go out with. You stay with us, dear. I'm sure you will be able to find a nice job right away. Your father and I are both looking out for one for you."

I made no comment.

Something hard came into her face and voice. "You know your father owes me considerable money; in fact, I lent him the forty dollars to send for you."

In my surprise I blurted out, "He only sent me thirty-five dollars."

"Probably he needed the five for himself." Then coaxingly, "But you and me and the family will get along fine, I know. Just you let me and your father be your advisors and listen to us like the good girl I know you are."

After what she'd told me, I thought I needed to do a little figuring myself but answered, "I am sure we will get along," and didn't feel I was telling an untruth. My words seemed to satisfy her, and she left – with my letters.

I had been worrying about my father's expense for my room, but now my worry was that he might not be paying for it at all. I wanted to get out. I packed what few belongings I would require immediately, set the little valise out of sight, and went downstairs the back way to ask the postmaster when the stage left for Coal Coulee and how much the fare was. If I got to Coal Coulee and hadn't enough money to hire a livery rig, I could walk the four and a half miles to the ranch.

He told me the stage left at six-thirty in the morning.

I had hardly got back to my room when my father came and asked me to join the crowd in Mrs. Steadly's apartment. I think he and Mrs. Steadly, knowing my weakness for horses, had cooked up a plan to divert me from my expressed intentions, for I was no sooner seated than my father said, "How would you like to ride in the relay races at the state fair this fall?"

"I don't know whether I'm fast enough at mounting for that," I answered.

"I'm sure you can match up with the best of them, and you'll have lots of time to practice between now and fall."

"Yes, lots of time to practice, if I had the horses."

Almost before the words were out of my mouth he assured me, "I can easily get you a string of good horses."

I wondered how that could be when he had had to borrow money for my fare to Montana. Mrs. Steadly saw I looked dubious and guessed the reason. "Your father and I have that all figured out," she insisted. "We even know where we can get some of the horses."

Father added, "If you see a horse that looks good to you, bring him around. I'll try him out. If he's got what it takes, I'll buy him for you."

That would have sounded like a very generous offer if Mrs. Steadly's bill hadn't been staring me in the face. But I said I'd be on the lookout. Fred Steadly sat close beside me on the davenport, telling me his grandfather had lots of fast horses, and he would take me over there – I might be able to pick all the horses I wanted right there from his bunch.

There was no use replying to that suggestion, for I knew the exceptionally fast horses for relay racing weren't to be picked up at random. But before the evening was over, Fred had me winning all the races. Everyone seemed very excited, but I told myself the whole thing was a castle in the air, and I'd be lucky if my father bought me one horse, let alone a string.

I kept looking at my father all the evening, wondering how such a fine-appearing, courteous person could be so unscrupulous about borrowing.

Father left as usual about nine o'clock, and I excused myself soon afterward. I had no watch, and I had to waken in time for the early stage. In my room I wrote a nice note to my father and one to Mrs. Steadly, thanking her for all she had done to make my visit pleasant. I asked her to thank Fred for being so kind to me. I left no note for him, feeling this would be too personal for a girl intent on reentering the novitiate. I wrote my notes before I went to bed for fear I might not have time in the morning.

In the morning I slipped out quietly, not waking anyone.

14

I was the only passenger on the stage, so I had an opportunity to ask the driver whether I could get a livery rig at Coal Coulee. He said he was sure I could. So now the only thing I had to worry about was the price. I didn't know until later that the driver owned the livery stable.

It was May. The season was late and seemed the more backward to me, coming as I did from Vancouver. New grass was just pricking through the winter brown, and chokecherry trees were coming into leaf.

The hills puzzled me. I remembered them green, with tall grass waving like grain. Now they were a dirty gray, with no grass at all that I could see. I asked the driver why they looked so bare, and he explained that everything close by was pretty well grazed off by the town herds. He called my attention to long lines of rock dumps burning in the distance and told me the sulphur in them smudged up all the houses in Coal Coulee no matter how often they were painted. He said he had been sheriff in that county for years and leaned over to rub his hand along his leg, saying he still carried a bullet in it.

He knew everybody, the old-timers and the new nesters whose fences made the prairie strange to me. "Yes, indeed," he assured me in answer to my question. "Your uncle Mike is right there on the homestead with your good old grandma."

He sent me on my way out of Coal Coulee with a slick buggy, a nice young driver, and a fast-stepping horse. As soon as we pulled out of the coulee and struck the rise overlooking the prairie, I got my bearings, and my heart began to jump. Here was where the rattlesnakes used to roll up in the picket rope while I stood terrified, trying to picket Hedge's crazy horses. The old road past his homestead had been abandoned, and the new road we were traveling was farther from the site. Not a building was left, but in the distance I saw a dark object and with a sudden sickness in my throat knew it for what it was: the old stove that Hedge had thrown out and forbidden my mother to use after she and Grandma had broken their backs lifting it into the buckboard. We passed the draw where the coyotes had howled around us on that terrible night trip with the sick baby.

My memories were flying ahead of the buggy. We were coming close to the house. I could see a man leaving the field with his team.

There was a fence around the yard. We pulled up beside the gate, and the driver waited while I paid him. The livery rig was one dollar, and the driver charged me twenty-five cents for bringing me out to the ranch. My grandmother was coming down the path, rolling her bare arms in her apron as the young man drove off. I hadn't written to her that I was coming. She may have been puzzled to see a strange young woman arriving in a hired buggy, but she was disturbed that a man should drive away just at mealtime without being invited to come in and eat. She looked after him as if debating how to call him back.

She didn't seem greatly changed to me; her cheeks and mouth were sunken, but her hair was only slightly gray.

"Don't you know me?" I asked. "Have I changed so much since you saw me?"

Her hands flew out of her apron, stretching toward me. "It's you, it's you! My prayers are answered – thank God – I've prayed for this – I've prayed that you would come back to me!"

Tears were running down her cheeks and down mine, too. We went together to meet Uncle Mike.

He knew me at once. "I would have known her anyplace," he said. "She looks so much like her father."

Grandma scouted the idea and insisted, "She looks like her mother."

Uncle Mike was limping and evidently in pain. His old injury from the mine was troubling him. Years ago his mine car had missed a sprag, one wheel had left the track, and he had heaved the car back by main strength. Ever since, his knee would slip out of place at intervals. He had been thrown from his seat the day before when his plow hit a rock, and his knee had slipped from its socket. I offered to lead his team to water.

"Better keep away with those good clothes! They'll slobber on you."

"I won't let them," and I took the halter shanks from his hands. He leaned against the gatepost to rest, and he and Grandma stood looking after me as I led the horses to the pump.

Up until now, Grandma had been able to pull Uncle Mike's knee back in place, but this time she couldn't. After dinner I tried, but I couldn't. Uncle Mike thought this was because it was swollen; in the morning the swelling would be down, and he was sure we could set it. But the next morning we failed again, and Uncle Mike said as soon as he finished seeding he would drive over to Sam Davis's place – Sam was as strong as a bull – and get his knee back in place.

After Uncle Mike had gone to the field, Grandma and I had a visiting good time; then I took off my good clothes and had the hay in the mangers for the horses when Uncle Mike came home, and I put the horses in the barn for him.

He was using a riding plow, something I knew nothing about. I offered to finish the plowing if he would show me how to operate the plow, but he wouldn't hear of such a thing. He had only a small patch to finish, he said, and then he'd go over to Sam's.

To his concern and dismay, Sam could do nothing, either, and Uncle Mike came home in distress. Grandma now insisted that he go to the doctor at once, and he agreed that there was nothing else to do – the longer the knee was out of place, the worse it got. He was disheartened at being knocked out just when he needed to get his crops in. I told him to show me which side of the tongue the horses were accustomed to working on, and I'd do the disking. I had never disked, but I had driven a mower and a rake from the time I was ten years old.

Grandma didn't raise any objections, but we could see she didn't like the idea; and Uncle Mike was reluctant to let me take over his work in the field. I persisted, and finally Uncle Mike and I sauntered down to the barn. He showed me which harness went on which horse and where the horses were accustomed to working (he used four horses on the disk), and when morning came I was all ready to go to work. Uncle Mike had good horses, well broken, and the disking went like clockwork.

In the middle of the afternoon, as I was swinging the horses around for the turn, I saw a livery rig drive through our gate and head straight for the field where I was working. I knew it was a livery rig because the horse's head was checked up. Liverymen always put a checkrein on horses they sent out that were inclined to hang their heads, but ranchers never did.

I suppose Fred Steadly was as much surprised to see me, all sunburned and dusty and riding behind four horses on a disk, as I was to see him. I dreaded his comment, but when he had recovered from his astonishment he said, "You are sure good! I bet you can do anything on a ranch!"

"No," I answered, "I'm not familiar with some of the new machinery. This is the first time I ever did any disking."

"Well, I'll say you're doing all right. I wish Mother could see you."

"I'm tickled that she can't!"

"Why?" he asked, surprised again.

"Oh, I suppose this isn't a city person's idea of being ladylike. But my uncle's knee was out of place, and he had to go to the doctor to have it set, so I'm doing the disking for him."

"Do you know why I drove out here?"

"I'm sure I don't."

"There's going to be a picnic and barbecue in the Falls on Sunday, and I thought you might like to go."

"I have to go to church on Sunday."

"That's fine – what time do you go? I'll come and get you, and after church is over, we'll go to the picnic – is it a deal?"

"I'm not sure. I had planned on going to six o'clock Mass, to be back in time to help Uncle Mike if he works on Sunday. He never used to. I won't know until he comes home."

"When do you expect him?" Fred drew his gold watch from his vest pocket. "It is four o'clock now."

"It depends on how much trouble the doctor has with his leg."

"I haven't anything to do. I'll wait awhile."

"You better go to the house and visit with my grandmother. I'll be working until six o'clock."

"How'll you know when six o'clock comes?"

"The horses will let me know."

Fred looked at me skeptically but drove off to the house. I went round and round the field for a couple of hours, while my thoughts went round and round about what Grandma and Uncle Mike would say about Fred rushing out to see me so promptly.

Fred made friends with Grandma while he was waiting, but Uncle Mike was half sick when he got home and in no mood to be bothered with Fred. He said he never did ranch work on Sunday – if a man couldn't make a living working six days a week, he better get another job. The decision about going to the barbecue rested with me.

Grandma had supper ready for us when I came in. Fred expressed surprise at the good fare ranchers had. He left early. Our roads were none too good, and he was no expert driver to be driving home in the dark.

He was hardly out of the gate when Uncle Mike blew up. "Of all the bloody simpletons I ever saw, he takes the cake. To come out here before you have time to turn around and expect you to go back to town with him! I hope you're not taking that fellow seriously."

"Don't worry, Uncle Mike. I'm not taking any man seriously. I'm going back to the novitiate as soon as they think my health is good enough."

"That would be the lesser of the two evils," he said, laughing in spite of himself.

Grandma didn't like to hear Uncle Mike speaking slightingly of my gentleman friend, much less of the novitiate. "I think, Michael, you should know more about such things before passing harsh judgments. I had a long visit with the young man, and he doesn't seem to be a bad sort. Now tell me, did the doctor have much trouble setting your knee?"

"He had one hell of a time. He pulled on it until he was tired and saw it was no use. 'We'll have to drive to Rocket,' he told me, 'where I can get another doctor to help me. I'm going to have to give you chloroform to get that knee set.'"

"They didn't give you *chloroform!*" Grandma exclaimed. "What did they charge you?"

"They took twenty-five dollars away from me without batting an eye and told me to come back again next week. That will cost me some more, I suppose."

"It had to be done," Grandma reminded him, "and it's worth that to have your knee in place again."

"Yes, but there goes my money for the new binder, and I can't break the colts now. I won't get a hell of a lot for them, selling them as they are."

"I'll break them," I said. "You come along and boss the job, and I'll get along all right."

"I can't let you do that – it's not a woman's work."

"I've done lots of work that wasn't a woman's work. I don't like housework, anyway. You tell me how you want the work done, and I'll help you with everything. They didn't teach us how to break horses at the novitiate, but they certainly taught us how to follow instructions."

Uncle Mike smiled at me, and some of the worried look left his face.

Disking was finished, and the next job was seeding oats. We took turns broadcasting them from the back of the wagon, sitting on a box with a pail of oats between our knees. Uncle Mike had two fields to prepare for alfalfa. He said we'd get the colts, Jimmie and Bobby, up, use them on the wagon hauling the fertilizer, then work them alternately on the disk half a day at a time to harden them.

I drove the colts in. They were gentle and well halter-broken, and it was no trick at all to put a halter on Jim and lead him into the barn. I kept levelheaded old Pete in his stall to use when I was ready for him. I fed Jim a few oats, and while he was busy with them, I tried a time or two until I got the harness over his back. I buckled the hames and bellyband before I pushed the breeching over his rump. A colt is touchy about his hind legs. I walked Jim around the corral until he was used to the harness and less jumpy, then I put on his bridle.

The manure was already loaded. Uncle Mike climbed painfully on the wagon seat before I began hooking up Jim and Pete. I worked fast, reaching across the tongue and hooking Jim's inside trace, and as soon as I had the team placed and Pete's tugs hooked, I handed Uncle Mike the lines. The last thing I did was to pull Jim's halter shank through the rings of his bridle and tie it to Pete's hames. A colt can't do much under these circumstances, no matter how he tries, and usually he walks along with the other horse with only a few shakes of his head and a jump or two.

Uncle Mike and I broke not only the two colts he wanted to sell but four three year olds he hadn't intended to handle until the following spring, and we did this without a single accident.

My health was better than it had been since I left Canada, but my nice convent complexion was ruined. Grandma grieved about this, but Uncle Mike said if a girl had to stay inside till she ruined her health to protect her peaches-and-cream complexion, to hell with the complexion. "Winter will take the tan off," he assured her.

A new mining camp had started at Rocket, with a big miners' boardinghouse. About the time our work on the ranch eased up, a woman came from Rocket to see whether she could get me to work at her boardinghouse. Uncle Mike was away on a trip to the doctor. He might have advised against my going, for he knew the woman and didn't think much of her, but Grandma may have thought working in a boardinghouse more ladylike than plowing and breaking horses, for she encouraged me to take the job.

The woman said she would pay me twenty dollars a month – and a month was just how long I lasted! By the last week I was so played out I could eat nothing but orange juice and milk. We baked bread every day and worked from five o'clock in the morning till eleven o'clock at night (if we were lucky), but if the bread happened to be slow in rising, we worked until midnight or one o'clock, or whatever time it took to finish the baking.

When my boss came to pay me, she handed me a ten-dollar bill, a five-dollar bill, and two silver dollars. She said she was paying her niece only seventeen dollars and wouldn't think of paying me any more!

That ended my career as a hired girl. I told the woman I'd go back to breaking horses, where I could earn two dollars a day. I broke all my uncle's horses to ride, and by the time I had finished with them, it was time to hay. I cut and raked all his hay, but Uncle Mike hired a man to do the heavy stacking.

There was a family near my uncle's, the Mollinellis, who were better musicians than ranchers. The father was Italian and often away on concert tours. His wife was Bohemian. Mrs. Mollinelli came one day to see whether I could cut her hay, which was mostly wild oats. She asked what I would charge. Uncle Mike spoke up, "Two fifty a day – she'll have to use one of my horses, because yours are more or less spoiled and aren't safe."

Mrs. Mollinelli agreed.

Working for her was no snap. Her horses were fractious, her machinery was a wreck, rocks stuck up all over the plowed field. There was only one sickle bar for the mower, and I had to sharpen that before I could cut a swathe. Sharpening sickles is hard on the arms, and I earned my $2.50 a day! The best horse they had caused me the most trouble. He was a big bright bay who had bluffed them out of even catching him. Since he was younger and faster than any of my uncle's horses, I had a hard time getting him into the corral, where I could drop a rope over his head. He reared and struck at my horse, then whirled and let fly with both heels. I let go of the rope and got out of range, but my old work horse wasn't any too quick and almost got kicked.

Eventually, I got the big bay snubbed to the snubbing post with a half hitch on his jaw. That was the beginning of the end of his wild life. I called his bluff, conquered him, made friends with him, and worked him on the stoneboat till he was ready to behave, and when I put him on the mower I didn't have a bit of trouble with him. He made a good work horse and pulled more than his share of the load all day long. It was really wrong to hook him up with the stiffened old plugs he had to work with who slowed him until he was likely to become balky.

I was in the field one morning at seven o'clock, but it began to rain, and I had to come in. Mrs. Mollinelli rushed out to find out what was the matter, and when I explained that one couldn't cut hay in the rain, she began to wring her hands and wail, "Two dollars and feefty cent a day! Am I to pay two dollar and feefty cent ven it rain?"

"Yes," I said, "because I will put in my time sharpening sickles."

There were at least six discarded sickle bars in the corner of the chicken house, each with one or more sections broken out. The tool box on the mower had new sections and proper tools for inserting them. I got a hammer and punch to remove the broken sections and replaced them with new ones while Mrs. Mollinelli watched in astonishment. Not one of the Mollinellis had ever repaired a sickle, even though the ranch was so rocky that the sickles broke frequently. They tossed a broken one aside and bought a new one.

I put five sickle bars in working order. At first Mrs. Mollinelli was delighted to have so many usable sickle bars on hand, but then she began to feel sorry for herself because she was married to a man who knew how to play the violin instead of knowing how to make farm repairs. I reminded her that all her family were good musicians, and it was much more wonderful to know how to play a violin than to know how to repair a sickle; but she still thought I was a genius, first for making a usable horse out of her big bright bay and second for making good sickles out of rubbish.

Mr. Mollinelli had come near getting himself lynched when he first came to the country.

Everybody was in the cattle business at that time. No one milked cows. They used canned milk. Few ranchers bothered with a garden – they depended mostly on canned tomatoes. But the Mollinellis planted a big, beautiful garden, and what a treat it was to the grasshoppers! The hoppers made short work of his round cabbages, and Mollinelli wrung his hands and raged and decided to burn up the hoppers. He set fire to the prairie and burned out all the ranchers for miles around. The fire not only swept their pastures but burned

218

their haystacks. Uncle Mike lost three stacks – one hundred and fifty tons.

The ranchers got together in their first rage and swore they'd lynch the locoed son of a so-and-so. Uncle Mike rode with the rest up to Mollinelli's place. They yanked him out of the house. "What the hell did you think you were doing?"

Mollinelli was still intent on his garden. "Dem dam' grassa de hop, he eat all my cabbeech, and for dat me burn all de son of a beech!"

The speech saved his life. It set some of the younger fellows laughing so hard they laughed themselves out of the lynching notion.

My job of cutting and bunching the hay was soon completed, and Mrs. Mollinelli was pleased in spite of the $2.50 a day. The day I finished, she and her daughter got out their violins after supper and played for me before I went home. Their music was beautiful. The daughter had learned to play the violin when she was four years old, too small to hold the instrument correctly. She let it lie across her lap and still held it so.

I rode home singing that night. Not that it was unusual for me to sing – I liked to, and I sang most of the time when I was working alone in the field. But this time I was singing because everyone seemed satisfied with the job I'd done, and I had a little money of my own. I knew what I was going to do with the money, or part of it: buy myself a divided skirt of good stout whipcord so my flimsy dresses wouldn't be flapping in the wind while I was trying to handle horses.

In all the years with Hedge, I had had money in my hand twice: once when the cowboys were lost at Gull Lake and gave me a quarter for showing them where the road was, and once when I found a sheepherder's horse and he gave me a quarter.

Finding the horse was a queer experience. I had been looking for our team that had strayed, riding a black mare bareback and tired of it, when I saw a single horse standing on the open prairie with nobody in sight. As I rode nearer, I saw it was saddled and bridled, but still I couldn't see a rider. I was puzzled. I got off my mare, and after half an hour or so the horse let me come up to him. I thought I might as well be riding a saddle as riding bareback, and the horse didn't act as if he wanted to buck, so I climbed on him and led my mare.

As I rode along, I noticed something strange about the hills. They were in motion, quivering, as though their entire surface was flowing. Nearsighted as I was, I couldn't make out why they looked that way and rode on. It was sheep. Thousands of them. A big outfit was moving its bands. A man left the sheep and walked toward me, and then I knew where the saddle horse had come from. The man said the horse had been trying to get back to his old range and had been lost for two days. I got off and turned him over to his owner, and the man gave me a quarter.

When I got back to the shack, I showed the quarter to Hedge. He saw me looking for a pet crow I had that usually came to me the moment I was in sight and followed me around. Hedge asked me if I wanted to know where it was and said if I'd give him the quarter he'd get the crow for me. I said I did, and he disappeared in the brush and came back with the crow.

I told Grandma and Uncle Mike about finding the horse when I showed them the money I'd earned at Mrs. Mollinelli's.

15

After breakfast the next morning, which was Sunday, someone drove up to our house in a buggy and got out. It was Roscoe Alsworth, one of our neighbors. The Alsworths had a big spread south of us. A section of their pasture land lay between us and the Mollinellis. Mr. Alsworth was a college man, different from most of the homesteaders around us, always well dressed and very courteous in his speech.

Uncle Mike came from the barn, greeted him, and asked him to put up his horse and come in. Alsworth excused himself, saying he hadn't time. He was going across the pasture to look at stock and repair the fence where a wire was down. He had a colt that he would like broken. He had seen me working Mrs. Mollinelli's big bay and had spoken with her. Might he speak to the young lady?

His horse was restless and kept backing as Alsworth stood holding the lines, so he stepped to the horse's head while he waited for me to come out.

I was so surprised that an important man like Mr. Alsworth should expect me to advise him that I couldn't talk naturally at first. His urbanity disconcerted me. When he asked what I would charge to break the colt to drive single and double, Uncle Mike spoke up, "Ten dollars is the going price," but I was so confused it took several promptings from him before I collected my wits enough to say I'd take the job.

They had the colt in the barn and ready for me when I rode over to the Alsworth ranch Monday morning. She was a fine dapple gray Percheron with a kind eye, not even halter-broken, but I knew as soon as I looked at her that she wasn't going to make me any trouble.

"I think she's going to be a holy terror, the way she's been raising Cain ever since I put her in the barn," Mr. Alsworth remarked.

"She is plain scared now, shut up in the barn alone – like a little child shut up alone in a big room. She is bigger than lots of other horses, but she is a baby in years and experience."

"I never thought of that. Maybe you are right," he admitted.

At the barn door I left him, because he was afraid to go inside. "You can't tell what she might do," he said, but I knew there was no danger unless I got in her way and let her run over me.

The family had all come out to the barn, expecting a hectic performance. They found cracks around the little windows used to put hay in the mangers so they could watch me handle the colt. I walked quietly in after asking everyone not to talk. I was going to try to teach the colt the meaning of two words: "Come here!"

As I went into the barn I made sure the door was safely closed, for a colt will jump into even a closed door when being forced to obey.

To make friends with her, I had a little pan with a few handfuls of oats. She was afraid to come so close, so I put the oats in the feed box and stepped back to let her eat them. I tried to get up to her head when she had quieted down enough so I could hold her attention, but she dashed away. Then I gave her a light tap with the whip, which I had had hanging around my neck.

A barn with mangers and harness hangers is no place to whip-break a colt. She is liable to run into such things and knock her eye out or otherwise injure herself. For this reason I couldn't use my whip at just the right moment, for instance, when she turned her rump to me and crouched ready to kick. Instead, I had to maneuver her into a favorable spot and see whether she would repeat the act. This maneuvering was less effective and took more time. I resolved hereafter to take any horses I was breaking to my uncle's nice round seven-foot pole corral with its good snubbing post. I'd have no worries then about a colt jumping out or hurting herself as she raced around.

This colt was such a docile animal that I soon had her following me around the barn, to the surprise of the Alsworths. Once she knew all I wanted was cooperation, I had no trouble harnessing her and hooking her up to an old stoneboat, and she walked off like a lady.

Mr. Alsworth went with me as I drove her around the field, stopping and starting to teach her the meaning of "Whoa!" and "Get up!" I drove her around until noon, then told Mr. Alsworth I thought half a day was enough for a colt.

He told me she was four years old, but I explained that she was young and soft, especially in her shoulders, which might get sore. It was never good to overtax a colt's capacity, mental or physical. I pointed out that his colt had already had too much for her mental capacity, since one thing a day was enough to teach her. We had whip-broken her, partly halter-broken her, taught her to throw her weight against the collar and pull, and taught her the commands "Whoa!" and "Get up!" This is a good deal when we come to think about it. A horse doesn't speak our language and must learn what we are talking about before she can obey.

Compared with a horse, a woman has little strength. I seldom used brute force on horses but tried to outsmart them without gaining their ill will.

It took me almost a week to get the Percheron colt in shape to turn her over to her owner with any degree of safety. She was too big for a saddle horse, but they wanted their money's worth and asked me to break her to ride. One evening after working her in the field all day, I put a bridle on her and climbed on her bareback (to her owner's surprise) and rode her around the barn. She was not too bridle-wise, having had a teammate to follow when she was hitched up. But I broke her to work single and double and also to ride. When I wasn't working the colt all day I put another horse on the disk and finished out the day, so Mr. Alsworth got quite a bit of disking, along with the horse breaking, for his ten dollars.

The evening I finished with the so-called terror, Mrs. Alsworth invited me to what I called supper but they called dinner. Not once while I had been working with the colt had I felt nervous. Now, as we walked from the barn to the house, my heart began to fail me. I looked at my divided skirt, which smelled to heaven of horse sweat, and wished I had refrained from the show-off stunt of climbing on the Percheron colt's back when she was wet from the field. How I wished I could get out of going to the house, where Mrs. Alsworth and her two daughters were so daintily dressed! The men had been working in the field alongside me in jackets and overalls, and their clothes didn't put me to shame, but the finery in the house certainly did. The table sparkled with silver, cut glass, and fine china. The food was well cooked and properly served.

I was embarrassed and self-conscious as Mr. Alsworth seated me, and I thought how the tables had been turned on me. All week I had lived in my world, where everything came naturally to me. Here I was a fish out of water. My hand trembled as I took the dishes passed to me. How I wished I could be at ease as these people were – attentive, overlooking nothing, in spite of constant talk of how clever I was, how delighted they were to have me teach them to handle a young horse, how little they had expected such quick results.

They had been complimenting me steadily, and I thought it was time for me to give them a little credit. I said, "I sure enjoyed your supper. It was very nice."

Mrs. Alsworth answered, "We always try to have our best meal at dinnertime. I seldom bother much about the other two meals."

I had been admiring her lovely dishes and said, "Your dishes are beautiful."

"I take great pride in my china," she said. "I must show you some of my treasured pieces."

She had a collection, some that had belonged to her grandmother and some to her mother, some that she had received as wedding gifts, and some that she had bought at various times. She handed me a delicately patterned cake plate. "You will recognize this piece as Haviland. It was very popular in your grandmother's time. She probably has some pieces like it, but all I have is this cake plate."

I didn't know whether to admit my ignorance and tell her I didn't know one make of china from another or to keep still and let her assume I knew something. I thought it might embarrass Grandma if I said she didn't have any Haviland when maybe she did. I liked pretty dishes, as any girl would, but I had concentrated on learning the breeds of stock and was a fairly good judge of horses and cattle. I could ride into a bunch of horses and pick out each mare's offspring by their build and action or that certain way they had of looking me over, even to the three and four year olds, and the same way with a bunch of cattle.

I needed to get home to do the chores, so I thanked my hostess and was about to leave when Mr. Alsworth put me on the spot by asking point-blank, "Do you think I'll ever make a successful rancher?"

I hated to answer after they had been so nice to me, but I thought of his motley bunch of cattle, scrubby things not fit for breeding stock, the culls somebody had unloaded on him. He urged me, "Go ahead. Tell me just what you think."

I did my best to be truthful without being too abrupt. "If you would hire a good foreman, one who really understands the cattle business, you would learn about it from him, and by the time your son was ready to take over, he could be as good as the best of them. I think one has to grow up with stock to really understand animals. You are smart, but you are just learning the cattle business. If you were in some business where your education would help you in your everyday work, you would get along wonderfully."

I felt that I had said it very poorly.

His wife interposed, "We sold a fine furniture business to buy this lonesome old ranch! I never wanted to buy a ranch, much less come and live on it."

Mr. Alsworth seemed to be afraid his wife might disclose how bad their financial position really was, for he spoke hurriedly, "I suppose you know we are trying to sell, and when we do, I think we will go back into the furniture business."

This was true. There were rumors going around that the Alsworths were going to get out.

"Really, folks, I think you would be more successful and happy in the furniture business. Ranch life doesn't seem to appeal to your family," and with that I backed out of the door, feeling sorry for these misplaced persons who had stepped out of a life they knew into one they knew nothing about. They had been on the ranch five years, and their fences were down and their buildings and machinery were wrecked. He would be in for an unpleasant surprise whenever a buyer looked his place over.

I had forgotten all about my poor health that had driven me from the novitiate. I knew I had gained weight, but I didn't know how much. Come to think of it, I hadn't known a sick moment since I came to Uncle Mike's ranch. I had to write the sisters and tell them.

When I got home from the Alsworths', I found that Fred had been waiting for me all afternoon. Grandma was delaying supper for me, too. She had worried about me, because the horse I was riding was an old saddle horse of my uncle's, an ornery devil that knew all the tricks and hadn't been ridden for six or seven years. He liked the life of a loafer and didn't intend to give it up without a struggle.

I sat at the table and talked while the others ate. After supper Fred took me for a drive. His technique hadn't improved a bit, and his driving made me nervous, though I made no comment on it. He hit rocks and drove into holes that should have been avoided. As he was taking me home in the dusk, he said abruptly, "When are you going to give me an answer?"

"Answer to what?" I asked. I couldn't remember his asking me anything.

"What do you think I've been chasing you for, ever since I met you? Why does any man court a girl?" he asked indignantly.

"Not being a man, I wouldn't know." I knew very well now but wasn't anxious to give a direct answer.

"You're crazy about ranching. My grandfather has one of the biggest, best-stocked cattle ranches in Montana, and you know it will someday belong to us kids. What more do you want? Who's going to make you a better offer?"

"Fred, I've let you and everybody else understand that I'm not looking for 'offers.' I'm going back to Vancouver to enter the novitiate."

"And I'm going to tell you that your father won't let you go and bury yourself in a convent."

I didn't answer. I was going to be eighteen in six months.

"Your father and my mother sure wish you would come back and live in town. You could live at the hotel and help Mother till you found a better job. Maid work isn't so bad, is it?"

"Not if you like it. I don't."

"I should think it'd be better than cleaning out a stable – you're a chambermaid for the horses, aren't you!"

"I made my board doing chores for my uncle, and I made ten dollars breaking the Alsworth colt. I'm not going to people's ranches to break any more horses – I'll bring them to Uncle Mike's corral, and then I'll be working on his place instead of somebody else's. He has weeds that should be disked under right now."

"So you aren't going to give me an answer?"

"Fred, I think I have given you an answer, but you can't take any answer but the one you want."

"All right, if that's the way you are going to treat me. I know other girls."

He stopped his horse without getting out to help me as he usually did. I hopped out and said, "Thank you so much for the ride," and went into the house. As I undressed for bed I thought maybe it would be best if he did find another girl.

Not that I didn't find a certain pleasure in his visits. They were a diversion. And it wasn't as though I knew how to dance and could go out and have a good time with a crowd. Fred at least kept things from being all work and no play for me.

He had driven away without saying good night. He didn't come back the following Sunday. I decided he had made good his threat to find another girl, and to my surprise, it didn't make me feel the least bit happy. I wrote the sisters a long letter, asking whether they thought I might be able to return soon. They answered that my lungs couldn't be wholly healed yet, and they would recommend that I remain on the ranch at least another year to insure not having to leave again.

I was deeply discouraged. A year seemed a long time to wait. I couldn't shake off my depression until a neighbor came to ask me if I would break three colts for him. I asked him whether he had a good corral and whether his colts were halter-broken. His answer was no to both questions, so I asked him to help me drive the colts to Uncle Mike's corral. He liked the idea, because my uncle's corral was made of poles, and his was barbed wire, which the colts might cut themselves on. I handled the colts much as I had handled the others and in three days had them ready to hook up half a day at a time.

Another Sunday came but no Fred. (I heard later that he had made a play for Minnie Alsworth but couldn't get her to say yes, either.) But the third Sunday, here he came! I treated him with more consideration than I usually showed him, which only encouraged him to come twice a week instead of once, bringing me flowers and candy. This went on all summer and fall until everybody expected us to be married.

Uncle Mike wasn't a bit pleased. He told me if I didn't care enough about the fellow to marry him, I had no business keeping him dangling and accepting his gifts. I respected my uncle's opinions, but I realized too that Fred gave me my only respite from hard monotony. While I was in a quandary over him, I accepted another horse to break, one that proved a different kind and took everything I had before I was done with him. Fred was off my mind for a while.

The colt was one of those buzzard heads, with a Roman nose and small three-cornered eyes and sly dodging actions like a coyote – a plain cayuse of the worst type. Uncle Mike and I watched as he trotted around the corral, looking for any opening.

Uncle Mike said, "Well, my lady, you've met your match. I wish my knee was in shape. I'd give that son of a so-and-so a good dressing-down before I'd let you go near him. Get me the whip. I'll put a popper on it that will give you a lot of help – and you're going to need help. I have no use for a man who will turn a bloody cayuse like that over to a girl to handle."

"Uncle Mike, the sisters used to say that nothing in this world is perfect. I've had it easy with horses so far. Maybe I was getting to think too well of my ability, and now it's up to me to prove it."

Uncle Mike sat down on a box in the shade of the gate post, and I went into the corral to let Mr. Cayuse find out who was to be boss from now on. It took half an hour of fast footwork followed by plenty of whip and commanding willpower before the knothead would follow me around the corral. I put a hackamore on him, led him to the barn, and gave him a few handfuls of oats. He wasn't much interested in the oats and much less interested in my friendship.

It had taken me twice as long to make this horse follow me as the average colt, and it took twice as long with every subsequent step;

but I didn't have much difficulty breaking him to work. The trouble with him was that just as you thought you had him broken you had to start in and do everything all over again. He was always on the lookout for a chance to act up or get away. I worked him harder and longer than any colt I'd broken yet. After I came in from a day's work, I would ride him around in the field for a while every night. I put a JIC bit on him. This was severe but necessary, because he was always angling to throw me and finally did after I thought I had him civilized.

One Sunday morning I was going to ride him to the mountains to see how my uncle's cattle were doing. I rode for about five miles with him on his best behavior – until we came to a bunch of colts running on the county road. Knothead wanted to follow them and got mad when I wouldn't let him. His jumping around had got my divided skirt wrinkled and twisted. I raised up in the saddle to straighten it, and there was his chance. Down went his head, and I went over it so fast I couldn't explain how it happened. I lit on my shoulder and skinned the right side of my face.

Knothead kept bucking to throw off the saddle, but he didn't run as I expected him to. He kept stepping on the long heavy reins and may not have known he was loose.

I got hold of him, dusted myself off, climbed into the saddle, and spurred him every time he made a false move. At the first spring we came to I washed off my face. I had no mirror, but I knew I looked terrible. My eye was swollen, my cheek was scraped. I decided not to stop at the ranch where my uncle had directed me but to let Knothead make the round trip in one day. It was him or me, and I figured it was no harder for him to make the long trip than for me to show up among strangers with my face and clothes a mess.

The cattle were badly scattered, and I did quite a bit of riding to look them over. I didn't get an early start home, and it was nearly eleven in the evening by the time Knothead and I turned in at our gate. He was gentle enough by that time. Neither he nor I had had anything but cold spring water since early morning.

Grandma and Uncle Mike were asleep. The dogs' barking wakened them. They knew someone was in the barn by the way the dogs were acting, and they were not expecting me home until the next day. Uncle Mike got up, lit the lamp, and was partly dressed before I had fed Knothead and unsaddled him. When he opened the door I called, "Go back to bed. It's only me."

"What in hell made you come home tonight? Didn't I tell you to stay at Billy Morgan's place?"

"Knothead had his innings today, and I didn't want to be seen with a face like this. I wanted to ride him to a standstill, and I did. Grandma could ride him, the way he is tonight."

"He sure put a hell of a face on you. How did it happen?"

"My skirt got pulled up, and I stood up in the saddle to pull it down. He pulled me down, head first." .

By this time, Grandma was up and dressed. She came to get a closer look.

"I told you you'd work around them broncos until you got hurt. It's a wonder you weren't killed. I've told you over and over, that's no work for a little girl, and now I hope you and your uncle will see that I'm right. Look at your face, now. I hope you aren't going to have ugly scars for the rest of your life!"

"Of course she isn't, Mother," Uncle Mike said. "Most of that is just skin rubbed off and dirt rubbed in. Why didn't you turn back home, wash your face off good, and put salve on it so the wind wouldn't dry it out?"

I had thought about turning back, but Knothead might have thought he had won; and besides, Grandma might have put up a stiff fight about my starting out again.

"The cattle are looking fine. I looked up all the cows that we were expecting to calve, and they all have calves except that old horned roan. She's dry, but she's certainly putting on beef!"

"I'm going to ship her with the steers in the fall. She's getting pretty old. She was such a good stock cow – she always raised a fine, big calf. This is the first year she ever missed."

Grandma was so busy washing the dirt off my face she forgot I hadn't had anything to eat since breakfast. She lifted the teakettle and found there was no more warm water. "Son, put a few more sticks on the fire. I need more water, and maybe Peggy would drink a cup of tea."

"I could go for most anything in the way of food right now," I said.

"Bless my soul, child, I was so taken up with this face of yours that I forgot about your stomach. Son, get that bit of leftover ham and the pie and fry her a couple of eggs. By the time they're ready I will have done all I can for her face."

Uncle Mike was a believer in the healing powers of carbolic acid. He mixed such a strong solution for the final rinse on my face that it hurt me more than the accident had; but by morning my face was much better, so his judgment was evidently right.

Farm work went on as usual for a time until one day when I was driving a four-horse team, harrowing, using three of my uncle's steady work horses and Knothead. The harrow had four sections. I was standing on a wide plank to weigh down the middle sections and had put a few big rocks on the two end sections. The wind was blowing, and across the field came a big tumbleweed. It rolled under the horses' bellies and landed against Knothead's hind legs. He threw both hind legs in the air and came down outside the traces, startling the gentle horses. They jumped and threw me off the plank.

It was easy to quiet my uncle's horses, but Knothead kept on jumping, kicking, and bucking. He couldn't get away because his head was tied to the next horse's hames, but I didn't like to take a chance on getting in front of the harrow to unhook the traces. I finally did: I unhooked all the horses, drove them around into position, and hooked them up again. I finished the job of harrowing without telling anyone about the tumbleweed incident, but it taught me it was well to follow my uncle's advice. It doesn't pay to try to gentle such animals. You can never depend on them. The moment anything goes wrong, such horses will quit you or kick you to death if they get a chance.

We were all glad when Knothead went home. I told his owner to keep him working or he would have to break him all over again and to hobble his stirrups when he rode him.

Cattlemen and cowboys could climb on any kind of a horse without any of the preliminaries I went through. They wouldn't think of asking anyone to break their horses for them, least of all a girl; but the tenderfoots who homesteaded made good business for me.

Uncle Mike sold the two colts I had broken for him (he got $125 for Jim) and bought his first binder. It was shipped knocked down, with a book of instructions. He and I were not familiar with binders, and we had difficulty putting it together and more difficulty making it work. Uncle Mike had learned to cuss driving mules in the mines. When he couldn't make the binder work, his cussing got on my nerves and on the horses'. They knew he was furious, and they wanted to get going. I knew they were as glad as I was when he said he couldn't stand on his knee any longer and went to the house.

I kept fitting the parts together until they were all working except the bundle tier. When Uncle Mike came back after a little rest, he saw our trouble at once and adjusted it. From then on he had very little trouble with the binder, but he didn't have much grain to cut. Uncle Mike drove the binder, and I did the shocking. In my first attempts I didn't know how to make the shocks stand up against the wind, and I had to do plenty of reshocking.

As long as I was busy with the harvest and the general fall work I was contented, but when the work slackened up and the weather turned wet so I had to stay indoors, I grew restless to get back to the novitiate. I wrote the sisters that I had gained ten pounds and was never ill. It was a long time before their answer came, instructing me to go to a certain doctor, show him my letter, and submit to an examination. My return would depend on his report.

I was delighted. I expected the doctor to say I was in perfect condition. But he told me nothing specific, just said, "You are doing fine. Keep on improving, and you will be all right."

As I rode home I was blue and discouraged. I had been planning to visit my father, and I remembered his suggestion that if I found a fast horse, I should bring it around and let him see it. I had run across one I liked the looks of early in the summer and tried it out. Mrs. Larson, who owned it, lived in Great Falls. She was willing to sell it but told me she didn't want me riding it anymore unless I intended to buy it.

I thought it would help shorten the time I had to wait for the sisters' decision if I had the horse for my own. Once when I was in Great Falls I had seen my father driving a trotting horse in a sulky. He didn't notice me. The horse was going at a fast clip, and my father was too intent on the horse to see anything else. I thought he might be assembling a string of horses. Uncle Mike was skeptical but didn't oppose my visit to my father. "It will surprise me if he buys the horse for you, but you can't tell – you might happen to strike him when he has a few dollars."

Fred had told me my father was living at the Arlington House and hadn't been with the Steadlys for some time. One of the girls I knew, Hilda Eckberg, rode to the Falls with me. She wanted to look

234

for a job. I went first to Mrs. Larson's to tell her I had brought the horse in for my father to see. After putting the horse in the barn, I went to look for the Arlington House. It was way down on the south side, and for some reason it looked unsavory and queer to me. I didn't want to go in. A policeman was standing on the corner below the hotel. I crossed the street, approached him, and told him who I was and why I was looking for my father. I asked him if he would go up to the room and ask my father to come down.

I waited.

After a time the policeman came out of the building alone. He came toward me with a peculiar expression and hesitated a moment before he spoke. "For some reason your father doesn't wish to see you. He is there," he added, in answer to my look of surprise, "and told me to tell you he was not – but he is. For some reason he does not wish to talk with you."

I turned away.

"Have you someplace to go?" he asked. "Are you staying in town?"

"I've been living on the ranch with my grandmother."

"Then my advice to you is to go back to the ranch and stay there." He added, "I am truly sorry for you, my child."

I got the horse from the barn and hunted up Hilda, and we rode home together. I left the horse at the Larson ranch. Hilda led her horse, and we walked the mile from the Larsons' to our place. All I told them at home was that I had taken the horse back to the ranch. Uncle Mike said he wasn't surprised.

16

The first September storms were over, but winter was on the way. These bland Indian summer days wouldn't last forever. It was time to bring the cattle down from the mountains. Uncle Mike said we would start in the morning.

We had had more than the usual run of worries that summer. For one thing, some neighboring corporation land had been fenced. For years these sections had been open, the mineral rights leased to the Canyon Coal Company, the pasture free to small stockmen and nesters. Shut off now from this range, the homesteaders were short of pasture. Two smart young chaps from the land corporation saw a chance to make a little money from the situation. They promised the homesteaders wonderful grass in the mountains and offered to take their stock to the upper range for fifty cents a head. They contracted for all the small herds around that part of the country and threw the cattle on our range, overstocking it. We were uneasy. The cattle that had looked good when Knothead and I made our long ride to the mountains might not be in such good shape at shipping time.

Another matter worried Uncle Mike. He had heard rumors that Billy Morgan was selling out. The Morgan ranch was Uncle Mike's stopover when he brought his stock out of the mountains. If he were cut out of this night camp, taking his stock to and from the mountains would be a more complicated business.

Uncle Mike and Morgan had known each other a long time. They had come from Helena together and filed on their homesteads together, and they both got out poles and timber from the mountains. For years their mountain trips had been an outing to look forward to, a few days of relaxation and companionship.

Uncle Mike had already written Billy to tell him we were coming and had received no answer. That meant "Come ahead." Billy wasn't one to waste words. If there had been anything unusual, he would have written.

We started before daylight, Uncle Mike in the buggy with his best driving mare, I riding Caper, a good cow horse. Grandma had put up an ample lunch for us, and we had the old coffee pot and plenty of coffee. We would make Billy Morgan's place by midmorning, with ten miles still ahead of us.

I had heard so much about Billy's wonderful ranch that his little two-room log cabin surprised me – a typical bachelor cabin with the characteristic cabin smell. Clutter and dust – rumpled clothing, slickers and sweaters hanging along the walls, a half-mended horse collar leaning against one wall, a rifle slung across deer-horn rests above the low window. He hailed us and made us welcome. As the men talked I drifted outside, intending to stand in the sun on the south side of the cabin. The sun beat down, and from the ground the odor of stale urine rose pungent and choking. I walked to the fence and rubbed Caper's nose.

I could hear the men's voices. Billy came to the door and tossed something to the dog, who sniffed it and turned aside. "All right, go to hell and starve to death then, you goddamn black son of a bitch," he remarked conversationally and turned back to the kitchen. Yes, he was going to pull out, he told Uncle Mike. Too many nesters coming in. No real cowhands left. The good times were gone – he was too old to handle the ranch, and he couldn't stand the saddle anymore. He was dickering with a fellow now who wanted to buy the place – no, nobody Uncle Mike knew, nor he either, somebody from across the Line.

Uncle Mike declined Billy Morgan's invitation to eat venison with him, saying we wanted to push on to the mountains. Billy followed Uncle Mike to the buggy, and I told him how my bronc had stood me on my head and kept me from stopping at his place earlier in the summer. He looked at me sourly, as though he didn't blame the horse, then unexpectedly smiled as we pulled out.

We ate our lunch at Billy Morgan's big spring and fed the horses their oats and let them graze two hours before we started working the cattle. It was surprising what a good job of herding Uncle Mike could do from a buggy. I did the cutting out and all the worst part of the driving. I would cut out a few head and run them through the gate, and Uncle Mike would close-herd them on the slope while I cut out a few more.

It was a beautiful day for the work. The sunny air held a hint of crispness. The tall pines, the yellow aspens, and the deep golden cottonwoods and box elders made a picture I wouldn't forget. We could look down on Billy's buildings, the wide meadows between spring-fed creeks, cottonwoods and willows along the banks making ideal shelter for stock. Since I had set my heart on becoming a sister, I had put Dave Treu out of my thoughts, but now I remembered him and wondered whether he had ever found his dream ranch.

Uncle Mike roused me from my daydreaming. "A penny for your thoughts."

"I was wondering why Billy would ever consider selling such a beautiful ranch. I should think this would be the spot he'd choose to die in."

"He can't run it. He's getting so crabbed and cranky that no one will work for him. That's why he thinks there are no more good cowhands. The only ranch hands that will stand for him are loafers and drunks who want a few meals and a grubstake – or just a few meals. He has been a good friend to me and still is, and I have been to him – I hope. But life has changed for him. He never married. He hasn't a chick nor a child nor a relative that I know of. He's too old to ride – that's why he has had to sell most of his stock, which is why the grass is so good here."

The fence below our range was a surprise to us. When we had

heard rumors that our stock weren't faring well, Uncle Mike had argued, "There are some old cows up there that will strike for home if they aren't getting good feed." The fence told us why none of them had strayed down to lower grassland.

The stock was in poor condition. Three of the old cows with big calves were almost down. It would be nip and tuck to get them home. Uncle Mike was disheartened. He could see that the easy days were over. With Billy Morgan's ranch sold and the corporation land gone, his best move was to sell off most of his stock – and they were in poor shape to sell.

We got to Billy's before dark and ate a supper of fried potatoes, venison, and canned tomatoes with coffee and canned milk. The kitchen table was piled so high with old papers, magazines, catalogs, and more magazines, piled up and pushed back and piled up again, that there were only two little alcoves between the stacks where the heaped papers had been pushed back to make room for plates. They must have accumulated for years. The bit of oilcloth that showed at the back was dust-covered but new-looking. In front, the oilcloth was worn and frayed and gashed with innumerable knife cuts, the pattern obliterated. On top of one stack was a spool of white thread, flyspecked, with a threaded needle stuck in it. Billy tried to push clear a third place, but I told him I'd sit on the couch and hold my plate on my lap.

We talked almost all night. I lay back on the couch for a few winks of sleep before morning. Beyond the kitchen door, Billy's bed stood unmade and disheveled, a grimy blue sheet blanket with a red stripe near the top to emphasize its grime, uncased pillows yellow and black with oily dirt. The men went into the bedroom. They were still talking when I drifted off.

We got the cattle home with the three cows still alive, but it was a slow, tedious drive. We cut out the calves, and I took on the job of weaning them and trying to save the weakened cows. Uncle Mike let the beef cattle rest and feed a few days, then drove them to Great Falls to ship to St. Paul. Our roads, always bad, sometimes became impassable during the winter, so while he was in town he paid his taxes and laid in his winter grub and coal, and when he came home he paid me.

"Get all supplies laid in before the snow flies," he used to say, but he traded wheat for flour, and sometimes we were so late getting our grain threshed that we could not haul flour until the roads drifted.

Uncle Mike was a great reader, especially during the winter. He was dependent on the mail. When the roads were drifted, his buggy was almost useless. It was no longer easy for him to ride horseback, but I could ride to Coal Coulee almost any mail day. I didn't expect the sisters to summon me to the novitiate during the winter, but I told him I hoped they would accept me in the spring.

"What are you going to do with the simpleton?" he asked, meaning Fred.

"My conscience hurts me for not telling him to find himself a real girl who could repay his devotion."

"Devotion is right, for that is all Fred could give any girl. Really, Peggy, I don't think that fellow has brains enough to pound sand into a rat hole."

"Son, that is unkind of you," Grandma chided him. "Fred is a nice enough fellow, but he has never had to do any work, and consequently he never learned how."

"It's high time he started – a man of twenty-seven who can't turn his hand to anything!"

"I understand his grandmother is leaving that big ranch to Fred and the other two children," Grandma remarked. "They will be well fixed."

"Yes, and isn't he going to make a hell of a manager for that big spread!"

"He'll have to learn like the rest of us," Grandma persisted.

"And lose it all while he's learning."

I was waiting anxiously to hear from the sisters after they received the doctor's report. I was sure they would tell me to prepare to enter the novitiate in the spring. No such word came. Instead, they wrote that the doctor thought I should remain in Montana, where my health was good.

Their advice seemed inconclusive and remote, and I had half a notion to go to Vancouver and talk with Sister Assistant Provincial. On second thought, I knew the trip would be futile. I had no chance of persuading the sisters if there was a reason against my admission, and I believed the doctor's report had clinched their decision.

I was discouraged when Fred arrived the next Sunday; and when he asked how I was, I told him my spirits were low, that I had no satisfying word from the sisters. He was all sympathy and kindness, and I was in a mood to accept sympathy. Telling him my troubles gave him more encouragement than I intended. After he left, I was disgusted with myself. Uncle Mike was right: I had no business encouraging Fred or even letting him come to see me when I was determined to be a sister and not anybody's wife.

The next time he came I told him he was wasting his time and money on me. Telling him was like throwing water on a duck's back. He brushed aside everything he didn't want to hear. He had told his mother and my father that I wasn't getting anywhere with the sisters. I supposed I could have been emphatic and walked off to my room; but I couldn't be mean to him when he had always been good to me. We continued through the winter as we had before until I was looking forward to his visits.

In the spring I wrote the sisters for a definite decision. I told them

I was busy helping Uncle Mike get his crop in and putting in a garden. The reply came, still indefinite: I was to help my uncle as long as he needed me, then have the doctor examine me again.

I wanted an answer, yes or no. For the first time I felt a flash of resentment. They were being evasive. They were stalling. Maybe I wasn't a suitable type for a sister. Girls were rejected whom I had considered angels. We did not know why. Such matters were never discussed. All we knew was that where a postulant had sat, there was now a vacant chair. As far as we were concerned, the dismissals were sudden and final. We did not see the rejected ones before they left, and we did not know where they went.

Pious and good, still they were rejected. Who was I to consider myself fit? I, who had always been ashamed of accepting Fred's attentions when my mind was fixed on the novitiate! The slight pleasure of his company and his candy and flowers were little worth their cost if through them I lost the great privilege of becoming a sister. Regret and remorse filled my thoughts. The lovely spring days brought me only restlessness and turmoil.

This was the time when I had been confident I should return to the novitiate. My life of hard knocks had taught me to take the blows without collapsing. If the sisters had told me to wait a year, two years, any required period, I would have accepted their decision without self-pity. But to be left in uncertainty without end, so that I could make no plans and could look forward to nothing but more uncertainty – it was too much. Daydreaming was insubstantial fare.

On the ranch, working alone, one has time to think; and I did a lot of thinking. I saw that the sisters were justified – from their viewpoint. I asked myself, "Why am I trying to force myself where I am not wanted and dismissing Fred, who offers me more than a welcome?"

Grandma saw that I was worrying. "I know that you are disappointed over that last letter," she said, "but God does everything for the best. If he wants you to be a sister, he will make it possible. If you can do more good where you are, you will become reconciled and be happy where God wants you. Try to look at it in that light."

"I might as well. There isn't much else I can do."

"Let's have that party for you I've been wanting to give ever since you came home. It may cheer us all up. Most of the ranchers have their spring work done, and I think everybody would enjoy a little get-together."

"All right, Grandma, go ahead. A little excitement will give me something to think about. I wish I had some colts to break."

"God forbid any more like the last one! He nearly broke you and put more gray hairs on my old head! Bad luck go with him, and the devil take him."

Grandma couldn't write, so I sent out the invitations for a week from the coming Saturday.

I felt sorry for poor Grandma. She worked hours to have everything just right; but I knew no matter how hard we tried, we couldn't match the Alsworths when it came to parties. But to my surprise, the Alsworth girls were so engrossed in Fred that they paid no attention to anything else.

Fred was wearing a new suit for the occasion and outdistanced all the country boys at the party. He knew how to put everyone at ease. As a hostess I was none the best, but Fred would step in and take care of anything I overlooked and do it without making my oversight obvious. We turned on an old Edison phonograph, and since I didn't dance I busied myself changing records. Everybody danced, the young folks and most of the older ones. I felt like a fish out of water. Fred was most considerate and whispered, "Never mind! I'll teach you to dance before we go to another party!"

I liked Fred better than I ever had before and told him after the party that I thought he had handled everything beautifully.

Grandma was proud of him, but Uncle Mike was disgusted.

"Women are such damned fools," he exploded as soon as we were alone. "They'll fall for a good suit of clothes every time! It's too damn bad Fred can't do something besides dance. He sure was high man here tonight, and there wasn't a man in the crowd who couldn't work circles around him!"

"Mike, son, you're too hard on Fred. You'll have to admit he was a great help in making the party a success. And he danced with every one of the ladies, old or young, whether she was a good dancer or not."

"Yes, Mother, I noticed that, and it was nice of him," Uncle Mike admitted. "Not every young man would do that."

Someone left our gate open, going home from the party, and our stock got out. I rode looking for strays all Sunday afternoon. The season was coming on fast, and Uncle Mike said the calves were raising the devil.

"We'll have to start them for the mountains," he said. "Maybe we better plan to start tomorrow."

There were only about half as many to put on summer range as we had had the year before. Uncle Mike had shipped them pretty close. I had nursed the three old cows along until I had them in fair shape, feeding them cooked mush and putting them in the barn every night. One evening I had gone riding with Hilda and stayed later than I intended. The night had been cold, and when I came in I asked Uncle Mike whether he had put the cows in the barn. He hadn't, and by morning one of them was dead. I pulled the other two through again, and he sold them that spring for twenty-five dollars apiece.

We didn't get started as early as we intended, for there were one or two strays still at large. I lost time hunting them up, but at last we had them all in and counted.

The trip was much as it had been before, with Uncle Mike in the buggy and me on his best saddle horse. We had heard repeatedly that Billy Morgan had sold out, and when we stopped at his ranch we learned that this was true. The buyer would be dropping in anytime now to close the deal. We turned the stock into Billy's lush pasture, perhaps for the last time. Billy was excited over the sale and more querulous and crabbed than ever. He had aged a lot over the winter.

We shoved the stock through the gate of the tight four-wire fence and hoped for the best. Some of the stockmen had been outraged at the condition of their cattle the fall before and wouldn't send them to the mountains again, at least not with the smart young capitalists. Some had even threatened to bring damage suits for the stock they had lost. Perhaps the range would not be so badly overstocked this season.

On our way down, we talked of Billy Morgan and how he had failed in the past few months. We would drop in on him again to thank him for his hospitality and all the favors of the past. Uncle Mike wanted to invite him to visit us after the new owner took over.

A saddle horse was standing at Billy's gate, and as we rode up we tried to figure out whose it was. "It's a damned fine horse," said Uncle Mike, "whoever it belongs to."

He was a handsome buckskin that, from his size, might have a touch of Morgan or Hambletonian blood. Every line showed breeding. We figured out that he might be a cross between an American saddler and a Morgan.

Billy hailed us from the door. "Put up your horses and come in and meet the new owner," he cackled.

We went in. The new owner rose to greet us.

It was Dave Treu.

Afterword

Peggy Bell's story of her youth ends at her eighteenth year, but her life after that was another story of struggle and the search for happiness. In 1976, at the age of eighty-eight, she penned these words:

Many years I have hoed my own row, mostly in the business world, and fared as well as the average, sometimes a wee bit better. I raised a family of five, two girls and three boys. Maybe some of my generation will do something worthwhile. I now have at age eighty-eight, three of my children living, seven grandchildren, twenty-one great-grandchildren, and soon will have five great-great-grandchildren. As they are mostly quite young yet, maybe they will do something great. They are smarter and have an education, that I didn't have. Oh, I almost forgot, I did get a good education in cowpunching, and to be good at that you must know something about horses.

A woman who had met Peggy a year earlier remembered, "At age 87 she was the essence of independence with her proud bearing, alert eyes, and firm handclasp. The Western flavor of her garb, including a fringed jacket, was beautifully appropriate."

There may have been a real Dave Treu, but Peggy didn't marry him. Nor did she ever return to the convent. After living with her grandmother and her uncle Mike Travers for a year or so, breaking horses and helping Mike with ranch work, she met and married a man named Phillip Criviansky of Sand Coulee. She was nineteen, and he was twenty-eight. Peggy described their lifestyle in her journal: "My husband, who was a butcher and a good one, stayed in Sand Coulee and ran the meat market. I lived on the homestead most of the year, running the ranch."

Although she always had a hired girl and usually a hired man, it was a hard life for Peggy, riding and running cattle, and her babies came rapidly, about a year apart, five in all. A photo shows them as scrubbed, blond, handsome children, posed with their goat and goat cart, perhaps for a parade, because a sign on the cart reads Great Falls 1917, but they scowl into the sun or at the photographer or both. They were not happy children; they were too often left to the care of an inexperienced hired girl, and they hungered for the love and affection of their cowboy mother. But the scars of Peggy's abusive childhood had remained, coloring her relationship with her own children.

Peggy's accounts of the early years of her marriage reflect the development of the homestead, the moving of cattle, descriptions of hired men, and her work on the ranch. She wrote very little about her children except to describe a couple of incidents, one of which was fear for their safety when one of the ranch hands got drunk and started shooting off a gun. She also wrote of occasions when the children were taken along on a trail ride in the wagon used for picking up calves that became too tired to follow the cows. The trunk Peggy used to separate the children from the calves also provided a change of clothing for everyone.

Because Phillip Criviansky came out to the homestead on Saturday evenings and returned to the meat shop on Sundays, Peggy was very much in charge of the family and the ranch. Criviansky, however, remained in charge of his wife. She told of a time she planned to go to a dance at Truly:

We all intended to go, but when I told my husband about us going he was thunder struck and said, "You can't go to a dance without me. Don't you know better than that?"

I answered, "You are not missing anything else – weddings, Christenings and all kinds of celebrations."

"That's entirely different. I have to go to such things for business reasons," he replied.

Then I reminded him it was only the Slavish people that he was going to *their weddings and Christenings, and he was doing business with the Americans, the Finlanders and the Italians, and he got their business without catering to them. He just said, "You are not going to any dances without me."*

He was getting mad, so we dropped the discussion, but it still stuck in my craw. How come he could go out and enjoy himself without me, and I could only work like hell without him.

Later the family moved to Great Falls for the winters for the children to go to school, but the marriage failed, and Peggy and Criviansky were divorced in 1928. Criviansky, who died three years later from a brain tumor, was remembered fondly by his children and grandchildren. The fourth of their five children, Stanley, died of spinal meningitis when he was eighteen.

In 1927 Peggy paid for her daughter Agnes to go to beauty school, and the two of them subsequently ran a shop in the days of marcels and cold waves. Theirs was a tempestuous relationship. Agnes and the other children still competed for their mother's affection, and when Margaret helped her son Phillip (apparently the only one of her children to whom she could show affection) financially, it created a further rift with her daughter that was never resolved.

In 1930, at the age of forty-two, Peggy married Shadrick Bell. Her son Phillip, who had moved to California and eventually died in his early forties while on a hunting trip to Alaska, took the Bell name. Later, when the youngest son, Martin, went to join Phillip in California, he also took the Bell name. None of the Criviansky children remembered Bell fondly, however.

Peggy was always writing. Martin says that his mother carried a notebook and was constantly recording events, keeping her writing in a small trunk that the children were not to touch. She wrote about Charlie Russell and Sacajawea and the experiences of her own early life. She had never told anyone about the sexual abuse she had endured from her stepfather, but now she struggled for the words to describe her ordeal. The writing must have been a catharsis for her, and in 1947 she attended a meeting of the Montana Institute of the Arts and approached H. G. Merriam to show him her manuscript. Merriam introduced her to Grace Stone Coates, who, sharply criticized for publishing her revealing poetry, may have stopped writing for some of the same reasons that were compelling Peggy to write.

In 1948, after rigorously revising her manuscript under the guidance of Coates, Peggy gathered her children around her kitchen table and asked each of them for two hundred dollars to finance a trip to New York for her to visit a publisher. The children were reticent about family secrets and uneasy about her plans for publication, but they gave her the money, and off she went. Apparently, she garnered an offer of an advance from Harper's, because Grace Stone Coates wrote to her, "CONGRATULATIONS again and again on the wonderful, wonderful results with Harpers. And the success of your New York trip – all coming to you for your determination and courage." And yet nothing came of the offer, if it was an offer. In a 1957 letter, Coates inquired how her book fund was coming, suggesting that Peggy still had no way of financing her publication.

Peggy had divorced Shadrick Bell, and in 1957 she married Roy Dobin. They enjoyed fishing and hunting together on her little ranch near Sims, Montana, where Peggy told people that she planned to open a little museum of Montana memorabilia, together with a pop and ice cream concession. Her love of horses was still one of the few consistencies in her life. She was active in the Montana Cowgirls Association in the 1960s, serving as its historian, and in 1962 she and two other Montana Cowgirls received charter life memberships in the Cowboy Hall of Fame in Oklahoma City. A newspaper article of the day reported that Margaret Bell Dobin, Elizabeth Giffin Cheney, and Fanny Sperry Steele received their Hall of Fame certificates at the annual meeting of the Montana Cowgirls

Association in Great Falls. Only a niece and Peggy's friend Evelyn Cole were there to see Peggy receive her award.

In 1964 Peggy was the grand marshal for the Bicentennial parade in Great Falls. That was also the year that she stood in line for two and a half hours to shake the hand of President Lyndon Johnson when he visited Great Falls. During this time she continued to write – more memoirs, stories, and a good many letters to editors and politicians. After a silence of fifty years, she began a correspondence with her half-sister Rose, a rewarding reunion for both. In 1969, when she was eighty-one, she wrote to Senator Edward Kennedy and challenged him to help the Indians. "Now Montana's water and air is polluted and the lush grass lands will soon become baren, from overgrazing, the greed of the white man will soon put himself out of business." There is no record of response from the senator.

Peggy made a last attempt at publishing in the 1970s with the schoolteacher who had agreed to edit her manuscript. She died on 19 September 1982 at the age of ninety-four. Her son Martin Criviansky Bell and daughters, Agnes Nilson and Catherine Thomas, were listed as survivors, along with two sisters, seven grandchildren, nineteen great-grandchildren, and seven great-great-grandchildren.

When our search for Peggy led us to Great Falls, where her story began and ended, her granddaughter Diane Volk was delighted to learn of her grandmother's memoirs and to share her story with her family. It helped explain to her some of the strained family relationships she had encountered as she grew up and that linger today. "I'm so sorry," Diane said, "that I did not know this story while Granny was still alive. I would have liked to have known her better, and perhaps been the one to bring more closeness to the family."

LEE ROSTAD